COUNTRY BREAKFASTS

Country Baking

Home for the Holidays

Country
Breakfasts

KEN HAEDRICH

BANTAM BOOKS

New York   Toronto   London   Sydney   Auckland

COUNTRY BREAKFASTS
A Bantam Book/November 1994

BOOK DESIGN BY ELLEN CIPRIANO

Library of Congress Cataloging-in-Publication Data

Haedrich, Ken, 1954–
    Country breakfasts / Ken Haedrich.
        p.   cm.
    Includes index.
    ISBN 0-553-37246-7
    1. Breakfasts.   2. Cookery, American.   I. Title.
TX733.H34   1994
641.5'2—dc20   94-17330
                                              CIP

Published simultaneously in the United States and Canada

Bantam Books are published by Bantam Books, a division of Bantam Doubleday Dell Publishing
Group, Inc. Its trademark, consisting of the words "Bantam Books" and the portrayal of a rooster, is
Registered in U.S. Patent and Trademark Office and in other countries. Marca Registrada. Bantam
Books, 1540 Broadway, New York, New York 10036.

PRINTED   IN   THE   UNITED   STATES   OF   AMERICA
FFG   0 9 8 7 6 5 4 3 2 1

This book is
dedicated to my son Ben.

When you finally leave the nest
I'll wish you the best
And leave you this one piece of
Advice to digest:
Life will be fruitful
Just like it's supposed ta
If you'll just keep your silverware
Outta the toasta.

CONTENTS

CONTENTS

CONTENTS

CONTENTS

· · · · · · · · · · · · ·

CONTENTS

CONTENTS

ACKNOWLEDGMENTS

A HANDFUL OF GOOD people made this book possible and supported me in one way or another through the writing and production of it. Thanks to:

My agent, Meg Ruley, for being there when I need her; and my editor, Fran McCullough: this is our third book together, and I couldn't imagine doing this without her. In California, Marion Cunningham has been a good friend over the years, someone I always enjoy talking to. In Chicago, Brenda McDowell, Lisa Piasecki, Lisa Carlson, and Lyn Fitzgerald have been loyal supporters and a pleasure to work with on special projects. And heaven knows what I would do without the sharp eye of my copy editor, Chris Benton.

Closer to home, my pal Cindy and I continue to plan the breakfast place of our dreams, the No Whiners Diner. My most memorable morning meals have been in the company of the Johnson boys—Sam, Mark, and Andy—the Three Stooges of American cooking. Nancy and Mike Phillips, organic farmers and good friends, were kind enough to contribute recipes to this collection. Our good neighbor Elzey Burkham is always willing to share his fax, oven, and blueberries (what the bears and our kids don't steal first).

Thanks to my mom and dad, Joe, Barb, Tom, Willy, Joanne, and Mary for many fond breakfast memories in Plainfield.

Finally, despite our differences on the subject of egg cookery, I can think of no finer breakfast companion than my mate, K.P., and our kids—Ben, Tess, Ali, and Sam.

J

INTRODUCTION

ALMOST FROM THE MOMENT I began telling folks I was working on a breakfast book, I started to hear echoes of my own voice confirming a suspicion I have held for a number of years: that for many of us breakfast is still the most important—and beloved—meal of the day. We may have grown accustomed to frozen waffles and instant coffee or count Dunkin' Donuts on our list of early morning rituals. But in spite of all that, we still long for the personal touch of an egg cooked just so, freshly brewed coffee, and the warm cozy feelings we get sitting down to eat real, fresh food with our family and friends. I believe breakfast can be that way and that anybody can prepare tasty, wholesome morning meals on a daily basis. That's what this book is all about.

Oliver Wendell Holmes once said, "Man's mind, stretched to a new idea, never goes back to its original dimension"—a principle that applies quite nicely to breakfast. Aside from a modestly equipped kitchen, one need only start imagining—*stretching* to—the many possibilities to become a more able and creative breakfast cook. By stretching I mean embracing the possibilities for the sake of good eating, not for the purpose of following some new trend or fashion. By its very nature quiet and serene, breakfast defies all attempts to become something nouvelle, cutting edge, fashionable. We're safe at breakfast, allowed to drop our defenses and worldly concerns.

We begin with the knowledge that breakfast—as much as dinner—should be an orientation of the season, the weather, larder, and appetite. What's in the fridge that demands our attention? What does the garden, the season, have to offer? We need to consider the "feel" of the day. Is it festive and leisurely, or does the schedule suggest something simple but still hearty? We factor these variables into the dinner equation more or less instinctively. It may, however, take a little getting used to in regard to the morning meal; breakfast tends to sneak up on us, whereas we have the whole day to plan for dinner. But that's nothing a little planning can't accommodate.

I'm a breakfast romantic, I'll admit, probably because I am happiest in the kitchen, fiddling around with new recipes and raw ingredients. I'm also an early riser. I've always found such peace in those predawn hours, before the waking world of bills and dirty laundry takes hold. But of course I know that most people today want good fresh food and accessible recipes that don't tie them to the kitchen any longer than necessary.

With the exception of yeast breads and yeast coffee cakes, and some of the heartier dishes reserved for weekends, most breakfast dishes can be accomplished in a relatively short amount of time. Fruit is a perfect example of an ingredient that seldom needs much in the way of enhancement or cooking to render it thoroughly enjoyable: fresh sliced peaches baked in cream; sautéed bananas with brown sugar and rum; caramelized grapefruit. We love all of them for breakfast. Egg dishes take from just a few seconds to a few minutes. Breakfast cereals cook in short order on top of the stove or in the slow cooker while you sleep. Muffins and biscuits can be tossed together in 10 minutes and baked while you get the kids ready for school. And you can make a pancake recipe from scratch in essentially the same amount of time it takes to do it with a boxed mix. Simple as these recipes are, most can be made at least partially ahead; usually the do-ahead steps are self-evident when you read a recipe, but sometimes I'll tip you off. Depending on your schedule, and the number of willing helpers you have, advance preparations can be done the night before or over a weekend. Organization is important. Planning a week of breakfast menus before shopping day will allow you the greatest variety in your morning menus and prevent last-minute trips to the grocery store for key ingredients.

A number of people have mentioned to me that they love breakfast so much they eat it for dinner—some because they're so pressed for time when they wake up that they just can't enjoy the morning meal, others simply because these are the foods they like most. When I was growing up, we often had pancakes for dinner on weekends, a tradition that lives on in New England to this day. I still like to eat omelets for dinner, with a salad and slices of toasted French bread—a feast I can have on the table in about 5 minutes. This is the flexible nature of breakfast, and you should feel comfortable working these recipes into your own life the way you see fit. Sometimes, when we have a lazy Saturday morning, I won't start the dough for a coffee cake until midmorning—and we have coffee cake when we'd normally eat lunch. If we have the ingredients on hand for a favorite hash, no one complains if we have that for dinner with poached eggs. After all, good food is good food, no matter what time of day you eat it.

Breakfast has charms and pleasures specific to every season, but there's something extraspecial about summer breakfasts. We have long winters here in New Hampshire, and by summer we're ready to be outdoors from dawn to dusk. My wife, Karen, and I like to begin our summer days with tea or coffee in the garden. It's such a delight just to sit there, bathing in the early morning sunlight and the fragrance of fresh herbs, while the kids play down by the stream and the bees and hummingbirds make their rounds. Simple breakfasts arise so naturally at this time of year: strawberry shortcakes, fresh blueberries or blackberries and cream, a berry muffin, or a creamy omelet made with the fresh herbs our kids like to gather. (Get a kiss from our little Alison in May or June, and there's always a whisper of chives or lovage on her breath.) Once the blackflies are gone, we love to take breakfast at the picnic table. If you've forgotten the fun of breakfast outdoors, make a point of trying it soon.

I believe you get out of breakfast, or any meal, what you put into it, the attitudes you bring to the table. And those who get the most out of it seem to have the capacity to invest mealtime with meaning beyond the purely physical objective of assuaging hunger.

One could argue that these times already demand enough of our time and attention. Who has the time for such food worship, especially when convenience foods are so widely available? But there's a price to pay when we separate ourselves too far, and too often, from the pleasures of the kitchen in the interest of speed and efficiency. Writing in his wonderful book *Southern Food,* John Egerton puts it this way: "So breakfast has been transformed—speeded up, trimmed down, liquefied, purified, packaged. If you miss it at home, you can catch it at a fast-food outlet on the way to work, or even from a coin-operated machine. A large and varied and delicious morning repast to be shared in good company, or even lingered over, along with an extra cup of coffee and the morning paper, has become a pleasure more to be remembered wistfully than experienced."

Convenience is both the cure and the curse of our times. Convenience is the sword that cuts the human link off the food chain. As poet Wendell Berry once wrote, "If you take away from food the wholeness of growing it or take away the joy and conviviality of preparing it in your own home, then I believe you are talking about a whole new definition of the human being."

A thoughtfully prepared breakfast is no cure-all. But it is a starting place, an opportunity to reconnect with our family or friends in an atmosphere of comfort and shared effort. The age we live in makes unreasonable demands on our time and energies. All of us are tied to schedules, to work that often demands more of us than we get in return. But we should not take that to mean we should leave our nourishment in the hands of others. Rather, we should look to the morning meal as one small refuge from these demands and dignify this time of day with our best effort, even if we eat alone.

May your morning meals be filled with good food, good company, and delight for the simple things in life.

Sunday Morning Specials: Pancakes, Waffles, French Toast, and Crepes

Most of us have mornings when we wake up and our stomachs demand some immediate and serious stoking; my kids, in fact, live in this state perpetually. These are the mornings when nothing but a tall stack of something from the griddle will do. You simply don't know the true splendor of pancakes and waffles until you've made your own grainy renditions from scratch and anointed them with real maple syrup or fresh fruit sauce and sweet butter. If they serve breakfast in heaven, this is what I imagine it's like; and if they don't, I'm hoping for a quick reincarnation.

I can understand the allure of boxed and frozen versions of pancakes and waffles, but making your own from scratch is so easy, and even if they aren't quite instant, they're quick to make indeed. We're talking less than 15 minutes from throwing together your batter to the time the batter hits the griddle with an inviting sizzle. Easy? My 12-year-old, Ben, and 10-year-old, Tess, can do it without missing a beat. And they love it. If you're a sleepyhead, think about farming the job out to your kids.

Waffles are trickier than pancakes because they take longer to cook, and you can prepare only as many as your waffle iron can cook at once—usually just a single serving. This can be a problem if you plan to serve them for company or all the kids are clamoring for waffles at once. Fortunately, waffles are supposed to be crisp, so you can hold them in a warm oven—where they'll retain their texture—for up to about 30 minutes; beyond that they start to dry out. Pancakes turn rubbery if you do that.

Put as much thought into your toppings as you do your pancakes and waffles. Real maple syrup isn't cheap, but a little of it can go a long way; if you warm it gently before you serve it, it will thin out and go even further. If real maple syrup seems too expensive, seasonal fruit sauces (see the box on page 23) are easy to make and bursting with flavor and color.

Unlike pancakes or waffles, crepes can be made well ahead and enjoyed with an astonishing assortment of sweet or savory fillings, so they're a particularly good choice for breakfast or brunch entertaining. Crepes can be prewrapped and warmed, or the ingredients can be assembled in one area and each person can create his or her own fantasies.

And let us not forget the estimable French toast, of which I offer you two favorites, including a tangy buttermilk variation served with a lemon-butter sauce and a dusting of powdered sugar.

Leftover Oatmeal Pancakes

Makes about 12 four-inch pancakes

It's a shame to waste leftover cooked oatmeal, but there are only so many creative things you can do with it. Kids can spot rewarmed oatmeal a mile away, so unless you plan to use it in yeast bread it's destined for the compost heap or garbage. But hold on! Here's the best thing to happen to cooked oatmeal since butter, light cream, and lots of brown sugar: a pancake that gives day-old oatmeal a fresh start in life. These are really delicious, light but oat-chewy, good enough that you may start making leftover oatmeal *on purpose*. They're moist too, perfect with the basics: butter and maple syrup. The batter is thicker than most; be careful not to thin it too much.

1 cup cold cooked oatmeal
1 cup unbleached flour
¼ cup sugar
1½ teaspoons baking powder

½ teaspoon salt
½ teaspoon ground cinnamon
2 large eggs
½ cup milk
2 tablespoons flavorless vegetable oil or unsalted butter, melted

Put the oatmeal in a large mixing bowl. Mix the dry ingredients in a separate bowl and pour them over the oatmeal. Using your fingers, rub the mixture gently to break up the oats. Set aside.

Crack the eggs into the bowl you mixed the dry ingredients in and whisk them until frothy. Whisk in the milk and oil. Pour the liquid into the dry mixture and stir briskly, just until evenly blended. Set the batter aside for 5 minutes and then check the consistency; it should be thicker than normal pancake batter but not as stiff as a board. If it is not the slightest bit loose, stir in a tablespoon or two more milk.

Preheat a griddle or skillet, oil it lightly, then cook the pancakes without crowding them, using about ¼ to ⅓ cup batter per cake. Cook for about 1½ minutes on the first side, flip, then cook for about 1 minute on the second side. Serve hot.

Pancake Savvy

In New Hampshire, where I live—heart of maple syrup country—pancakes are king. And facing off to a tower of flapjacks, stuck with blueberries and drenched in sweet cream butter and a small pond of real maple syrup, is my idea of heaven on earth. Even before I moved to New Hampshire some 13 years ago, I was hooked. I even served them at my first wedding, personally presiding over the grilling of hundreds of hotcakes. That marriage was destined to fizzle, but my love for pancakes has never wavered.

Having traveled to the fringes of pancake creativity and back again, I'm convinced that all white-flour pancakes can't stack up to whole grain pancakes. Pancakes, regrettably I think, don't often break out of the white-flour buttermilk sort, much to our gastronomic loss. Whole grains open up new vistas. They add flavor, color, and texture to your hotcakes and a veritable gold mine of fiber as well.

It's a popular misconception that whole grains and light, fluffy pancakes are a contradiction in terms. Hogwash! If you *have* had the misfortune to meet pancakes of the hockey puck persuasion, probably a violation of the Basic Pancake Tenets, not the whole grains, caused the problem. So perhaps this is a good time to review some of the key points.

First, mixing. The History of Failed Pancakes is littered with mixing abuses, most of which are the direct result of overzealous beating. Mad stirring, which on the surface looks like purposeful cook's work, is a detriment to light pancakes because it develops gluten in the flour. Gluten is a protein that becomes elastic when mixed—the stuff that allows your yeasted breads to rise but makes for a tough flapjack, one that resists a lofty "spring" on the griddle.

The proper consistency of pancake batter is neither too thin nor too thick. Even with precise measurements, as I've given here, there's liable to be some variation in consistency between your batter and mine. The grind of flour you use (coarse or fine) and where it has been stored can affect consistency. Generally speaking, a thin batter will result in moist, thin pancakes; a thick batter, drier, cakier, thicker pancakes.

Because whole grain pancakes are slow to absorb moisture, I like to let the batter sit for at least 5 minutes before I cook a trial pancake. At that point, if I need to, I can make the necessary adjustments, thinning the batter with a splash of milk or adding a bit of flour to thicken it.

Cooking any pancake requires the right pan, good timing, and a steady flipping hand. For the pan, the more metal you put between the heat and your batter, the better. Plain cast iron is great because it spreads the heat evenly, minimizing hot spots that can cause uneven cooking. A regular skillet will do, but a low-sided pancake pan or griddle is better since there is more room to maneuver a spatula.

I am partial to my trusty, 15-year-old Farberware electric griddle. I just set the temperature at 400° and go. The standard test for checking to see if any griddle is hot enough is to throw a drop of water on the surface. If the water sizzles and stays put, it needs more time to heat up. If it vaporizes on contact, it's too hot. But if it skitters and dances across the surface, it's just right.

Oil your skillet lightly, rubbing the oil on with a wad of paper towels; don't press hard, or the heat will travel up through the towels and burn you. Ladle on the batter, using about ¼ cup per pancake. Pancakes are ready to flip when little air holes appear on the surface, the perimeter appears dryish, and the pancakes are nicely puffed, usually about 1 to 1½ minutes. Turn them only once, cooking not quite as long on the second side. Avoid any inclination to press, poke, or prod them—acceptable macho behavior at a cookout, but not here. Have warm plates, soft butter, hot coffee, and juice standing by; pancakes wait for no one, and holding them in a warm oven or nuking them in the microwave will diminish the pancake experience manyfold.

However, since the batter can be prepared up to a day ahead, even someone on a tight schedule can enjoy pancakes. If your mornings are hectic, prepare your pancakes the night before. Just mix the dry ingredients (cover and leave at room temperature), separately mix the wet ingredients (cover and refrigerate), and blend them when you get up. If egg whites are called for, beat them in the morning.

Oatmeal Corn Cakes

Makes 14 four-inch pancakes

Someone once said about my family that we should have been horses for all the oats we eat. It's true. Here's another oat hotcake we love, a little moister and less cakey than Leftover Oatmeal Pancakes (preceding recipe). The cottage cheese gives them just a slight tang; the oats, a bit of chewiness. Serve with any syrup or sauce you like—applesauce is wonderful—then sprinkle with granola.

1 cup rolled oats (*not* instant)
⅓ cup packed light brown sugar
1 cup small- or large-curd cottage cheese
1 cup milk
3 large eggs
⅔ cup unbleached flour
⅓ cup yellow cornmeal, preferably stone-ground
1 tablespoon baking powder
½ teaspoon salt
¼ cup unsalted butter, melted and cooled, or
    flavorless vegetable oil

Put the oats and brown sugar in a food processor and process until the oats are finely chopped but not as fine as flour. Add the cottage cheese, milk, and eggs and puree until smooth. Reserve.

Toss the flour, cornmeal, baking powder, and salt in a large mixing bowl. Make a well in the dry ingredients, then stir in the liquid. When the batter is still a little lumpy, gently stir in the butter. Let the batter rest for 5 minutes (it should be thickish) while you preheat a griddle. Ladle the batter onto the greased griddle and cook for about 1½ minutes, flip, and cook for about 1 minute on the second side. Serve hot.

Buckwheat Flapjacks

Makes about 16 five-inch pancakes

There's nothing subtle about the flavor of buckwheat; alone, it tastes wild and somewhat grassy. In moderation, however, it can be used successfully in pancakes. My trick for taming the flavor of buckwheat is combining it with twice as much unbleached flour and some cocoa powder. The cocoa doesn't so much obscure the buckwheat flavor as rein it in and mellow it out. I've made these for a number of avowed buckwheat haters—including Karen, my wife—and the response is predictably one of pleasant surprise. Serve with maple syrup and sour cream.

1 cup unbleached flour
½ cup buckwheat flour
1½ tablespoons unsweetened cocoa powder
2½ teaspoons baking powder
½ teaspoon salt
2 large eggs
2 cups milk
3 tablespoons sugar
¼ cup flavorless vegetable oil

Sift the flours, cocoa, baking powder, and salt into a large bowl. Whisk the eggs in a separate bowl, then whisk in the milk, sugar, and oil. Make a well in the dry mixture, add the liquids, then blend with a few deft strokes. Set the batter aside for 5 minutes to thicken, then adjust the consistency with a touch more milk if it seems too thick.

Cook the pancakes on a preheated greased skillet or griddle for about 1½ minutes, flip, and cook for about 1 minute on the second side. Serve hot.

Blueberry Banana Pancakes

Makes 12 to 14 four-inch pancakes

We love these in the summer, with fresh blueberries right off our bushes. They're still good with frozen blueberries, however; use them straight from the freezer, without thawing them. Try other berries here too, in place of or in addition to the blues. Serve with maple syrup and plain yogurt on the side.

1 cup unbleached flour
1 cup whole wheat flour
1 tablespoon baking powder
½ teaspoon ground nutmeg
½ teaspoon ground cinnamon
½ teaspoon salt
¼ cup sugar
1 large or 2 small very ripe bananas
1¼ cups milk
2 large eggs
½ teaspoon vanilla extract
⅓ cup flavorless vegetable oil
1 cup blueberries

Combine the dry ingredients in a large mixing bowl and toss to mix. Puree the banana in a food processor, gradually adding the milk, then the eggs and vanilla. Make a well in the dry ingredients, add the liquid, and stir just to blend. Stir in the oil, then fold in the berries. Let the batter rest for 5 minutes, then cook on a preheated greased griddle or skillet for about 1½ minutes, flip, and cook for about 1 minute on the second side. Serve hot.

Banana Walnut Hotcakes

Makes about 16 four-inch pancakes

Everyone needs a few good recipes for those brown, overripe bananas we occasionally discover hidden behind the pile of unpaid bills that we throw on top of the fridge. Here's a great one. Almost nobody—kids, friends, lovers—seems to have a quarrel with the flavor of banana, so these are universally popular. Dress them up with maple syrup, butter, extra chopped nuts, and more banana slices, but use prime bananas for the garnish, not the same gooey ones you put in the batter.

1 cup walnut pieces
1 cup whole wheat flour
1 cup unbleached flour
1 tablespoon baking powder
½ teaspoon salt
½ teaspoon ground cinnamon
¼ teaspoon ground nutmeg
2 large very ripe bananas
1⅔ cups milk
¼ cup sugar
2 large eggs
½ teaspoon vanilla or lemon extract
¼ cup flavorless vegetable oil

If you want to use toasted walnuts—nice because they have a deeper flavor, but not necessary—spread them on a baking sheet and toast in a preheated 350° oven for 10 minutes. Slide them onto a counter and cool. In any case, chop the nuts finely by hand and set them aside.

Mix the dry ingredients in a large bowl and set aside. In a food processor, combine the bananas, milk, sugar, eggs, and vanilla. Process to a smooth puree. Make a well in the dry ingredients and blend in the liquid, beating just until smooth. Stir in the oil and reserved nuts. Cook the pancakes on a preheated greased griddle for about 1½ minutes, flip, and cook for about 1 minute on the second side. Serve hot.

Gingerbread Corn Cakes with Warm Applesauce

Makes about 18 four-inch pancakes

These soft, spicy hotcakes were made to be eaten with apples in any form, especially the Cranberry Applesauce on page 226. They're also excellent with the Cider Jelly on page 223. Yet another option is the easy sauce here, made with nothing more than applesauce and molasses and a small amount of sugar and water to bring it to the right consistency. The sauce is no problem; in the time it takes the first batch of pancakes to cook, you can have this into the saucepan. If you don't have any soft butter on hand for the pancakes, just swirl a couple of tablespoons right into the sauce as it warms. Then you don't even need to put it on the cakes themselves.

¾ cup whole wheat flour
½ cup unbleached flour
¼ cup yellow cornmeal, preferably stone-ground
2½ teaspoons baking powder
1 teaspoon ground ginger
½ teaspoon ground cinnamon
½ teaspoon ground cloves
½ teaspoon ground nutmeg
½ teaspoon salt
2 large eggs
¼ cup unsulphured molasses
1⅔ cups milk
¼ cup flavorless vegetable oil

In a large bowl, combine the dry ingredients. Toss to mix well. In a separate bowl, beat the eggs lightly. Whisk in the molasses and milk.

Make a well in the center of the dry ingredients and pour in the liquid. Whisk several times, just until smooth; do not overmix. Stir in the oil. The batter will be thin at this point, but it will thicken as it stands. Let rest for 5 minutes. If it still seems a bit thin, thicken it up by whisking in a few tablespoons of flour.

Cook on a preheated greased griddle or skillet for about 1½ minutes, flip, and cook for about 1 minute on the second side. Serve hot with the following sauce.

 THE SAUCE

1½ cups sweetened or unsweetened applesauce
3 tablespoons unsulphured molasses
1 tablespoon sugar if you're using unsweetened applesauce

Puree the ingredients in a food processor, adding just enough water to bring it to the consistency of a thickish sauce. Transfer the sauce to a small saucepan. Heat, thinning if necessary with a little more water.

Orange, Rye, and Fennel Seed Cakes

Makes about 18 four-inch pancakes

These are light, cakey pancakes—perhaps not what you would expect from a rye pancake. They have a decidedly wholesome flavor and nubby texture. But the real surprise here is how the flavors of the orange and fennel seed perfectly complement each other. Serve with maple syrup or the Sweet Tahini Sauce on page 227.

1 cup unbleached flour
⅔ cup rye flour
2½ teaspoons baking powder

½ teaspoon salt
1 teaspoon crushed fennel seeds (see note)
3 large eggs
¼ cup sugar
1½ cups milk
¼ cup sour cream
finely grated zest of 1 large orange
¼ cup flavorless vegetable oil
orange slices for garnish

Combine the dry ingredients in a large bowl and mix well. In a separate bowl, beat the eggs and sugar with a whisk. Whisk in the milk, sour cream, and orange zest. Make a well in the dry ingredients, pour in the liquid, and stir just until blended; do not overmix. Let rest for 5 minutes to thicken, then stir in the oil.

Cook on a preheated greased griddle or skillet for about 1½ minutes, flip, and cook for about 1 minute on the second side. Serve hot, garnished with half-moon slices of orange.

Note: To crush fennel seeds, simply roll over them repeatedly with your rolling pin on a hard surface.

Lemon Feather Cakes

Makes 14 four-inch pancakes

These are in the featherweight class, ethereal hotcakes with an almost sponge-like texture. The clear, clean lemon flavor makes them the perfect cake to dress up with fresh berries, warmed in a saucepan with a little sugar just until the berries throw off their liquid. If you want to get really fancy, I recommend a warm blueberry sauce—made as I just described—with a big dollop of whipped cream on top of everything. Or keep it simple and just scatter some toasted pecan halves over the cakes.

4 large eggs, separated
¼ cup sugar
½ cup sour cream
½ cup milk
1 teaspoon lemon extract
finely grated zest of 1 lemon
1½ cups unbleached flour
1 teaspoon baking soda
½ teaspoon salt
½ teaspoon ground nutmeg

In a large mixing bowl, beat the egg yolks and sugar with an electric mixer for about 3 to 4 minutes, until thick and lemon colored. Set the whites aside in a separate bowl. Wash and dry the beaters and keep them handy.

Whisk the sour cream, milk, lemon extract, and lemon zest into the egg yolk mixture and set aside. Sift the dry ingredients into a bowl and reserve. Using the clean beaters, beat the egg whites until they hold soft peaks. Whisk the dry ingredients into the liquid just until smooth. Fold in the egg whites. Cook the pancakes on a preheated greased griddle or skillet for about 1½ minutes, flip, and cook for about 1 minute on the second side. Serve at once.

Pop's Yeasted Whole Grain Pancakes

Makes about 14 four-inch pancakes

I love these mixed grain yeasted pancakes so much I decided to name them after myself. When you have the time, yeast is an excellent way to raise a pancake; maybe it's my imagination, but the flavor of these is smoother and more earthy than comparable pancakes leavened with baking powder or soda. Because the batter

· · · · · · · · · · · ·

actually rises like a sponge you'd prepare for a yeast bread dough, the texture of the pancakes isn't quite so delicate; they're ever so slightly bready, though still very soft and tender.

⅓ cup lukewarm water
1 ¼-ounce envelope (about 2¼ teaspoons) active dry yeast
1½ cups milk
½ cup packed light brown sugar
3 tablespoons unsalted butter, cut into several pieces
2 large eggs, lightly beaten
1 cup whole wheat flour
½ cup unbleached flour
½ cup yellow cornmeal, preferably stone-ground
1 teaspoon salt

Measure the water into a measuring cup and sprinkle the yeast over it. Mix gently, then set aside for 5 minutes to dissolve.

In a small saucepan, gently warm the milk, brown sugar, and butter until the butter is almost melted. Pour it into a medium bowl and let cool to body temperature. Blend in the beaten eggs and dissolved yeast.

In another bowl, sift the dry ingredients; if there are any flecks of grain left in the sifter, just add them to the bowl. Make a well in the dry ingredients, add the liquid, and whisk for about 15 seconds to smooth the batter out. Cover the bowl with plastic or the lid from a pot and set aside in a warm spot for 30 minutes.

After the 30 minutes have elapsed, *do not stir the batter down*. Gently scoop the batter onto a preheated greased griddle, cook for about 2 minutes, flip, and cook for about 1 or 1½ minutes on the second side. Serve hot with butter and maple syrup.

·   ·   ·   ·   ·   ·   ·   ·   ·   ·   ·   ·   ·

Gail's Baked Apple Pancake

Makes 4 servings

My Tennessee friend Gail Damerow is a writer, editor, homesteader, and ice cream freak—she wrote *Ice Cream! The Whole Scoop* (Glenbridge Publishing, 1991). She's also an accomplished breakfast cook who loves to prepare this dramatic puffed oven pancake. This is sweet, soft, and delicate, almost like a skillet soufflé. It's lighter than typical stovetop pancakes, more like biting into a golden brown apple cloud. Serve with hot apple cider and perhaps a slice of warm ham.

2 large eggs, separated
3 tablespoons sugar
3 tablespoons milk
3 tablespoons unbleached flour
¼ teaspoon baking powder
⅛ teaspoon salt
1 large tart apple, peeled, cored, and grated
1 tablespoon fresh lemon juice
1 tablespoon unsalted butter
½ teaspoon ground cinnamon
2 tablespoons chopped walnuts

Preheat the oven to 375° and get out a 10-inch cast-iron skillet. Beat the egg whites until foamy, then add 1 tablespoon of the sugar and continue to beat until they hold soft peaks. In a separate bowl, beat the yolks until pale. Add the milk, then whisk in the flour, baking powder, and salt. Fold in the beaten whites, grated apple, and lemon juice. Melt the butter in the skillet, remove from the heat, and scrape the batter into the pan. Mix the cinnamon and walnuts with the remaining 2 tablespoons sugar and sprinkle over the top. Bake for 15 to 18 minutes, until the pancake is puffy and browned. Cut into wedges and serve at once.

Oatmeal Apple Fritters

Makes about 18 small fritters, serving 6

I like to make these in the fall, when the good local apples start coming in and summer's lighter breakfasts give way to more substantial ones. These are crispy little apple cakes, made with a rough-textured flour of ground walnuts and oatmeal. The difference between fritters and pancakes: fritters are fried in a bit of oil, whereas pancakes rest on a thin protective film of oil to keep them from sticking. The extra oil used for fritters makes them crisper than a pancake—the edges are the best, crispiest part—but you must take care that the oil is hot enough when you add the batter; if it isn't, the oil just soaks into the batter and makes the fritters sodden. These are great with a mug of warm cider.

½ cup rolled oats (*not* instant)
½ cup shelled walnuts
½ cup unbleached or whole wheat flour
1 teaspoon baking powder
¼ teaspoon salt
½ teaspoon ground cinnamon
3 large eggs
⅓ cup sugar
⅔ cup milk
2 tablespoons unsalted butter, melted
1 large apple, peeled, cored, and chopped, not too finely
¼ cup flavorless vegetable oil, approximately

Put the oats and nuts in a food processor and chop to a fine meal. Empty into a bowl and mix in the other dry ingredients. Set aside.

Using an electric mixer, beat the eggs and sugar on high speed for about 3 minutes, until light and lemon colored. Stir the milk into the dry mixture and set aside for several minutes, until the liquid is absorbed. Fold the egg mixture into the oat mixture, then stir in the melted butter and fold in the chopped apple.

Heat a tablespoon of the oil in a nonstick skillet over medium heat. When the oil is hot, scoop heaping tablespoons of batter into the pan; you should be able to cook 3 or 4 at a time without crowding them. Cook for about 1 minute on the first side, until golden and crusty, flip, then cook for about 1 minute on the second side. Serve hot with maple syrup and sour cream or yogurt.

Corn Fritters in Cornmeal Batter

Makes 18 fritters, serving about 6

These small fried cornmeal pancakes are made with a base of cornmeal porridge—cooked cornmeal and milk. The batter is then lightened with beaten egg whites, so these are especially soft and tender. These cornmeal fritters have the handy feature of being able to go with sweet or savory accompaniments. A plateful with maple syrup and a dab of sour cream is fine indeed, but they're equally at home with a splash of salsa and herb-laced sour cream. I like them with breakfast ham or bacon and a creamy scrambled egg or two, but they go with just about everything. For something more on the savory side, add a tablespoon each of minced parsley and onion.

⅓ cup yellow cornmeal, preferably stone-ground
1¼ cups milk
2 tablespoons unsalted butter, cut into several pieces
3 large eggs, separated
¼ teaspoon salt
2 tablespoons unbleached flour
1 teaspoon baking powder
1½ cups thawed frozen or freshly scraped corn kernels
6 tablespoons flavorless vegetable oil

Combine the cornmeal and milk in a small saucepan over medium heat. Cook the mixture, stirring almost continuously, until it becomes about as thick as porridge; it will take about 3 to 5 minutes. Scrape the mixture into a bowl, then whisk in the butter, egg yolks, and salt.

Using an electric mixer, beat the egg whites until they hold stiff peaks. Fold about a third of the whites into the cornmeal mixture, then fold the rest of them in until evenly blended. Combine the flour and baking powder. Sift it over the batter and fold it in. Fold in the corn.

Heat a tablespoon of the oil in a skillet over medium to medium-high heat; a nonstick skillet is best here. Drop heaped tablespoons of batter into the oil; do about 3 fritters at a time. Fry for about 2 minutes on the first side, then flip and cook for another minute on the second side. Repeat for the remaining batter, adding about a tablespoon of oil to the skillet for each batch. Serve them as they come off the skillet or hold them in a low oven until they're all cooked. Or fire up several larger skillets and cook them in a couple of quick volleys.

THE NO-MAPLE OPTION

It's heresy, in my neck of the woods, even to think about pancakes without real maple syrup. Nonetheless, there have been times when I've swallowed my regional pride in search of satisfying alternatives. For instance, I make a warm honey, butter, and orange juice emulsion for the Orange, Rye, and Fennel Seed Cakes on page 15 by whisking together about ½ cup honey with 2 tablespoons unsalted butter and about a tablespoon of orange juice concentrate in a small saucepan until warm.

In the summer we make a lot of impromptu fruit sauces with fresh seasonal berries. The Blueberry Banana Pancakes on page 12, for example, shine under a blanket of fresh blueberry sauce. My standard method is to put about 2 tablespoons of water—just enough to cover the bottom—in a small nonreactive saucepan. Then throw in a generous cup of berries and cook, partially covered, until they start breaking down and releasing their juices. If the berries seem to need it, I add a little sugar or lemon juice to bring out the flavor and cook them over moderate heat, uncovered, until the sauce thickens just a little. You don't really need to use cornstarch to thicken the sauce, because it should be thin enough to soak into the pancakes. Serve the sauce chunky or smooth, pureed in the food processor or blender. Strain, if desired, to remove small seeds from blackberries or raspberries.

Yogurt is a great topping base. Try whisking about 3 parts yogurt with 1 part of either honey and molasses or maple syrup and spoon that onto your cakes. For a richer version, replace the yogurt with sour cream or whipped cream.

In addition to sauces, it's appetizing to dress up your pancakes with related garnishes. Sliced bananas will enhance the Banana Walnut Hotcakes on page 13. And a scattering of toasted pecan halves will be appreciated on the Lemon Feather Cakes on page 16.

Ben's Favorite Whole Wheat Waffles

Makes about 10 waffles

If I can brag here for just a minute, my 12-year-old son, Ben, is a born cook and—like his old man—loves breakfast. There is almost nothing he likes as much as waffles. This recipe was transcribed from a long sheet of ragged, oil-stained paper that's been floating around our kitchen for about six years, getting lost now and then but always resurfacing. At the top of the page it says "my favorites." Ben thinks that the whole wheat flour gives them extra crunch, and I agree. We do these up with strawberries and whipped cream on Karen's birthday in early summer, with ice cream and fresh fruit for birthday breakfasts, and with just plain butter or sour cream and maple syrup for every day.

3 large eggs
2 cups milk
2 tablespoons sugar
2 cups whole wheat flour
1 tablespoon baking powder
½ teaspoon salt
1 teaspoon ground cinnamon
½ teaspoon ground nutmeg
6 tablespoons unsalted butter, melted, or
    flavorless vegetable oil

In a mixing bowl, beat the eggs with the milk and sugar. Set aside. In a large bowl, toss together the dry ingredients. Make a well in the center and stir in the liquid just until the batter is smooth; do not overbeat. Let the batter sit for a minute or two, then gently stir in the butter or oil.

Cook the waffles on a preheated waffle iron for approximately 4 to 5 minutes, until brown and crisp; the timing will depend on the type of waffle iron you use. Serve right away, topped as you like and dusted with a little extra nutmeg.

Classic Sour Cream Waffles

Makes 5 servings

What's a classic waffle? One whose crackling, crisp, golden brown crust breaks into a tender, cakelike interior. One so good you could eat great stacks of them, awash in warm maple syrup, fresh berries, and yogurt. Like this one. These waffles will hold for up to 30 minutes in a very low oven if you want to serve everyone at once. Beyond that, however, they start to dry out.

1½ cups unbleached flour
½ cup whole wheat flour
2 teaspoons baking powder
1 teaspoon baking soda
½ teaspoon salt
3 large eggs, separated
1½ cups sour cream
1⅓ cups milk or light cream
½ cup (1 stick) unsalted butter, melted and cooled

Sift the dry ingredients into a bowl and set aside. In a large bowl, beat the egg yolks, sour cream, and milk. Gradually whisk the dry mixture into the liquid just until smooth. Gently stir in the melted butter. Let the batter sit for several minutes.

In a separate bowl, beat the egg whites until stiff. Fold the whites into the batter. Ladle the batter into a preheated waffle iron and cook for 4 to 5 minutes, until the surface of the waffle is golden brown and crisp.

. . . .

Scotch Oat and Corn Waffles

Makes about 10 waffles, serving 5

Steel-cut oats, also known as *Scotch oatmeal,* are chopped kernels of oat grain. Some would argue that they're the purest and best-tasting type of oats, though there's no question they have a chewier, nuttier texture than rolled oats. Here the oats are soaked ahead to soften them a bit but not so much that they become mushy. The heat of the waffle iron seems to toast the oats near the surface, because they have a decidedly crunchy exterior; at least that's the way it works with my waffle iron, and I hope with yours. Remember that because most waffles have a fair amount of butter or oil in them, you don't really need to add butter to the top; just a dab of yogurt is good.

½ cup steel-cut oats
boiling water
1¼ cups unbleached flour
½ cup yellow cornmeal, preferably stone-ground
1 tablespoon baking powder
½ teaspoon salt
2 tablespoons light brown sugar, packed
3 large eggs
1½ cups milk
½ cup chopped raisins
7 tablespoons flavorless vegetable oil or unsalted butter,
   melted and cooled

Put the oats in a heatproof bowl and pour enough boiling water over them to cover by an inch or so. Cover and set aside for 45 to 60 minutes. When the grain has softened but is still pleasantly chewy, drain it in a sieve, gently pressing out most of the liquid with the back of a spoon.

Mix the dry ingredients in a bowl, breaking up any lumps of sugar with your fingers. In another large bowl, whisk the eggs until frothy, then blend in the milk, raisins, and oats. Gradually whisk the dry ingredients into the liquid, then blend in the oil until the batter is uniform. Set aside for 10 minutes while you preheat a waffle iron.

Ladle the batter into the preheated waffle iron and cook for 3 to 5 minutes, depending on your iron (mine always takes about 4½ minutes), until the waffle is golden brown and crisp. Serve the waffles as they come off the iron or hold them in a 200° oven for up to 30 minutes, uncovered.

Orange French Toast with Toasted Almonds

Makes 4 to 5 servings

Some people save French toast for weekends, but it's so simple to make that there's really no reason to. In fact it's no more difficult than breaking a few eggs and heating a skillet. We love this version, spiked with orange zest. The extra egg yolks make the toast pillowy soft and tender. Use just about any bread; a light egg bread is good, but so is whole wheat or caraway rye. Orange extract is available at health food stores.

1 cup shelled almonds
2 large eggs
4 large egg yolks
1 cup milk or light cream
1 tablespoon sugar
1 teaspoon orange extract
½ teaspoon vanilla extract
¼ teaspoon ground cinnamon
unsalted butter for the griddle
8 to 10 slices of bread

Preheat the oven to 350° and spread the almonds out on a large baking sheet. Toast the almonds for 8 to 10 minutes, until fragrant. Dump them onto a cutting board and let cool. Chop by hand, not too finely, and set aside.

In a large bowl, whisk the eggs and egg yolks until frothy, then blend in the milk, sugar, orange and vanilla extracts, and cinnamon. Melt a little unsalted butter in a skillet. As the butter melts, dunk 2 or 3 pieces of bread in the custard—as many pieces as will fit comfortably in the skillet at once—then place them in the skillet. Fry the bread over medium heat for about 1½ to 2 minutes on the first side, flip them once, and fry almost as long on the second side. Repeat with the remaining slices. Serve buttered, with a little warm maple syrup or honey, garnished generously with the toasted almonds. If you like, grate just a touch of lemon zest over the top.

Banana-Stuffed French Toast with Banana Cream

Makes 4 servings

I love plain French toast, but I think of this version in a class by itself. And it isn't the least bit involved; any klutz can pull this off. You begin with a loaf of unsliced white or light whole wheat bread. The loaf is sliced into thickish slices, each with a hinged "pocket" where you tuck sliced bananas, brown sugar, and chopped nuts. And you know the rest from there—just dip and fry. We serve this with a big dollop of banana-flavored whipped cream plunked on top, but you can get really carried away and serve it with coffee ice cream (for a special brunch) or just plain maple syrup if your situation calls for a bit more restraint.

1 whole loaf of light bread, unsliced
4 small or 2 large just-ripe bananas
¼ cup packed light brown sugar
½ cup chopped pecans or walnuts
3 large eggs
¾ cup milk or light cream
1 tablespoon sugar
½ teaspoon vanilla extract
¼ cup unsalted butter

BANANA CREAM

1 small ripe banana
1 cup heavy cream
⅓ cup confectioners' sugar

Slice the loaf as follows: If you're using a round loaf, start about a third of the way into it so you aren't using the small ends. Using a sharp serrated knife, slice all the way through the loaf. Move the knife over ¼ inch and make another slice, but don't cut all the way through; leave a little ½-inch hinge. Now move the knife over another ¼ inch and cut all the way through the loaf. You will now have 2 slices of bread connected by a crust hinge. Repeat to make 3 more bread pockets.

Peel the bananas and cut each one into 3 lengthwise slices; if you're using large bananas, cut them in half first. Lay 3 slices inside each pocket, making a banana sandwich. Sprinkle the tops of the bananas with a tablespoon of brown sugar and about 2 tablespoons of chopped nuts.

In a large bowl, lightly whisk the eggs until frothy, then whisk in the milk, sugar, and vanilla. Set aside. Put 1 tablespoon of the butter in a skillet just slightly larger than your bread and place it on the burner with the heat off.

Make the banana cream: Mash the banana with a potato masher and scrape it onto a plate. Cover with plastic and place in the freezer. Pour the cream into the same bowl you mashed the banana in and beat it with an electric mixer until it holds soft peaks. Add the confectioners' sugar and beat until it stiffens a little more, then beat the banana in on low speed. Cover and refrigerate.

Begin heating the butter over medium heat. Once it has melted, quickly rewhisk the egg mixture, then dip both sides of the sandwich into it, letting it saturate for 5 or 6 seconds. Place the sandwich in the skillet and fry over medium heat for 2 to 3 minutes on each side, until golden brown. If you would like to serve these all at once, put them on serving plates and hold in a preheated low oven. Add another tablespoon of butter to the skillet and repeat for the remaining sandwiches. (Note: The reason these are cooked in a small skillet is to reduce the amount of butter smoking from the hot skillet. A larger skillet can be used so you can cook a couple at a time, but expect some smoking.) Serve hot, with maple syrup and a big dollop of the banana cream on top.

Phyllo Apple Crepes with Vanilla Custard Sauce

Makes 3 servings

The packaged phyllo dough we've all used over the years to make such Greek delights as baklava and spanakopita also makes an excellent surrogate crepe wrapper. As you would imagine, the thin phyllo makes a very different kind of shell than a tender crepe; it is characteristically crisp-brittle, closer to puff pastry than a real crepe. Here the sheets are filled with gently sautéed apple slices, caramelized in brown sugar and dusted with cinnamon. Once baked, they're brushed with honey and lemon and then served with cold Vanilla Custard Sauce, without which they just aren't the same.

> 6 tablespoons unsalted butter
> 3 large Golden Delicious apples, peeled, cored, and cut into
>   ¼-inch-thick slices
> ¼ cup packed light brown sugar
> ½ teaspoon ground cinnamon
> ½ cup finely chopped walnuts
> 6 full sheets of packaged phyllo dough
> 2 tablespoons honey
> juice of 1 lemon
> 1 recipe Vanilla Custard Sauce (page 227), chilled

Gently warm 2 tablespoons of the butter in a large skillet. Add the apple slices and sauté them over medium-low heat for 30 seconds, turning with a spatula. Push the apples to one side and stir the brown sugar into the skillet. As it starts to caramelize, toss the apples in it just to coat them. Remove from the heat and immediately scrape the apples into a bowl. Gently toss in the cinnamon and walnuts. Melt the rest of the butter in a small skillet and set it aside. Preheat the oven to 375° and lightly butter a large baking sheet.

Lay the sheets of phyllo out flat and cut them in half across the width. Place one stack on top of the other. Lightly brush the top sheet of phyllo with melted butter, then remove it from the pile and place it on the counter with a short edge facing you. Butter a second sheet and lay it on top of the first. Cover the main pile of phyllo with a piece of plastic wrap while you assemble each crepe.

Starting about 1½ inches in from the short edge closest to you, lay an overlapping line of apple slices across the width, stopping about 1½ inches from both sides. Fold the long sides over until they meet the filling, then fold the bottom margin up over the apples. Roll the crepe up until it is sealed, then place it on the baking sheet seam down. Brush the exposed surface with a little butter. Make 5 more crepes in the same manner. Bake for 35 to 40 minutes, until golden brown. While they bake, warm the honey and lemon juice with any butter that remains in the small skillet.

When the crepes are golden, remove them from the oven. Brush each one with some of the warm honey mixture. Wait 5 minutes, then brush again. Spoon some of the custard sauce onto each serving dish and place 2 crepes on top of it.

Basic Crepes

Makes 12 crepes

Crepes were once all the rage—special crepe pans, a zillion crepe cookbooks, and all that—but now they've settled back down to a more comfortable status as just plain good food. Crepes aren't something most of us make often, but there are those special times when crepes are just the sort of indulgence to celebrate the first native strawberries (Sugar-Dusted Strawberry Crepes, page 36) or some other notable event. The crepe pancakes themselves are a snap to prepare; the fillings can be as simple as a spoonful of jam or more involved, like creamed vegetables.

I like a basic 8- or 9-inch nonstick omelet pan for making crepes. The batter is scooped into the pan, which is twirled slightly to spread it out, then the excess batter is poured back into the bowl. Pouring the batter out leaves a sort of tail or handle that's useful for flipping the crepes, the only tricky part of the operation. A spatula can be trouble because it's hard to maneuver under the pancake without tearing it. I find flipping the crepes by hand the easiest way to do it; to prevent the crepe from burning my fingers, I run my fingers under cold water, then quickly dry them off right before I flip the crepe—works like a charm. The first crepe or two are usually experimental (they tend to get a bit mangled), but after that it's smooth sailing. Sprinkle any botched crepes with sugar and eat them right out of hand.

> 3 large eggs
> 1½ cups milk
> 1 cup unbleached flour; for whole wheat crepes, use ½ cup
>   unbleached and ½ cup whole wheat flour
> 1 tablespoon sugar (omit for savory crepes)
> ¼ teaspoon salt
> 1 tablespoon unsalted butter, melted, plus a little extra for
>   the pan

Put all of the ingredients except the butter in a blender or food processor and puree until smooth. Add the butter and puree briefly again. Pour the batter into a large measuring cup or pitcher and let sit at room temperature for 30 minutes, or overnight in the refrigerator, covered.

When you're ready to cook the crepes, heat an 8- or 9-inch nonstick skillet over medium heat. Rub a little butter in the pan with paper towels, then ladle a scoop of the batter into the pan. Immediately tilt and twirl the pan to spread the batter evenly around the bottom of the pan, then pour off the excess; from the time the batter hits the pan until the time you pour off the excess, no more than 3 to 5 seconds should pass.

Cook the crepe on the first side for 45 to 60 seconds, then loosen the "tail" (where you poured off the excess) with a knife; flip the crepe and cook on the other side for about 30 more seconds. Slide the crepe out of the pan onto a baking sheet lined with wax paper. Continue to cook the crepes in this manner, brushing the pan with butter after every other crepe. Place a piece of wax paper between crepes. The crepes can be used right away, or you can let the stack cool, then cover it with plastic wrap and refrigerate overnight. They can also be frozen for several weeks—well wrapped in plastic—then thawed at room temperature.

Variations: *Cornmeal Crepes:* substitute ⅓ cup yellow or white cornmeal, preferably stone-ground, for an equal amount of unbleached flour.

Vanilla Crepes: Put the milk into a saucepan. Scrape the seeds from half a vanilla bean into the milk; add the pod to the milk too. Heat the milk to near boiling, then remove from heat. Cover and cool to room temperature. Remove the pod, then proceed as directed.

Cornmeal Cheese Crepes with Peach Salsa

Makes 4 servings

Once you get into the swing of making crepes (if you aren't already), you'll find yourself making them over and over again. Why? Because they're so adaptable, so easy to tuck with leftovers, a bit of ham, cheese, or cooked vegetables for a simple breakfast. Here we sprinkle delicate cornmeal crepes with a little sharp Cheddar cheese and a scattering of corn. They're then folded into quarters, fried in a little butter until the cheese is just starting to ooze, and served hot with a sprightly salsa featuring fresh summer peaches. It's a combination that works well, these sweet and savory flavors of deep summer bringing out the best in each other. Do try to make the salsa a day ahead, both to simplify life on the day you plan to serve this and so the salsa flavors have time to mingle and mellow.

 SALSA

   3 medium-small ripe peaches
   ½ teaspoon sugar
   1 large green or red bell pepper, finely chopped
   4 to 5 pickled hot cherry peppers, drained and finely chopped

1 red onion, finely chopped
½ cup chopped parsley or part parsley and part cilantro
3 tablespoons fresh lemon juice
3 tablespoons fresh lime juice
a big pinch of salt

 ## CREPES AND FILLING

1 recipe Cornmeal Crepes (page 32)
2 cups frozen or fresh corn kernels
½ pound grated extrasharp Cheddar cheese or smoked
    Cheddar cheese
2 to 3 tablespoons unsalted butter for the pan

First make the salsa: Peel, pit, and slice the peaches, cutting the slices crosswise into small pieces. Drop them into a bowl and sprinkle with the sugar. Prepare the remaining salsa ingredients, adding them to the bowl with the peaches as each one is ready. Stir to blend thoroughly, then cover and refrigerate.

Prepare the cornmeal crepes if you haven't already. Set aside. If the corn is frozen, boil it in a little water for several minutes, until done. If you're using freshly scraped corn, boil it in a little water for about 1 minute. Either way, drain the corn thoroughly. Spread briefly on a triple layer of paper towels to dry further, then empty it into a bowl.

Working with 1 crepe at a time, sprinkle half of the surface thoroughly but not too heavily with grated cheese. Scatter about 2 tablespoons corn over the cheese, then fold the uncovered half over the covered half. Fold the crepe again, forming a quarter wedge. Repeat for the remaining crepes; there should be enough filling for 12 crepes.

Melt some of the butter over medium heat in a large skillet. Add the crepes and fry on each side until golden, about 1½ minutes per side; don't crowd them in the pan. Keep them warm in a low oven while you fry the remaining ones, then serve hot with the salsa on the side. For a nice presentation, put 3 crepes on each serving plate with the points touching and a big pile of salsa right in the middle.

Crepes with Cherry Preserves and Toasted Almonds

Makes 4 to 6 servings

One of the best ways to eat crepes is with a simple filling of your favorite preserves; just spread it on straight from the jar and you're in business. Then it's a simple matter to fry them in a little butter and add an accenting flavor. Here I use cherry preserves and scatter the top with chopped toasted almonds. These are excellent just the way they are, dusted with confectioners' sugar, but there's room on the plate between the crepes for a quick compote of pitted cherries and fresh summer berries.

1 recipe Vanilla Crepes (page 33)
1 cup shelled almonds
1 10-ounce jar cherry preserves
unsalted butter for the pan
confectioners' sugar for dusting the top

Prepare the crepes and set them aside; they can be made a day ahead if you like. Spread the almonds on a baking sheet and toast them for about 8 to 10 minutes in a preheated 350° oven, until fragrant. Turn the almonds out onto a counter or plate and let them cool, then chop them finely by hand and set aside.

Spread about 1 tablespoon of preserves over the surface of a crepe. Fold the crepe in half, enclosing the filling, then fold in half again to form a quarter wedge. Repeat for the remaining crepes, laying them aside on a sheet of wax paper.

Melt about 1 tablespoon of butter over medium-low heat in a large skillet. Add as many crepes to the pan as will fit comfortably, then fry for about 1½ minutes on the first side, until lightly browned. Flip the crepes and fry on the second side for about 1 minute more. Repeat for the remaining crepes.

Serve the crepes hot or warm, 2 or 3 per person. Sprinkle with the chopped almonds and dust the top of them with confectioners' sugar; arrange the wedges on opposite sides of the plate, with the tips just touching.

Sugar-Dusted Strawberry Crepes

Makes 12 crepes

There are a number of ways to make strawberry crepes. The simplest way is just to spread them with strawberry preserves, fold them into quarters, and fry in a little butter. Eat as is or add sliced strawberries and whipped cream. This recipe is a little more elaborate—a fresh strawberry puree is added to whipped cream, then the cream and sliced strawberries are rolled up in the crepe. The top is dusted with confectioners' sugar; it's like eating a sugar-dusted strawberry cloud. There's nothing here that can't be done the afternoon or evening ahead of your planned breakfast, and nothing so complicated it can't also be done the same day. The one requirement is really good and ripe native strawberries; without them this just isn't worth the effort.

    1 recipe Basic Crepes (page 31)
    1 quart strawberries
    1 tablespoon granulated sugar
    1 tablespoon cornstarch
    1½ cups heavy cream
    ¼ cup confectioners' sugar, plus more for dusting the crepes
    ½ teaspoon lemon extract or a little finely grated lemon zest

Prepare the crepes if you haven't already and set them aside; they should be at room temperature when you prepare this recipe. Clean and hull the strawberries, setting aside half of them. Coarsely cut up the remaining half and put them in a bowl, tossing with the tablespoon of sugar. Set aside for 10 minutes, then mash to a coarse puree with a potato masher or fork. Transfer the puree to a nonreactive saucepan, add the cornstarch, and bring to a boil over medium heat. Boil, stirring, for 1 minute, until the mixture has thickened and become translucent. Scrape into a bowl and cool in the refrigerator.

Meanwhile, whip the cream until it is somewhat thick. Add the ¼ cup confectioners' sugar and continue to beat until thickened but not grainy. Add the lemon extract and fold in the cooled strawberry puree.

Assemble the crepes right on the wax paper. Cut several strawberries into slices and make an overlapping line of them down the center of a crepe. Top with several big dollops of the strawberry cream, then roll it up; you may find the wax paper handy for rolling the crepes rather than handling the crepes themselves. Roll 2 crepes onto a plate side by side, dust generously with confectioners' sugar, and serve.

GOOD GRAINS:
BREAKFAST CEREALS AND DUMPLINGS

WHEN DR. SYLVESTER GRAHAM —father of the flour and crackers that bear his name—was mugged by bakers in Boston for preaching the healthy gospel of whole grains, he overlooked a maxim and selling point good cooks have known for thousands of years: that the way to a man's heart is through his stomach. Had the good doctor simply focused on the intrinsic good flavor of whole grains, maybe handed out some recipe leaflets to promote his cause, there's no doubt his whole grain campaign would have had immediate and impressive results. Instead, most people passed him off as a crank.

Sadly, I think whole grain cereals still suffer from poor public relations. As kids, weren't we told to eat our porridge because it was *good* for us? Didn't anybody consider that if it *tasted* good we would have gladly eaten it? Lodged in our collective memory, then, is the uncomfortable notion that we *had* to eat grains; and coercion is shaky ground on which to build any relationship. Even granola, the most mainstream of the generic whole grain cereals, still has a reputation for being hippie food, though I haven't seen a hippie around in ages. Frankly, much of the whole grain cereal I remember as a kid did taste terrible—porridges as stiff as plaster and granola leaden with oil and sickeningly sweet.

So I think it's time we started taking whole grain cereals, hot and cold, seriously—not as health food but as just plain good food. Today we must bring a new sensibility to whole grains. Starting with good, preservative-free grains, we understand that the flavors of whole grains must speak for themselves. Our cooking methods should preserve the goodness that is there. Embellishments, like fruits, nuts, sweeteners, and milk or cream, should enhance and not overpower.

Here are recipes for hot cereals using a spectrum of inexpensive whole grains:

wheat, brown rice, rye, cornmeal, oats, and others. Some of them are coarse, some fine, depending on the texture of the grain you start with. All are no more difficult to prepare than boiling water. There are instant versions using convenient couscous, smooth cornmeal mushes, and hearty mixed porridges with a hodgepodge of good grains. This is deeply satisfying food for body and soul.

Granola is making a comeback these days. My kids and I eat it like there's no tomorrow—and there usually isn't unless I double the recipe. We still give granola for Christmas presents, take it on ski trips, and pack it into little bags for long rides in the car. I offer two choices, including one sweetened with maple syrup and a low-fat version sweetened with fruit juice. Take your pick.

Dumplings are a good old-fashioned dish we'd do well to revive for breakfast; I think of them as a sort of leavened hot cereal. When we do think of dumplings, they're normally of the savory kind, but here are a few sweet ones that you'll find make a hearty, filling morning dish.

Most dumplings are cooked in pretty much the same manner: liquid is brought to a simmer, then the biscuitlike dough is added by the spoonful. The dumplings are covered, so they cook by steam from above as well as below. They swell some, so leave several inches between them.

Grains are at the base of the new food pyramid issued by the government, so we should incorporate as many servings per day into our diet as possible. Giving grains a regular slot in your breakfast routine makes good nutritional sense and leaves you with an exciting array of tasty dishes to choose from.

Maple Cinnamon Granola

Makes about 3 pounds

There are probably as many granola recipes as there are ex-hippies. This one is typical of ex-hippies who like maple syrup and who are lucky enough to live where it's produced; the less fortunate will have to substitute honey. The salted peanuts give you that wonderful sweet and slightly salty contrast that wakes up the taste buds, but you can go with unsalted roasted peanuts or roasted cashews if you prefer—or walnuts or almonds for that matter. This recipe makes a lot, but it keeps almost forever in sealed bags. Unsweetened shredded coconut is available at health food stores.

> 2 pounds (about 10 cups) rolled oats (*not* instant)
> 1 cup raw hulled sunflower seeds
> ½ cup sweetened flaked coconut or unsweetened
>   shredded coconut
> 1 teaspoon ground cinnamon
> 3 tablespoons water
> ½ teaspoon salt
> 1 cup maple syrup
> ½ cup flavorless vegetable oil
> 1 teaspoon vanilla extract
> 2 cups raisins
> 2 cups roasted salted peanuts or other nuts

Preheat the oven to 300° and lightly oil 2 large jelly roll pans; your pans should have raised edges so the stuff doesn't fly all over the place when you stir it. In your largest bowl, mix the oats, sunflower seeds, coconut, and cinnamon. Bring the water to a boil in a small saucepan and stir in the salt to dissolve. Once it dissolves, add the maple syrup and oil and bring to a simmer. Remove from the heat, whisk in the vanilla, and immediately pour over the oat mixture in a stream, tossing the mixture at the same time so everything moistens evenly. Roll up your sleeves and continue to mix—rubbing everything together—for another minute.

Divide the granola between the pans, spreading it out evenly. Roast the granola for about 45 minutes, stirring every 15 minutes. Rotate the sheets from side to side or top to bottom each time you stir it so everything cooks evenly. Cool the granola on the sheets, then store it in 2 large plastic bags. Mix half of the raisins and peanuts into each bag when you package it.

Apple Apricot Granola

Makes about 9 cups

Granolas are supposed to be healthy, but the fact is they often contain excessive amounts of fat and sugar, which add little to the finished product. Here's a granola that uses no added fat and takes its sweetening, in large measure, from concentrated fruit juice. It tastes wonderful; you won't have a clue that anything is missing. The fruit juice permeates the granola with an almost tropical essence, and the pieces of dried apricots and apple add a delicious, colorful touch. This makes an excellent topping for fresh fruit salad or yogurt and would be a great gift for a friend, packed in a cellophane bag tied with a pretty ribbon. Unsweetened shredded coconut is available at health food stores.

> 7 cups rolled oats (*not* instant)
> 2 cups thinly sliced almonds
> 1½ cups sweetened flaked coconut or unsweetened shredded coconut
> 1½ cups good-quality apple-apricot juice, such as After the Fall brand
> ½ teaspoon salt
> ⅓ cup mild honey, such as orange blossom or clover
> finely grated zest of 1 lemon or orange
> ½ teaspoon vanilla or almond extract
> 1½ cups chopped dried apricots
> 1 cup chopped dried apples

Mix the oats, almonds, and coconut in a very large bowl and set aside. Lightly oil 2 large jelly roll pans and preheat the oven to 325°.

Bring the juice to a boil in a large saucepan and boil for 5 to 10 minutes, until reduced by about half; to check, simply pour it directly from the pan into a glass measuring cup. When it is reduced by about half—don't fret if you're a little over or under—stir in the salt to dissolve it, then the honey and zest. Heat very briefly, just to loosen the honey. Remove from the heat and stir in the vanilla.

Divide the granola between the pans, spreading it evenly. Roast the granola for about 40 minutes, until golden brown. After the first 15 minutes, stir the granola every 10 minutes with a spatula. Take care to bring the stuff near the edges inward and on the bottom upward. Also, switch the positions of the pans top to bottom or side to side. Cool the granola on the sheets. Mix in the chopped dried fruits before storing in airtight containers.

Annie's Toasted-Nut Muesli

Makes 4 to 5 servings

Muesli is a Swiss breakfast food, a sort of damp granola if you will. Unlike granola, however, the oats are not generally toasted; they're just moistened with milk. This recipe is an old family favorite of my friend Annie, who grew up in Switzerland in the town of Trübbach. This is the basic muesli Annie's mother used to make, generally topping it off with whatever fresh fruit was in season—strawberries, fresh peaches, or other berries. If you can find them, Annie says red currants are particularly good. Yogurt or yogurt cheese (page 230) is an especially good topping for fresh fruit. To save a little time in the morning, you can toast the nuts the day before.

½ cup shelled hazelnuts
½ cup shelled walnuts
½ cup raisins
1 cup rolled oats (*not* instant)

milk, about 1 cup
1 tart, juicy apple, such as Granny Smith
juice of ½ lemon
2 tablespoons honey or maple syrup

Preheat the oven to 350°. Spread the nuts on a large baking sheet, keeping the hazelnuts and walnuts in separate sections. Toast them for approximately 10 minutes, until fragrant. The walnuts may actually toast more quickly than the hazelnuts, whose skins should appear blistered for the most part. If this is the case, just slide the walnuts off the sheet into a separate pile on the counter and toast the hazelnuts a minute or two longer. Slide the hazelnuts onto a kitchen towel, fold the towel over them, and rub off the skins; don't worry if a few pieces of skin adhere on some of the nuts. Set the nuts aside to cool.

In a small bowl, barely cover the raisins with warm water and set them aside to plump. Put the oats in a large bowl and add just enough milk to cover. Cover with plastic wrap and refrigerate for 15 minutes.

After 15 minutes, peel the apple and grate it into a bowl. Squeeze the lemon juice right over the grated apple, tossing to mix. Mix the apple with the oats, then chop all of the nuts coarsely and add them too. Drain the raisins and stir them in along with the honey. Let everything sit for a few minutes, then stir and serve with fresh fruit and yogurt if you like.

Baked Corn and Oat Cereal

Makes about 10 cups

When we think of homemade dry cereals, we generally think of one thing— granola. Here's a slightly different approach—a dry cereal made of corn bread croutons. The corn bread is baked in a jelly roll pan, cooled, then cut into squares. The squares are dried in the oven—as you would croutons—cooled, and then stored in an airtight container. I like to mix this with blueberries in the summer and dried sweetened cranberries in the cooler months; but don't add the dried fruit to the same container as the cereal, because it tends to rehydrate the cereal, which then loses its crunch.

> 1½ cups unbleached flour
> 1 cup white or yellow cornmeal, preferably stone-ground
> ½ cup rolled oats (*not* instant)
> ⅓ cup packed light brown sugar
> 1 tablespoon baking powder
> ¾ teaspoon salt
> 1 large egg
> 1¾ cups water
> finely grated zest of 1 lemon (optional)

Lightly butter a 12- by 18-inch jelly roll pan. Line it with a sheet of wax paper and butter the paper. Preheat the oven to 400°.

Mix the dry ingredients in a large bowl. Whisk the egg in a separate bowl, then blend in the water and lemon zest if you're using it. Make a well in the dry ingredients, add the liquid, and stir to blend. Let the batter sit for 2 or 3 minutes, then scrape it into the pan. Bake for 20 minutes.

Turn the bread out onto a rack and peel off the wax paper. Cool to room temperature, then slice the bread into approximately ¾-inch squares. Set the oven at 275°.

Spread the squares on 1 or 2 large cookie sheets. Bake for 35 to 45 minutes, until the cubes are thoroughly dry. If they start to turn noticeably browner, they're done; best if you catch them before they get too brown. Cool the cubes right on the sheets. When cooled, immediately store in an airtight container.

Cornmeal Mush, Creamy and Fried

Makes 4 or more servings

Cornmeal cooked in nothing more than boiling water makes a soul-satisfying hot cereal: cornmeal mush. The name *mush* doesn't really do it justice and in fact sounds less than appetizing—certainly not as romantic as *polenta,* which it is. Mush can go one step farther than a hot cereal. Poured into a pan and chilled overnight, it becomes firm enough to cut and fry in butter. These firm slabs soften a little in the frying, but they do hold their shape and make a fine accompaniment on the breakfast platter for eggs, potatoes, meats, or what have you. It will keep in the refrigerator for a number of days, so you can use it throughout the week. Or you can cut and freeze the pieces individually, then fry them straight from the freezer.

1 quart water
1 teaspoon salt
1½ cups yellow cornmeal, preferably stone-ground
1 tablespoon unsalted butter

If you plan to fry the mush, butter a 9- by 13-inch casserole and set it aside.

Heat the water in a medium-size saucepan. Add the salt. As the water heats, add the cornmeal in a gradual, steady stream, whisking all the while.

When the mixture reaches a boil, switch to a wooden spoon. Reduce the heat to medium-low and cook the mush, stirring continuously, for about 10 minutes—if you're eating it hot—stirring in the butter during the last minute. Serve with maple syrup or brown sugar and milk.

If you're making fried mush, cook the cornmeal for another 3 or 4 minutes, stirring. Scrape it into the buttered pan and immediately smooth it with a spoon. Cool to room temperature—it must be thoroughly cooled—then cover with foil and refrigerate overnight.

To make fried mush, cut the firm-cooked cornmeal into whatever-size pieces you like. Dust the pieces in a little cornmeal. Melt some unsalted butter in a cast-iron skillet, then add the pieces and fry over medium-high heat for a couple of minutes on each side, until nicely browned. Serve hot, with sweet or savory foods.

Fried Cornmeal Mush with Maple-Hazelnut Syrup

Makes 5 or 6 servings

Fried cornmeal mush is a good foundation for sweet and savory breakfast foods alike. Here I serve it almost like pancakes, topped with a nutty maple sauce. Three or four of these on a plate, with a fruit compote or fresh sliced pears in the center, make an unexpected and exciting meal for a special weekend brunch with friends. Serve with a dollop of sour cream or mascarpone on the side.

½ cup shelled hazelnuts
⅓ cup maple syrup
¼ cup unsalted butter, cut into ½-inch pieces, plus more for frying
1 recipe Cornmeal Mush, refrigerated overnight (preceding recipe)
extra cornmeal for dusting the mush

Preheat the oven to 350°. Spread the hazelnuts on a baking sheet and toast them for approximately 12 minutes, until the skins have blistered. Place a clean kitchen towel on a counter and slide the nuts onto it. Fold the towel over the nuts and rub them vigorously to remove the skins. Don't worry if a few pieces of skin adhere to some of the nuts. Cool the nuts, then chop them finely by hand or in a food processor.

To make the sauce, gently heat the maple syrup in a small saucepan; do not let it boil. Add the butter a few pieces at a time, adding the rest as it melts. Stir in the nuts and remove from the heat.

Cut the mush into large serving-size pieces; 3 by 3 inches is a good size. Put some cornmeal on a plate and dredge 3 or 4 of the pieces in it. Melt about a tablespoon of butter in a large skillet. When the pan is hot, add the pieces and fry over medium-high heat for about 2 minutes on each side, until browned. Reheat the sauce, serving the fried mush with a spoonful of the sauce on top of each piece. Repeat for the remaining pieces, adding fresh butter to the pan for each new batch.

· · · · · · · · · · · · · ·

Spiced Pumpkin Cornmeal Mush

Makes 2 or 3 servings

This may indeed be the best way in the world to enjoy hot cereal; my 12-year-old son, Ben, an expert on this and all other matters, tells me so. And I agree. You will need to scout around for one essential ingredient: sweetened pumpkin butter. Plain pumpkin puree, even homemade, just doesn't pack the same amount of pumpkin punch as pumpkin butter. (If you can't find sweetened pumpkin butter at a local gourmet or health food store, send for the Pecan-Pumpkin Butter made by Muirhead; see Sources. It's sensational.) There are all sorts of fun ways to eat this: with maple syrup, brown sugar and butter, sweetened dried cranberries (which I would stir right into the mush a minute before it comes off the heat), and light cream or milk to moisten it. Put a dollop of pumpkin butter in the center of each bowlful and serve.

1½ cups water
¼ teaspoon salt
½ cup yellow cornmeal, preferably stone-ground
¼ teaspoon ground cinnamon
⅛ teaspoon ground nutmeg
⅛ teaspoon ground cloves
⅛ teaspoon ground ginger
⅓ cup sweetened pumpkin butter
1 tablespoon unsalted butter
¼ teaspoon vanilla extract

Start bringing the water to a boil in a small saucepan. Add the salt. As it heats, gradually whisk in the cornmeal; once the cornmeal has been added, switch to a wooden spoon. Reduce the heat to medium-low and stir the mush, continuously, for 5 minutes. (Use caution, because if you don't keep up with the stirring, the mixture may start to bubble up. Wear an oven mitt to protect yourself from possible splatters.) Stir in the spices and cook for another 5 minutes, stirring; it will become rather thick. About a minute before removing it from the heat, stir in the pumpkin butter and butter. Remove from the heat and stir in the vanilla. Serve at once.

Three-Grain Porridge

Makes 4 to 5 generous servings

I eat this hearty hot cereal when I'm in the mood for some serious whole grain nourishment. Unlike the usual creamy porridges, this one is nubby because you begin with whole or cracked grains. I actually got the idea from a wonderful diner in Hanover, New Hampshire, called Lou's. I was sitting a booth away from a fellow and his wife when the waitress plunked this huge bowl of nubby, steaming hot cereal in front of him. From the look he gave his wife and then me—by this point I was staring with genuine curiosity—you could tell this wasn't his usual bowl of Maypo. The man actually said to me, "It looks, well, healthy . . . at least." Anyway, I gleaned what I could about the cereal from the menu description and came up with this version. Keep in mind that you have to start this the night before; you just boil the grains and water for 5 minutes, then let it sit overnight. Simple and tasty.

4½ cups water
½ cup cracked wheat
½ cup pearled barley
½ cup steel-cut oats
scant teaspoon of salt

Bring the water to a boil in a medium-size saucepan. Stir in the grains and salt and bring the water back to a boil. Boil for 5 minutes, covered, then remove from the heat; do not remove the cover. Set the saucepan aside in a coolish spot for the night, but don't refrigerate it.

To serve the next morning, heat a little water in a skillet and add as much cereal as you want to serve. Heat, stirring, for 2 or 3 minutes, until heated through. Serve with brown sugar or maple syrup and milk or light cream. Or eat it any way you like—with cinnamon, raisins, chopped nuts, or just plain. Transfer any leftovers from the original saucepan to a bowl, cover, and refrigerate. You can reheat this in the same manner, storing it in the fridge for up to 4 days.

. . . .

Cream of Brown Rice Cereal

Makes 3 to 4 servings

I've fiddled around with all sorts of whole grain porridges, some of which were great and some of which even I—a regular whole grain champ—couldn't face first thing in the morning. This happens to be one I liked for its simplicity and subtlety— just ground short-grain brown rice cooked in water and a little milk. The texture is smooth and soft, like Cream of Wheat. It's wholesome, but it doesn't require the jaws of a granary rat or overwhelm you with untamed earthy flavors. You do have to stir the cereal pretty regularly while it cooks, but even those of us who suffer from early morning diminished mental capacity can handle moving a whisk in circles. Dress this up with brown sugar or maple syrup, milk or light cream, and maybe a few raisins or chopped dates.

1 cup short-grain brown rice
3 cups water or part water and part milk, approximately
¼ teaspoon salt

Using a blender, process the rice until it resembles a fine meal. It shouldn't be powder-fine but more the texture of the cornmeal you find at a health food store. Combine the rice meal, 2½ cups of the water, and the salt in a medium-size saucepan. Cook over medium to medium-low heat for about 10 minutes, whisking often to keep it from sticking. As it starts to thicken—after about 10 minutes— gradually add more water or milk. Continue to cook and whisk for about 10 minutes more, adjusting the consistency of the porridge with more liquid if necessary. The finished consistency should be smooth and creamy, neither too thick nor too thin. Serve piping hot.

Creamy Couscous with Dates and Walnuts

Makes 3 to 4 servings

I'm afraid my introduction to couscous wasn't in some Moroccan market or other exotic venue. It was on the pages of a favorite kid's book we used to have with a character named Couscous the Algerian detective. Besides being a detective, couscous is also a popular grain product now that instant varieties have become available; the stuff cooks in just minutes. It makes an easy, substantial breakfast cereal too—not unlike Cream of Wheat—here combined with a little vanilla for those who really like soft, comforting foods in the morning; Real Men and other ascetics can leave it out.

    1 cup instant couscous
    1 cup water
    ¼ teaspoon salt
    1 to 1⅓ cups milk as needed
    1 teaspoon vanilla extract (optional)
    chopped dates and walnuts for garnish

Put about a third of the couscous into a blender or coffee grinder and process to a flourlike texture (these fine particles help give the cereal a creamy consistency). Set aside. Bring the water to a boil in a small saucepan and stir in the salt. Stir in the couscous you haven't ground, cover, turn to the lowest possible heat, and cook for 2 minutes. Stir in 1 cup of the milk and the ground couscous and cook over medium heat, stirring, for about 3 or 4 minutes more, until it thickens to the desired consistency; thin with more milk if you want it more creamy than firm. When you remove the couscous from the heat, mix in the vanilla. Serve hot, topped as you please: with chopped walnuts and dates, brown sugar, and milk or light cream.

. . . .

Creamy Grits

Makes about 6 servings

I'm a Yankee, and like most Yankees my knowledge of grits is not all that impressive. I tried grits occasionally back in my navy days in Mississippi, but frankly I couldn't see what all the fuss was about. I couldn't tell if I just didn't care for grits or if the navy cooks hadn't quite gotten the knack of preparing them.

My awakening occurred only recently, when my friend Hoppin' John Taylor—author of *Hoppin' John's Lowcountry Cooking* (Bantam, 1992)—sent me a bag of his corn grits, stone-ground to his specifications, which is to say fairly coarse. His grits taste unlike anything I had in the navy or any of the commercial brands on the market. They're fresh tasting and nubby, and they make the most wonderful creamy grits you've ever had. (See Sources for ordering information.) You can use the following method to cook other brands of grits, but both the overall cooking time and the amount of water will probably be less. Besides eating them plain, grits are great with sauces; I love them served with Eggs Creole (page 74). They're good with breakfast fish or meats and with butter and maple syrup or brown sugar.

1 quart water
2 tablespoons unsalted butter
¼ to ½ teaspoon salt to taste
1 cup grits
2 to 3 cups milk, half-and-half, or light cream as needed

In a large saucepan, bring the water to a boil, adding the butter and salt as it heats. When the water reaches a boil, stir in the grits. Bring the grits back to a boil, then reduce the heat and cook at a low boil, stirring often, for 10 minutes. Stir ½ cup of the milk or cream into the grits. Reduce the heat to low and continue to cook, stirring, for 10 minutes more. As the liquid cooks off, continue adding milk about ½ cup at a time, stirring often to prevent sticking. Total cooking time should be about 1 hour, perhaps a little more. The finished consistency should be slightly soupy but still thick enough that it doesn't run on the plate. With commercial brands of grits, the cooking time will be less, as will the amount of extra liquid needed.

. . . .

Oatmeal Breakfast Dumplings

Makes 6 dumplings

I love these when I'm in the mood for oats—which is pretty often—but want something a little lighter and more interesting than plain hot oatmeal cereal. These oat cakes are spiked with walnuts and raisins and simmered gently in light cream; use milk for a less rich version. If you like, substitute some other nuts for the walnuts and dried apricots, apples, or prunes for the raisins. Because the cream base is sweetened, it isn't necessary to serve the dumplings with additional sweetening. I can eat two of these pretty easily, as can my older son, Ben. The little guys usually eat just one.

1 cup unbleached flour
1 cup rolled oats (*not* instant)
1½ teaspoons baking powder
¼ teaspoon salt
¼ teaspoon ground cinnamon
⅛ teaspoon ground nutmeg
2 tablespoons cold unsalted butter, cut into ¼-inch pieces
¼ cup finely chopped walnuts
¼ cup finely chopped raisins
1 large egg
⅓ cup milk, approximately
2 cups light cream or milk
⅓ cup packed light brown sugar
¼ teaspoon vanilla extract

In a large mixing bowl, toss together the flour, oats, baking powder, salt, cinnamon, and nutmeg. Stir. Add the butter and cut or rub it into the dry ingredients until it is thoroughly incorporated. Mix in the nuts and raisins.

Beat the egg with a fork in a glass measuring cup, then add enough milk—it should be about ⅓ cup—to make ½ cup liquid. Make a well in the dry ingredients, add the liquid, and stir until everything is blended.

Bring the cream, brown sugar, and vanilla to a simmer in a medium-size nonreactive saucepan. Reduce the heat to the lowest setting. Divide the batter in half with a large spoon. Use a serving spoon to take 3 equal spoonfuls from half of the batter and drop them into the simmering cream; leave about 3 inches between the dumplings so they have room to expand.

Cover the saucepan and simmer the dumplings for 8 minutes without removing the lid. To serve, spoon the dumplings into separate bowls, each with a little of the hot cream they were simmered in. Repeat the process with the remaining batter.

Whole Wheat Sour Cream Dumplings in Blueberry Sauce

Makes 8 dumplings

These are southern-style fruit dumplings—drop biscuit batter poached in a potful of simmering fruit. They're particularly nice in summer, when fresh berries are in season. We grow our own blueberries, but we also pick tons of wild blackberries in late summer, so I can tell you these are wonderful that way too. They're actually quite good with frozen berries; since you're cooking the fruit, the difference between fresh and frozen is not so obvious. Serve these in wide soup bowls, with a big spoonful of lemon yogurt to one side. The recipe can easily be halved (see note) if you're serving a smaller group.

1 quart blueberries
1½ cups water
⅔ cup sugar
1 cup whole wheat flour

½ cup unbleached flour
½ teaspoon ground cinnamon
½ teaspoon baking soda
¼ teaspoon salt
2 tablespoons cold unsalted butter
1 large egg
½ cup sour cream, approximately
2 to 3 tablespoons milk as needed

Combine the blueberries, water, and sugar in a large nonreactive pot or Dutch oven. Bring the mixture to a boil, then reduce the heat and cook at a low boil for 10 minutes. Stir the blueberry mixture occasionally while you make the dumplings.

In a bowl, mix the dry ingredients. Add the butter and cut or rub it into the dry mixture until it is thoroughly combined.

Using a fork, beat the egg in a glass measuring cup. Add enough sour cream to make ⅔ cup. Then make a well in the dry mixture and add the egg mixture and 2 tablespoons of the milk. Stir until you have a uniform, thick batter; if it seems dry, add the last tablespoon of milk.

Lower the heat under the blueberry mixture so it barely simmers. With a serving spoon, put 8 equal spoonfuls of batter into the berries, leaving room between them for expansion. Cover and simmer the dumplings gently for about 8 to 10 minutes. To serve, spoon 1 or 2 dumplings into each bowl with some of the blueberries.

Note: To halve the recipe, use the same amount of blueberries, water, and sugar. Halve all of the dumpling ingredients, using a full egg; add enough sour cream to make ⅓ cup. Then adjust the consistency with a little extra milk if necessary.

Eggs Just So

To a breakfast lover, one of the most beautiful phrases in the English language is *fresh eggs—$1.00 a dozen*. You still see these signs here in rural New Hampshire, small outposts where the resident hens soak up plenty of sunshine and feast on insects and grain. It might be a farm or just a small homestead where you drop your dollar in an old coffee can, but the eggs are uniformly good—brilliant golden yolks, firm body, and an incomparable flavor that elevates any egg dish a notch closer to perfection.

Farm fresh or from the market, Americans are eating far fewer eggs than we used to—about half as many as in 1970. The reason, of course, is concern over cholesterol. It may be heartening to note, then, that estimates of cholesterol found in eggs have recently been revised downward to 213 mg from 274. And studies have shown that eating eggs does not raise cholesterol in people with normal levels. Which is another way of saying there is definitely room for eggs in the diets of most healthy people, given an otherwise varied diet and a reasonably active life.

You can tell a lot about cooks by the way they make eggs. Some may think of egg cookery as a snap—"easy as scrambled eggs"—but that just isn't so. Eggs are extremely sensitive to mistreatment, and they magnify our abuses in boldface. Even a few extra seconds on the heat can turn soft curds into tough little nuggets. It takes a practiced hand—a knowledge of the relationship among your pan, the heat source, and the type of fat you may be using—to turn out creamy scrambled eggs and tender omelets. Cooked eggs don't hold well—something else a good cook honors. Think about it: when was the last time you had a chafing-dish egg that was anything but disappointing?

Eggs are an incredibly versatile food, and the variety of preparations in this chapter is testimony to that. They can be boiled, fried, poached, baked whole or in custards, souffléed, and turned into omelets or frittatas—a sort of egg pancake baked in a skillet with fillers like vegetables or even pasta. Eggs lend themselves to sweet and savory applications. Because the flavor is subtle, eggs mingle equally well with fruit, fresh herbs, vegetables, or cheese. They enrich a dish, lighten it, add color and tenderness—but they never overwhelm it.

Remember to consider textures when you're planning an egg dish as part of a larger menu. Egg dishes are soft and cry out for a crisp, crunchy, or otherwise contrasting counterpoint—toast is the obvious choice, but we also love whole wheat English muffins, firmer hashes, chili, and a host of other foods that eggs can go with or on. Eggs are old hat, but there's really no end to new ways we can enjoy them.

Basic Omelet

Makes 1 serving

There are a number of ways to make an omelet and many different personal styles. My wife and I have major differences on the subject. My omelets, for instance, are in and out of the pan in less than a minute—as I claim they should be. If Karen, on the other hand, starts making an omelet for breakfast, it *may* be done by lunch, but perhaps dinner, which is to say she likes her eggs essentially cremated; she enjoys them that way, and that is fine with me, but as you might guess, I seldom ask her to make me an omelet.

Here is your basic unfilled omelet, which my little kids call a rolled egg. I rarely eat unfilled omelets myself, and I offer this more to familiarize you with the technique than anything else. From this you can move easily into one of the filled omelets that follow. Since eggs aren't expensive, it might be worth a buck to buy a dozen and practice several in a row when no one is looking and you won't be disturbed; there's nothing more unnerving to a cook-in-the-making than a roomful of stifled guffaws or inquisitive kids wondering aloud why you're yelling things at your skillet that you usually only yell at Daddy when he forgets to pay the phone bill and they turn off the service.

Most people are terrified of making an omelet, at the risk of failure I suppose. You ask them why they don't make omelets, and they mumble something about being all thumbs or never having gone to omelet-making school—as if it were something only the gifted could learn. If little kids took the same attitude about learning to tie their shoes, we'd all be tripping over our laces. So just do it.

> 2 large eggs
> 1 teaspoon water (optional; some say it helps tenderize
>   the eggs)
> pinch of salt
> 1 tablespoon unsalted butter

Lightly beat the eggs, water, and salt in a small bowl. Place an omelet pan over medium-high heat and add the butter. When the butter starts to sizzle, but before it starts to brown, add the eggs. Immediately begin stirring the eggs with a fork in a circular motion; the tines of the fork should be parallel to the surface of the pan as you stir. As the eggs begin to set, in about 10 seconds—they will begin to form large curds that will bunch up if stirred more—stop the circular motion and push down on the forming curds with the tines of the fork to spread the curds out and facilitate even cooking. When you have a flat, even layer of egg, let it sit undisturbed for about 10 seconds, until the top looks almost fully set.

At that point, slide a spatula down the edge of the pan closest to the handle to begin folding the omelet in thirds. First, fold one-third of the omelet back over itself, as you would the first fold of a letter. Grasping the handle in an underhand fashion, palm up, tilt the pan so the unfolded third of the omelet slides onto your plate. Then tilt the pan even farther, folding the omelet out of the pan onto itself.

To make a filled omelet, have your filling ready and warm (or at room temperature if it is not a cooked filling). As soon as the eggs appear nearly set on top, spread your filling evenly across the center of the omelet, perpendicular to the handle. If you're using cheese, sprinkle it over the filling.

Next, as in the basic omelet, slide a spatula down the edge of the pan, close to the handle, and fold one-third of the omelet over the filling. Grasping the handle palm up, tilt the pan so the unfolded third of the omelet slides out of the pan onto the plate, then tilt the pan even farther, folding the omelet onto itself.

Spring Herb Omelet

Makes 2 omelets

Because they're the first herbs to appear in our garden, lovage and chives get quite a workout in our spring kitchen. Lovage is not a widely appreciated herb, but we love its powerful, celerylike flavor; I can seldom resist popping a leaf into my mouth on my rounds through the garden. Here I combine the lovage with three cheeses—ricotta, Parmesan, and provolone—which provides the proper creamy vehicle for the chives and lovage. Though this omelet is good alone, I try to make it when there's leftover tomato sauce in the fridge since tomatoes and lovage go so well together; I just reheat the sauce, adding the finely minced stalks from the lovage and a tiny splash of balsamic vinegar. Sauce each omelet—above or below—with about ½ cup of the sauce. Excellent with toasted slices of French or Italian bread.

⅓ cup ricotta cheese
⅓ cup loosely packed grated Parmesan cheese
¼ cup grated provolone cheese
2 tablespoons minced fresh chives
1 tablespoon minced fresh lovage
freshly ground black pepper to taste
pinch of salt
1 cup tomato sauce (optional)
2 Basic Omelets (see preceding recipe)

In a small bowl, mix the cheeses, herbs, pepper, and salt. Set aside. Prepare the sauce, bring slowly to a boil, and remove from the heat.

Prepare an omelet. Spoon half of the filling down the center of the omelet. Roll the omelet up, then turn off the heat and leave it in the pan for about 30 seconds to warm the filling. In the meantime, spread ½ cup of the sauce in a circle on your plate, then gently roll the omelet onto the sauce. Serve at once. Make a second omelet or cover and refrigerate the filling and sauce and use within 2 or 3 days.

. . . .

Eggplant and
Parmesan Cheese Omelet

Makes 1 omelet

Here is an omelet for eggplant lovers. Pieces of eggplant are cooked in a little olive oil until soft, with a bit of onion and garlic. This is rolled up in the omelet with the Parmesan cheese, then the omelet is gashed on top and moistened with reduced cream. In the summer, I sometimes add chopped fresh basil to the eggs before they go into the pan, and serve with a little pile of tomato sauce to one side.

1½ tablespoons olive oil
1 cup diced peeled eggplant in ½-inch cubes
1½ tablespoons minced onion
pinch of salt
1 garlic clove, minced
2 tablespoons heavy cream
1 Basic Omelet (page 56)
¼ cup grated Parmesan cheese

Heat the olive oil in a medium-size saucepan. Stir in the eggplant, onion, and salt. Cover and cook over medium heat for 5 minutes, stirring occasionally. If after several minutes the skillet appears dry because the eggplant has soaked up all the oil, press on the eggplant with a spatula to force some out of it. When the eggplant is soft but not mushy, stir in the garlic, cook for another 30 seconds, then scrape the filling onto a small plate.

Put the cream in your smallest skillet or saucepan and place it on a burner. Turn the heat on for 10 seconds or so to warm up the pan.

Prepare the omelet, adding the cooked filling and most of the Parmesan. Roll the omelet up, but leave it in the pan with the heat turned off. Quickly bring the cream to a boil and reduce it slightly. Slide the omelet out of the pan and make a ¼-inch-deep gash 3 inches long on top of the omelet. Pour in the reduced cream, then sprinkle the top of the omelet with a little more Parmesan cheese. Serve at once.

· · · · · · · · · · · · · · · ·

Guacamole Omelet on a Bed of Lettuce

Makes 2 omelets

Here's an attractive and delicious way to present an omelet—flanked closely on either side by crunchy lettuce greens (I like the heart of romaine or green leaf best). If you don't think you can handle lettuce before noon, this might change your mind (and if not, just wait until lunch or dinner to try this). The presentation is completed with a few tortilla chips for crunch, a topping of salsa, and an olive and parsley garnish. If it sounds or looks complicated, it really isn't. The guacamole is simple and straightforward; keeping the texture a little chunky, I think, adds more interest than smushing it into a baby food–like puree.

1 ripe Haas avocado (the small, pebbly-skinned type)
salt to taste
juice of ½ lemon
1 garlic clove (optional)
a handful of crisp lettuce leaves

4 good-quality pitted green olives
a small handful of parsley
¼ teaspoon grated lemon zest

¾ cup grated sharp Cheddar cheese
2 Basic Omelets (page 56)
½ cup salsa, approximately
handful of tortilla corn chips

Halve the avocado and scoop the flesh out into a bowl. Add a few pinches of salt to taste and most of the lemon juice, stirring and breaking the mixture up a little with a fork. If you want to add just a whisper of garlic, put the clove into a garlic press and press gently, expressing the first bit of juice into the guacamole. Set aside. Stack the lettuce leaves on top of one another and shred them with a sharp knife. Set them aside as well.

Make the garnish by finely chopping the olives, parsley, and lemon zest. Set aside in a small bowl.

Prepare an omelet as directed. When it is just about set, sprinkle half of the Cheddar cheese over the entire surface. Make a line of half the guacamole down the center of the omelet, then fold the egg over and slide it out of the pan as directed. Put a small pile of lettuce neatly to each side of the omelet. Spoon a little of the salsa over the omelet and dot the lettuce greens with it, then sprinkle half of the olive garnish over the omelet. Arrange a few chips at each end of the omelet. Repeat for the second omelet. Serve hot.

Blue Cheese and Walnut Omelet

Makes 2 omelets

Blue cheese is a good waker-upper, and it blends beautifully with ricotta and a scattering of walnuts. It takes a few extra minutes to toast the walnuts, but if you have the time, it's worth it. (Just spread them on a baking sheet and toast at 350° for 10 minutes.) Serve this with something crunchy; well-toasted bread is just the thing. In summer I would serve sliced cherry tomatoes on the side.

⅓ cup crumbled blue cheese
⅓ cup ricotta cheese
¼ cup chopped toasted walnuts
1½ tablespoons chopped parsley
pinch of cayenne pepper
2 Basic Omelets (page 56)

Blend all the filling ingredients in a small mixing bowl. Prepare an omelet as instructed, add half of the filling, and fold the egg up to enclose it. Turn the heat off and let the omelet sit in the pan for about 30 seconds to heat the filling. Repeat for the second omelet or save the filling in the fridge, covered, for another day.

OMELET PANS

You can make an omelet in almost any pan, but as with anything else, everybody seems to have an opinion on this subject. That includes me. Over the years I've progressed from one sort of pan to another, as the opportunity presented itself, making plenty of good omelets along the way. That's the whole point—a good omelet.

In the beginning I used a cast-iron skillet for omelets. More to the point, I used cast iron for everything I cooked, a habit that left my arms the size of country hams. Making an omelet was more like a weight-training session than cooking, so I gave it up. The other drawback of cast iron is that it absorbs and releases flavors; if I had made curry the night before, I would taste it in the morning.

Today our family has two primary omelet pans, one of rolled nonporous steel, the other nonstick. One isn't necessarily better than the other—they both get you there. But they have different requirements. My steel pan is used only for omelets, since using it for anything else might compromise the highly seasoned surface; when bits of egg or omelet filling do

stick, I sprinkle salt in the skillet and rub them off with a paper towel. Nonstick surfaces are much less finicky; when stuff gets stuck, it washes right off. Of course, that's why nonstick pans have such a large following. This is the pan the rest of my family prefers.

It may seem like a minor point, but I personally favor the steel pan because the surface has less "drag" than the nonstick pan; you feel this when you stir the eggs, which won't be quite as maneuverable. You don't feel that with the steel pan. It's the difference between skating on blades that are slightly dull and skating on blades you've just had sharpened. But both make good omelets.

Unlike a traditional skillet with straight sides, an omelet pan has low, gently sloping sides. This design allows you to stir the eggs with the back of a fork without burning your hand on the sides. It also eliminates the corners where the eggs can stick and provides you with a smooth surface for rolling the omelet out of the pan. The standard pan—one large enough for a 2- or 3-egg omelet—is about 10 inches in diameter and roughly 7½ inches across the bottom.

Creamy Scrambled Eggs with Variations

Makes 3 to 4 servings

Not everyone agrees, but I think scrambled eggs should be creamy and tender, not cooked into tiny little pellets you have to balance on your fork. Creamy eggs require a gentle, deliberate cooking style and a little bit of cream if your diet allows. The eggs are cooked over low heat and stirred regularly to prevent large curds from forming too soon. Total elapsed time will be anywhere from 5 to 8 minutes in a nonstick skillet—which I recommend—over medium-low heat. Other types of pans will work too, but most bare metals will cook the eggs more quickly. I like a trick I picked up in one of Julia Child's cookbooks: hold back a tablespoon or two of the beaten egg and stir it into the scrambled eggs to "cream" them just before serving. Consider the variations at the end of the recipe. You can tailor your eggs to the season or the rest of the menu with fresh herbs, vegetables, and other additions. I always scan the fridge for little odds and ends of meat, vegetables, whatever, before I make scrambled eggs.

> 8 large eggs at room temperature
> 1 or 2 tablespoons heavy cream to taste (optional)
> ⅛ teaspoon salt
> freshly ground pepper to taste
> 1 tablespoon unsalted butter

In a bowl, gently whisk the eggs, cream, salt, and pepper just until blended. Melt the butter in an 8- or 9-inch nonstick skillet over medium-low heat. Just when the butter melts, pour all but a tablespoon or two of the eggs into the skillet. Using a wooden spoon or plastic spatula, gently stir the eggs, scraping the bottom and sides of the pan as you do so; the stirring doesn't have to be continuous, but almost so. You may have to make minor adjustments to the heat if the eggs seem to be cooking too slow or too fast. As the eggs cook, they'll gradually form a large mass of creamy curds; cook them to your liking, then, about 15 seconds before you take them off the heat, stir in the little bit of egg you held back; this will give them an even creamier texture. Serve at once. If you cover them and stir every 30 seconds these will hold for a few minutes (in case you forgot to start the toast or something like that).

Variations: *With Fresh Herbs:* I do this in summer. Stir 2 tablespoons minced fresh herbs into the eggs a minute before they come off the heat. Parsley and basil can be used freely, alone or in combination with dill, lovage, and cilantro. These are excellent in baked puff pastry shells.

With Freshly Cut Corn Kernels: While the eggs cook, steam or lightly sauté a cup of corn kernels for a couple of minutes. Stir into the eggs with chopped parsley or cilantro during the last minute of cooking. Top with salsa.

With Sun-Dried Tomatoes and Bacon: Crumble several pieces of crisp-fried bacon and add to the eggs during the last minute with ¼ cup drained, chopped, oil-packed sun-dried tomatoes.

With Cheddar and Sage: Add ½ cup cubed Cheddar cheese and a big pinch of minced dried sage (or fresh when available) during the last minute of cooking.

With Mushrooms: Sauté a big handful of sliced mushrooms in butter. When they throw off their liquid, add a little dry white wine and cook until the liquid evaporates. Stir the mushrooms into the eggs during the last minute.

Perfect Poached Eggs

Makes 2 or more eggs

For a long time I never made poached eggs, and I think it had something to do with this whirlpool business. When I first started cooking, I remember reading a recipe for poached eggs that instructed the reader to make a whirlpool in a pan of simmering water, at the same time gently sliding an egg into the vortex. The theory was that the vortex would hold the egg in a perfect circle as it simmered, giving the egg a perfect round shape. Compounding my confusion was the fact that you weren't supposed to stop swirling the water, so I couldn't figure out how to slip the eggs in; it was like trying to run into a jump rope that was going full tilt. To make a long story short, my egg hit the water and flew all over the place, just like one of those splatter paintings you used to make at the state fair, where you'd drizzle the paint on a board traveling at 2,500 RPM. Eventually I found that adding vinegar to the water precludes the need for whirlpools because it keeps the eggs stable so long as the water doesn't boil vigorously when the eggs go in. And you need to use really fresh eggs. Poached eggs are good for feeding a crowd because you can make a lot of them in one pan or make them ahead and gently rewarm them in simmering water for a minute. Time them to suit you, simmering just until the whites are set, or longer to cook some of the yolk as well.

To make poached eggs, fill a deep nonreactive skillet with enough water to come within ¾ inch of the top. Bring it to a simmer, stirring in 2 tablespoons of vinegar; do not add any salt. Before you begin cooking the eggs, break as many eggs as you'll be needing into small individual bowls or ramekins. Slide the eggs into the simmering water. Gently shake the handle of the skillet from time to time; this will wash water over the top of the eggs to help cook them. And it will coax the eggs off the bottom of the skillet if they have any inclination to stick. As the eggs are cooking, place a bowl of warm water nearby.

Simmer the eggs for 2 to 4 minutes, depending on how well done you want them. Remove the eggs with a slotted spoon and dip them into the bowl of warm water to wash off any lingering vinegar. Serve at once or hold in cold water and rewarm when needed; refrigerate if you're holding them for more than half an hour or so.

Poached Eggs Provençal

Makes 4 to 6 servings

I don't know about you, but we often find ourselves up to our suspenders in fresh tomatoes come August—and we don't even grow them! Somebody gives you a bag here, another there, and before you know it either you're in the tomato sauce business or they're rotting in the bushel basket. Here's a good way to get rid of several pounds in one fell swoop. All you do, basically, is make a fresh tomato sauce with lots of basil and poach some eggs right in it. They can be served alone, but they're best on toasted slices of French bread, topped with the fresh sauce. Chopped parsley, olives, and grated Parmesan are the finishing touches. These are excellent with Olive Oil Roasted Potatoes (page 100).

> 4 to 5 large vine-ripened tomatoes to taste
> 3 tablespoons unsalted butter or olive oil
> 1 medium-size onion, minced
> 1 garlic clove, minced
> salt to taste
> ½ cup packed fresh basil leaves, chopped
> freshly ground pepper to taste
> 4 to 6 large eggs (1 per person)
> 7 or 8 good-quality black or green olives, pitted
> several parsley sprigs
> 4 to 6 thick slices (1 per person) French bread, toasted
> a little grated Parmesan cheese (optional)

Bring about 2 quarts of water to a boil in a medium-size saucepan. Add the tomatoes, a couple at a time, and let them cook for 30 seconds. Remove to a plate with a slotted spoon. Score the tomatoes around their midsections with a serrated knife, then pull off the skins; they should peel right off. Halve the tomatoes where you've scored them, then gently squeeze out the juice and seeds. Coarsely chop the pulp and put it in a measuring cup; you should have 3½ to 4 cups.

Heat the butter or olive oil in a large enameled or other nonreactive skillet; an

11- or 12-inch pan is not too big. Add the onion and sauté over medium heat for 7 to 8 minutes, stirring often. Stir in the garlic, sauté for another minute, then stir in the tomatoes and a few pinches of salt. Cover and cook over medium-high heat for 10 minutes, stirring occasionally. Stir in the basil and cook for another 7 or 8 minutes, uncovering the skillet for the last few minutes if the sauce is on the wet side; ideally, it should be neither too thick nor too wet when you add the eggs. Season the sauce with salt and pepper.

Turn the heat down quite low. Break one egg into a small bowl. Smooth out a shallow depression in the sauce with a spoon and slide the egg into it; repeat with the remaining eggs. Make sure there is a thin layer of sauce, not just bare skillet, at the bottom of the depression. You should be able to put 4 or 5 eggs around the perimeter and 1 or 2 in the center. Cover and poach the eggs for about 4 minutes or until the whites are set. As they poach, mince the olives and parsley together.

To serve, put a slice of toast on each serving plate. Put one egg on top of the toast and spoon some sauce over and around the egg. Sprinkle the minced parsley and olives on top, followed by the Parmesan cheese.

Variation: If you like scallops, this can become a wonderful seafood stew to serve with the eggs. Simply cook the sauce down a little longer to remove excess liquid, then stir in about ½ pound large or small scallops. Cover and cook for about 2 to 3 minutes. Stir again to distribute the liquid, then add the eggs and poach them.

Breakfast in Bed

The best hotels know a few things about our yearning to be cosseted and our willingness to pay dearly for it. Take morning room service, for instance. How else can you explain $15 omelets, a $7 pile of hash from a can, $3.50 for a cup of coffee? What is it about the freedom to linger in bed over a pot of decaf, home fries, and eggs that we choose to look the other way in the face of what amounts to highway robbery?

Breakfast in bed touches something deep in us, carrying us back to a time of innocence and strong family ties. When you had the flu, didn't your mom or dad bring you a tray of toast and hot tea? And even though the toast was dry—Can't I just have a *little* jelly?—didn't this small act of love, this one kindness, nourish you down to the very depths of your soul?

We can't go back to the innocence of youth, erase our adult knowledge of the impermanence of things. But we can still express our love for someone special—a spouse, parent, sibling, or friend— with a simple gesture like breakfast in bed. Can't cook? Doesn't matter. Breakfast in bed isn't about virtuosity at the range.

It's the thought that counts. Besides, you can hide a lot of incompetence behind pretty napkins, a glass of freshly squeezed orange juice, and a little vase of fresh flowers. Incompetence, somebody said, is the mother of originality. Dare to be original.

You don't need a reason to serve breakfast in bed. Any reason or no reason is good enough. There's something extraspecial about being honored with a breakfast tray just for being yourself, no strings attached.

What should you make? That all depends on the season, your confidence as a cook, and perhaps most important, the kind of foods your beloved enjoys. Does he wake up with a gaping black hole for an appetite? Is she a nibbler, fond of tea and scones? Is it cold out? What fruits are fresh and in season? Try working all these factors into the breakfast equation, but don't let them intimidate or stymie you. Use your best judgment and proceed with confidence.

Tend to the little details. Buy a favorite blend of coffee. If you're a poet, pen a few thoughtful lines on a card and deliver them on the tray. Or steal somebody else's lines. Deliver the morning paper, the latest issue of a favorite magazine, and send the kids out to play. Keep it fresh, personal, pretty, and you won't go wrong.

Poached Eggs on Pesto Bruschetta

Makes 4 servings

Everybody loves pesto, the fresh basil sauce that could make corrugated cardboard taste scrumptious. The ingredients here are all but staples of the summer kitchen: eggs, pesto, tomatoes, and French bread. You toast the bread, spread it with pesto, add a slice of tomato, and top with a poached egg and a dusting of cheese; simple. You can skip the tomato slice altogether or make a fresh tomato sauce to surround the bread on the plate. I love both ways. If you don't have a favorite pesto recipe, a good one is included here.

> 4 good-size slices of French bread, cut on the diagonal about
>   1 inch thick
> about ½ cup pesto (recipe follows)
> 4 large eggs
> 4 tomato slices (optional)
> ¼ cup grated Parmesan cheese

Preheat the oven to 450°. Lay the slices of bread right on the oven rack and toast for 10 to 15 minutes, until golden brown, turning them over after about 5 minutes. As the bread toasts, bring a skillet full of water to a near boil for poaching the eggs, according to the instructions on page 64.

When the bread is toasted, turn the oven off. Spread one side of each piece generously with the pesto, lay the pieces on an ovenproof plate, and keep warm in the oven while you poach the eggs.

Top each piece of pesto bread with a slice of tomato and a poached egg. Dust each serving with a little Parmesan.

PESTO

Makes about 1 cup

2½ cups lightly packed fresh basil leaves
2 to 3 garlic cloves to taste, peeled
⅔ cup good-quality olive oil
¼ cup shelled walnuts or pine nuts
⅛ teaspoon salt
¾ cup grated Parmesan cheese

In a blender or food processor, process the basil, garlic, olive oil, nuts, and salt until smooth, stopping occasionally to scrape the sides down. Scrape the mixture into a small bowl and stir in the Parmesan cheese. Refrigerate until needed, tightly covered.

Baked Eggs with Parmesan and Sun-Dried Tomatoes

Makes 4 servings

Baked eggs are a joy, a private little circle of white and yolk one can spoon at slowly, relishing each bite. They're wonderfully soft and tender, like a soft-cooked egg, but without the risk of those annoying fragments of eggshell. You can enjoy baked eggs plain, cooked in nothing but a buttered ramekin, but it's even better to dress them up a little, as I do here. I just dust the buttered ramekins with grated Parmesan cheese, then drop in a few pieces of sun-dried tomatoes. Starting the eggs in a boiling water bath on top of the stove puts just enough moisture in the air around the ramekins to keep the tops of the eggs from drying out. Serve baked eggs right in the ramekin, placed on serving plates, with your other favorite side dishes. Or turn them out onto hash or a piece of toasted and buttered French bread. I have also eaten these in the center of a plate of rewarmed spaghetti, tossed with bacon bits and more Parmesan cheese. Plan to serve them as soon as they are done, because they'll continue to cook in the ramekin if you don't.

> 1 tablespoon soft unsalted butter
> ½ cup grated Parmesan cheese
> 1 teaspoon dried basil, crumbled, or 1 tablespoon
>   chopped fresh
> 2 oil-packed sun-dried tomatoes, drained and
>   finely chopped
> 4 large eggs at room temperature (if they're cold, warm them
>   briefly in a bowl of hot water)

Preheat the oven to 425°. Butter 4 ramekins and dust the insides of each one with about a tablespoon of the cheese. Sprinkle a little basil and sun-dried tomato in each one, then crack an egg into each ramekin. Sprinkle the tops of the eggs with the rest of the cheese.

Put about 1 inch of hot water into an ovenproof skillet and add the ramekins. Bring just to a boil, then remove from the heat and place the skillet in the oven. Bake the eggs for 4 to 5 minutes, until done to your liking—at the very least the whites should be set, but the yolks can be either runny or set. Serve at once.

Tunisian Eggs

Makes 2 servings

Claudia Roden's wonderful *Mediterranean Cookery* (Knopf, 1992) is the closest I've come to that part of the world in a long time. Armchair travelers like me can't help delighting in her obvious love of that region of the world, its people, and of course the food. This dish is adapted from a recipe in her book, something called *chakchouka* in Tunisian. A lovely summer breakfast, it is an uncomplicated sauté of onions, garlic, peppers, and tomatoes with spices. After the vegetables are softened in olive oil, eggs are broken on top and gently cooked for a few minutes, just until set. In my adaptation, I embellish the finished dish with red pepper flakes, chopped olives, and parsley—all of which combine to add a fresh, bracing bite. Serve with slices of French bread, warmed or toasted.

2½ tablespoons olive oil
1 large green bell pepper, thinly sliced
1 medium-size onion, halved and sliced
2 large vine-ripened tomatoes
2 garlic cloves, thinly sliced
½ teaspoon paprika
½ teaspoon ground cumin
salt and freshly ground pepper to taste
2 large eggs
7 or 8 good-quality black or green olives, pitted and
     coarsely chopped
2 tablespoons chopped parsley
hot red pepper flakes for garnish

Heat the olive oil in a medium-size skillet, preferably nonstick. Add the sliced pepper and onion and sauté over medium-low heat for about 10 minutes, stirring occasionally.

Meanwhile, bring several inches of water to a boil in a small saucepan. Drop in the tomatoes and let them cook for 30 seconds. Transfer the tomatoes to a plate and score the skin around the circumference with a serrated knife. When cool enough to handle, peel, halve, and squeeze out the seeds, then cut the tomatoes into large, coarse chunks and set them aside.

After 10 minutes, stir the garlic, paprika, and cumin into the sauté. Cook for a few seconds, then stir in the tomato chunks and salt and pepper. Cover and cook over medium heat for 1 minute. Smooth 2 sections of the sauté with the back of a spoon, then crack an egg into each section. Reduce the heat to low, cover, and cook the eggs for 5 to 6 minutes, just until set. Serve the eggs and sautéed vegetables garnished with the olives, parsley, and red pepper flakes.

Eggs Creole

Makes 4 servings

This is my interpretation of a good breakfast served at Commander's Palace, the venerable New Orleans restaurant. Mind you, I didn't actually ask for the recipe. And my memory of the dish may, in fact, have been clouded by a bottle of celebratory champagne we drank with our meal. Nonetheless, I would call this a fine dish in its own right and quite possibly a fair representation of the original. At Commander's, poached eggs are served on a bed of grits with the sauce on top. I like it that way, or on a bed of warmed polenta squares (page 45), or just on toasted slices of French bread. In any event, the sauce is the key element—in this case a spicy, tomato-based sauce with peppers, onions, and celery. If you make the sauce the day or evening before, this can be ready in minutes. I like steamed asparagus spears on the side.

2 tablespoons olive oil
1 medium-size onion, finely chopped
1 large green bell pepper, finely chopped
1 celery rib, finely chopped
1 bay leaf
1 garlic clove, thinly sliced
1 tablespoon paprika
1½ teaspoons unbleached flour
¼ teaspoon cayenne pepper
1 cup chicken broth
1 cup canned tomato puree
1 teaspoon Worcestershire sauce
salt to taste
hot grits (page 51) or warm polenta squares (page 45)
poached eggs, 1 or 2 per person (page 64)
2 tablespoons chopped parsley (optional)

In a medium-size saucepan, heat the olive oil. Add the onion, pepper, celery, and bay leaf and sauté over medium heat, stirring, for 5 minutes. Stir in the garlic and sauté for another minute.

Mix the paprika, flour, and cayenne together and stir it into the sauté. Cook, stirring, for 1 minute, then add the chicken broth, tomato puree, and Worcestershire sauce. Lower the heat and simmer, covered, for several minutes. Season to taste with salt; it may take a bit to balance the tomato puree. Simmer, uncovered, for 10 minutes, adding water a tablespoon at a time if it gets too thick; it should be saucy when you serve it—not too thick or too thin.

To serve, spread a layer of hot grits or lay a piece of warm polenta on a plate. Top with 1 or 2 poached eggs, then spoon a generous portion of hot sauce over the top. Garnish with the parsley if you like.

Leftover Pasta and Artichoke Heart Frittata

Makes 6 generous servings

Leftover pasta is a great filler for a frittata, but it does need a little something else to add interest and flavor; here I use marinated artichoke hearts and Romano cheese, and they fit the bill just fine. What sort of pasta can you use? Just about any, really: small shells, spirals, and spaghetti are some of the more common ones I've used in this dish. (It was, in fact, inspired by a dish of spaghetti and artichoke hearts I had in a fine Italian restaurant.) Be sure to use a well-seasoned cast-iron skillet or a nonstick skillet so the slices can be removed easily from the pan. This is wonderful plain or with a little hot tomato sauce on the side.

8 large eggs
3 tablespoons olive oil
2 to 2½ cups cooked pasta
1 6-ounce jar marinated artichoke hearts, drained
1 garlic clove, minced (optional)
1 teaspoon dried basil, crumbled
½ teaspoon salt
½ cup finely grated Romano cheese

Whisk the eggs in a mixing bowl until evenly blended and set them aside. Preheat the oven to 350°.

Heat 2 tablespoons of the olive oil in a cast-iron or nonstick ovenproof skillet. Add the pasta and cook over medium heat, stirring, for 1 minute. Add the artichoke hearts and stir in the garlic if you're using it. Reduce the heat to low. Blend the basil and salt into the beaten eggs. Stir the remaining oil into the pan, then slowly and gently pour the eggs into the pan. Leave the pan on the heat for 1 minute—do not stir once you've poured the eggs into the pan. Sprinkle the cheese over the eggs and bake for 20 minutes, just until the eggs are set; check just below the surface with a fork. Do not overbake. Slice into wedges and serve hot.

HEARTY COMPANIONS:
BREAKFAST MEATS,
FISH, AND HASH (ONE MEATLESS)

FOR REASONS OF AFFORDABILITY, ethics, or health, Americans are eating less meat these days, but in the case of breakfast I think boredom has something to do with it too: a lot of us have fallen into the bacon or sausage rut. Here is a generous handful of meat, fish, and hash recipes that will help lift you out of that rut and bring newfound appreciation for this neglected part of the morning meal.

Today's meats tend to be less fatty than they once were, sometimes with a corresponding loss of flavor, a dilemma cooks can skirt with the judicious use of herbs, seasonings, and wine. Ham steaks are good, but glazed with a reduction of apple cider and dusted with fresh parsley and lemon thyme, they're sensational.

Outdoorsmen know what a fine morning meal can be made of eggs and panfried fish in the wilds. At home, though, we tend to relegate fish to the dinner table. Fresh or leftover, fish is a valuable asset to the breakfast cook. The flavor is tempered in a well-made hash, making it palatable for even an early breakfast. And it really adds a lot to a gratin of hard-cooked eggs, moistened with a cheese sauce. By itself the taste of fish is sometimes more agreeable after we have been up for a while, and engaged in some outdoor activity.

Portions for most of these recipes are modest, in keeping with today's scaled-down consumption of meats. To round out the menu, choose fresh biscuits or perhaps one of the vegetable dishes in The Savory Side. Many of the fruit dishes in Fruits Simple and Sublime add a pleasant, sweet counterpoint to savory meats. And with hash, poached eggs are wonderful, of course.

Baked Ham and Turkey Loaf

Makes 8 to 10 servings

I'm not much of a meat eater, so it isn't all that often that I make a meat loaf. And when I do, I don't care for it warm. I think the flavor and texture are both better the next morning, once the loaf has had a chance to sit overnight. This is a good morning loaf because it contains a nicely balanced blend of half ham and equal parts pork and turkey. I like it cut into thin slices, served with egg dishes—in summer with sliced fresh tomatoes on the side. Or you can lightly brown both sides in a buttered skillet. Unless you have a meat grinder, call ahead and have your butcher grind the meats for you.

1½ tablespoons unsalted butter
1 medium-size onion, finely chopped
1 medium-size green bell pepper, finely chopped
2 garlic cloves, minced
2 teaspoons dried thyme, crumbled
1 pound ground boiled ham
½ pound ground turkey
½ pound ground pork
2 large eggs, lightly beaten
½ cup fine dry bread crumbs
¼ cup milk or cream
1 tablespoon Dijon mustard
¼ cup minced parsley
¼ teaspoon salt
½ teaspoon freshly ground black pepper

Preheat the oven to 375° and lightly butter a 5- by 9-inch nonreactive loaf pan.

In a medium-size skillet, melt the butter over moderate heat. Add the onion and green pepper, cover partially, and cook until softened—about 10 minutes—stirring occasionally. Stir in the garlic and thyme and cook for another minute.

Transfer the contents of the skillet to a large bowl and stir in the remaining ingredients, using your hands to blend the ingredients thoroughly. Transfer the mixture to the prepared loaf pan, pat it down, and form a rounded top with your hands. Bake for 1¼ to 1½ hours, until a meat thermometer inserted in the center registers 165°.

Remove from the oven and tilt the pan to pour off the fat. Transfer to a rack and let the loaf cool to room temperature in the pan (you can, of course, serve it warm). Remove the loaf from the pan. Wrap well and refrigerate. This will keep well for 2 or 3 days.

Hot Pork and Bulgur Sausage Patties

Makes about 15 patties

Most pork sausage is fatty, high in calories, a nightmare for cholesterol watchers. And we love it, don't we? This version is no fat-free hero, but it's a tasty, satisfying sausage for those who love pork sausage but need to exercise restraint. Approximately half of the bulk in this sausage is cooked bulgur, which stretches the pork without adding fat, cholesterol, or many calories. It doesn't taste like pork—it's pretty neutral, in fact—but it does have a complementary, slightly chewy texture. The seasonings are flexible—you can add or substitute other herbs you like, such as oregano, the savories—but don't skimp; with this much bulk you need to use a free hand with the seasonings. If you don't like the heat, however, just leave out the pepper flakes. This makes a lot of patties, so whatever you won't be using within 3 days should be formed into patties, wrapped in freezer wrap, and frozen in sealed plastic bags. Use within 2 months.

¾ cup bulgur
1½ cups plus 1 tablespoon water
¾ teaspoon salt
1¼ pounds ground pork butt
2 teaspoons finely chopped dried sage (or fresh, if available)
1 teaspoon dried thyme, crumbled
1 teaspoon paprika
1 teaspoon hot red pepper flakes (optional)
¼ cup chopped parsley
freshly ground black pepper to taste

First cook the bulgur: Combine the bulgur and 1½ cups water in a medium saucepan. Add ¼ teaspoon of the salt and bring to a boil. Stir, reduce the heat, and cover. Cook over low heat for approximately 15 minutes, until all the water is absorbed. Remove from the heat.

Meanwhile, put the pork in a bowl with the seasonings and tablespoon of water, using 6 or 7 good turns of the pepper grinder. Measure out 2 cups of the bulgur and add that too; save any remaining bulgur for another use. Using your hands, mix and knead the ingredients until everything is well blended. Make a patty and fry it on both sides in a skillet with a little oil. Cool slightly, then taste and correct the seasonings if necessary. Use about 3 tablespoons of mix for each sausage patty, frying them for a couple of minutes on each side, until no longer pink in the center. Freeze whatever you won't be using within 3 days.

Cider-Syrup-Glazed Canadian Bacon

Makes 6 servings

Breakfast meats often work well with a sweet counterpoint. In this version I play the saltiness of the Canadian bacon against a light glaze made from quickly reduced apple cider and maple syrup. Once the glaze reaches the proper consistency, the bacon is dredged in it, warmed briefly, and served; the whole process takes only about 8 minutes.

scant cup of apple cider
2 tablespoons maple syrup
½ tablespoon unsalted butter
6 slices of Canadian bacon at room temperature

Bring the cider to a boil in a 10-inch nonreactive skillet. Boil it down rapidly until it turns into a near glaze, about 5 minutes; you will notice it turn a shade or so darker, and the boiling will sound higher in pitch. Just as it reaches that point, stir in the maple syrup and butter and turn the heat as low as it will go. Quickly dredge both sides of each piece of bacon in the glaze, then leave the pieces in the pan. Heat for about 1 minute, turning the pieces once, then serve.

Roast Beef Hash

Makes 4 to 5 servings

I don't think I've ever been served an authentic (not canned) beef hash in a diner. There was a hotel restaurant in Boston once where the hash was homemade, but it's a shame you can get good hash only at a place where breakfast costs the equivalent of a day's pay. Good roast beef hash is the sort of dish the country was built on: you cooked a roast, then you had hash the next morning. We should get back in the habit. Here is the way I do it, though hash aficionados all seem to have their little worries that the beef and potatoes be cut just so, that you use gravy and not cream, that you flip it over so the other side gets crusty too. Good grief—just get it all in the pan, and you can't go too wrong. Serve with—you guessed it—poached eggs.

    4 medium-size all-purpose potatoes, peeled and cut into
        ¼-inch dice
    ¼ cup flavorless vegetable oil
    1 large onion, finely chopped
    1 pound leftover roast beef, finely chopped (the food
        processor does a good job)
    1 teaspoon dried thyme, crumbled
    salt and freshly ground pepper to taste
    ¾ cup heavy cream or 1¼ cups leftover gravy, warmed to
        thin it out

Cover the potatoes with salted water and bring to a boil in a small saucepan. Boil for about 5 minutes or so, until tender, then drain.

Heat 2 tablespoons of the oil in a large, heavy skillet and add the onion. Sauté over medium heat for about 7 minutes, stirring often. Add the remaining 2 tablespoons oil to the pan, then stir in the potatoes, beef, and thyme. Stir in salt and pepper to taste. Cook, stirring, for 2 minutes, then pour the cream evenly over the hash. Mash the hash down a little with a fork to give it the proper slightly mushy texture, then let it cook over medium heat for another couple of minutes before serving. If you want a good bottom crust, put the whole skillet—uncovered—in a 425° oven for about 15 minutes—no longer, or it will dry out.

Barbecued Chicken Hash

Makes 5 servings

Move over, beef hash—here's some serious competition. There's nothing like a bottle of barbecue sauce to perk up the flavor of chicken. Throw in a few jalapeño peppers, some spuds, and grated cheese, and you've got an easy hash that will leave your crowd begging for more. Serve with poached eggs (page 64) and the Millet Corn Muffins on page 137.

6 medium-size all-purpose potatoes, peeled and cut into
  ½-inch dice
¼ cup flavorless vegetable oil
1 large onion, chopped
1 garlic clove, minced
3 cups cooked chicken in small pieces
¼ cup chopped pickled jalapeño peppers
1 teaspoon dried oregano, crumbled
salt to taste
⅔ cup smoky barbecue sauce
1½ cups grated Cheddar or Monterey Jack cheese

Preheat the oven to 400°. In a large saucepan, cover the potatoes with lightly salted water. Bring to a boil and cook for almost 10 minutes, just until tender. Drain and reserve the potatoes.

Heat the oil in a large cast-iron skillet. Add the onion and sauté over medium heat for 7 minutes. Add the garlic and cook for 1 minute more. Stir in the potatoes, chicken, jalapeño peppers, and oregano. Salt the mixture to taste, undersalting it slightly. Pour the barbecue sauce over the hash, then mash it lightly with a potato masher or fork. Leave on the heat for another minute, then sprinkle the cheese over the top and bake for 20 minutes. Serve at once.

Red Flannel Hash

Makes 6 servings

Red flannel hash is a New England tradition, as one old Maine columnist once wrote, "an Oriental-looking, taste tantalizing dish. . . . As a man comes through the woodshed with the milk pails on his arm, he inhales the smell and a smile lights his face." The red in red flannel hash is beets; where the flannel comes in is anybody's guess, since like all hashes this is somewhat lumpy, not smooth. Some—men with milk pails on their arms?—argue for an all-beets red flannel hash, but I find half beets and half potatoes more to my liking. This is served with poached eggs (page 64).

    3 medium-size beets, scrubbed
    3 medium-size all-purpose potatoes, peeled and cut into ½-inch dice
    3 tablespoons unsalted butter or flavorless vegetable oil
    1 large onion, finely chopped
    2 cups (about 1 pound) chopped cooked corned beef
    salt and freshly ground pepper to taste
    ¼ cup heavy cream

Preheat the oven to 400°. In a large saucepan, cover the beets with lightly salted water. Bring to a boil and cook for about 15 to 20 minutes, until tender. Drain and cool the beets. When they're cool enough to handle, slip off the skins and cut them into approximate ½-inch dice.

In a small saucepan, cover the potatoes with lightly salted water and bring to a boil. Cook for about 10 minutes, just until tender, then drain the potatoes and set them aside.

Melt the butter in a large cast-iron skillet. Add the onion and sauté over medium heat for 7 minutes. Stir in the beets, potatoes, and corned beef. Salt and pepper the hash to taste, then mash the mixture down gently with a potato masher or fork. Sprinkle the cream over the top. Leave the hash on the heat for another minute or two, then transfer to the oven and bake for 20 to 25 minutes. Serve piping hot.

Meatless Bulgur Hash

Makes 5 to 6 servings

Given the number of people who are eating less or no meat these days, this meatless hash is worth having in your repertoire. Bulgur, as you probably know by now, is cracked roasted wheat. It has a nutty flavor that may never pass for meat, but it adds a pleasant chewy texture of its own. We eat this often, just as you would any beef hash: with poached eggs and ketchup. Or with salsa—we love salsa on this. For a little added richness you can, if you like, grate a nice melting cheese—like a sharp Cheddar or Monterey Jack—over the top and stick it in a hot oven for a few minutes just before serving.

2 cups water or vegetable broth (see note)
1 cup bulgur
½ teaspoon salt
5 medium-size all-purpose potatoes, peeled and cut into
   ½-inch dice
3 tablespoons flavorless vegetable oil
1 large onion, chopped
1 garlic clove, minced
1 tablespoon soy sauce

Bring the water to a boil in a small saucepan. Stir in the bulgur and salt. Return to a boil, then lower the heat to a low simmer and cover. Cook for 15 to 20 minutes, until all the water is absorbed. Remove from the heat.

Meanwhile, cover the potatoes with salted water and bring to a boil in a large saucepan. Cook for about 10 minutes, until tender. Drain, reserving both the potatoes and the potato water.

Heat the oil in a large cast-iron skillet and stir in the onion. Sauté over medium heat for 7 minutes, then stir in the garlic and sauté for another minute. Add the cooked bulgur and potatoes. Stir the soy sauce into ½ cup of the reserved potato water and pour it over the hash—not in one spot; try to cover a lot of ground. Cook for another minute, then serve right away.

Note: For a fuller flavor, you can cook the bulgur in vegetable broth. If you don't keep any on hand—who does?—just dissolve a cube of vegetable bouillon in the water before you add the bulgur. Any health food store should carry vegetable bouillon cubes.

SOME THOUGHTS ABOUT HASH

When was the last time you had real hash, not the stuff from a can? Too long, probably. We had great hash when I was growing up. My mom used to keep an old hand-cranked meat grinder in the pantry, on a high shelf. I loved the ritual of lifting that heavy box off its top shelf, clamping it down to the counter, and feeding in the leftover pieces of corned beef my mom had trimmed. Made the best corned beef hash a fellow can imagine, and we would always top it with the requisite poached eggs. To this day I am in perfect ecstasy over good homemade corned beef hash.

Details are few, but one suspects that the history of hash in this country follows a trail of left-overs roughly paralleling America's meat-and-potatoes tradition. Hash is *the* leftovers dish par excellence, incorporating—in the highest tradition of American cookery—the twin culinary virtues of thrift and ease of preparation: just heat some fat in a skillet, add an onion, then toss in the remnants of last night's boiled dinner.

Even if hash is entrenched in the meat-and-potatoes tradition, there are a number of other fine hashes—based on fish, chicken, and grains—to consider. The surfeit of beef available to our fore-fathers gave them occasion to make hash much more than we do today. And because beef is no longer the inexpensive meat it was, the thrifty cook is well advised to weigh other options.

My hash experiments have led me to take exception to some of the standard hash-making techniques. For instance, I can't for the life of me flip an entire skilletful of hash at once to brown the other side—advice many cookbooks dole out with rather annoying nonchalance. I think it's easier just to flip it here and there, in sections, when hash needs browning. Normally I don't think this is even necessary.

For light eaters, hash alone may be plenty for breakfast; trencher-men will want to round it out with eggs, biscuits or toast, and juice.

Smoked Trout Cakes with Rémoulade Sauce

Makes 6 to 8 patties

Smoked trout isn't cheap, but it's really no more expensive than crab, and it makes the most delicious breakfast or brunch patties you ever did eat, better than any crab cake I've come across. It's the smokiness of the trout that gives you the feeling of eating in the great outdoors; one bite and you can hear the deer and raccoons stirring, as the morning sun beams shafts of light through the glade of pines surrounding your campsite. These trout cakes are truly unforgettable in the right company, that being the mustardy rémoulade sauce, poached eggs (page 64), and biscuits. If corn is in season, cook up a few ears and serve them on the side. Now, that's heaven.

1 large egg
2 tablespoons mayonnaise
2 teaspoons Dijon mustard
¼ teaspoon salt
juice of ½ lemon
⅛ teaspoon cayenne pepper
¼ cup minced fresh chives
1 tablespoon minced parsley
6 or 7 slices of slightly stale (not sweet) white bread as
    needed
2½ cups flaked smoked trout (a 1-pound fillet will be
    plenty; see Sources for ordering if unavailable locally),
    all but the tiny pin bones removed
2 to 3 tablespoons unsalted butter as needed for frying

In a large bowl, beat the egg lightly, then whisk in the mayonnaise, mustard, salt, lemon juice, cayenne, and herbs. Trim the crusts off the bread if they are very tough, then stack 4 of the pieces and cut them into ¼-inch strips one way and then the other, leaving you with small cubes. Measure out 1 cup (somewhat packed) of bread cubes and stir them into the mayonnaise mixture; set aside. Grate the remaining slices of bread on the large holes of a box grater to make small crumbs and set aside.

Finely chop the trout by hand, then blend it thoroughly with the moistened bread cubes. Form the mixture into 6 large or 8 smaller patties about ¾ inch thick, dust them on both sides with the remaining bread crumbs, and lay them on a small baking sheet lined with wax paper or plastic wrap. Cover the patties with plastic wrap and refrigerate for 30 to 60 minutes before cooking. While you're waiting, make the rémoulade sauce (recipe follows).

To cook the patties, melt about 1 tablespoon of the butter in a skillet. Fry several patties at a time over medium heat for about 3 to 4 minutes on the first side, until golden brown, and 2 to 3 minutes on the second side, turning only once. Wipe out the skillet with paper towels before frying successive batches. Serve hot, with a little of the rémoulade sauce on the side.

 RÉMOULADE SAUCE

    1 cup mayonnaise
    2 tablespoons Dijon mustard
    1 tablespoon minced onion or fresh chives
    1 tablespoon minced dill pickle
    1 tablespoon minced parsley
    1 tablespoon chopped drained capers (optional)
    2 teaspoons minced jalapeño peppers (optional)

Blend all the ingredients in a small bowl. Cover and refrigerate until using.

In the summer, I always add ½ teaspoon each fresh tarragon and chervil to this sauce; in winter months I substitute extra parsley.

Cornmeal-Sage-Dusted Fried Trout

Makes 2 servings

On those occasions when I enjoy a piece of fish for breakfast, I like it served simply, especially when the fish in question is freshly caught trout from Stinson Lake, just a stone's throw out our back door; the flavor of fresh trout is so delicate and sweet that you only confuse matters if you get too elaborate. Here I just drape the trout in a simple coating of cornmeal—which gives the skin a delicious crunch—and season it with a touch of sage, because I like the way cornmeal and sage taste together. This is an excellent camp breakfast, but at home or camp, always serve this with some kind of potato—one with a little bit of richness is good since the fish is so lean and light.

> 2 pan-size trout, about 8 to 12 ounces each, gutted, scaled,
>   and heads removed
> salt and freshly ground pepper to taste
> ½ cup yellow cornmeal, preferably stone-ground
> 2 teaspoons minced fresh or dried sage
> 2 tablespoons flavorless vegetable oil or olive oil
> 3 tablespoons unsalted butter
> milk

Rinse the fish well, including the cavities, under cold running water. Pat them dry with paper towels, then lightly salt and pepper the cavities.

Mix the cornmeal and sage on a dinner plate and set aside. Heat the oil in a large, heavy skillet over medium heat. Cut the butter into several pieces and add it to the pan too. As the butter melts, dip both sides of the fish in milk, then lightly salt and pepper the fish. Dredge both sides of the fish in the cornmeal and lay the fish in the skillet. Fry on the first side for approximately 4 minutes, then gently turn them and fry the second side about the same amount of time; the heat shouldn't be too high, or you'll burn the skin, so keep an eye on it. Drain the fish for about 10 seconds on paper towels, then serve hot.

Gratin of Fish and Hard-Cooked Eggs

Makes 6 servings

This creamy dish really hits the spot on a chilly, raw morning. It isn't unlike a hash, though the texture is somewhat different, saucier and with larger pieces of food rather than everything cut into small bits. I know of no better way to make use of leftover fish, and if you cook the eggs the night before—when you realize you're going to have fish left over from dinner—this is very quick to assemble. The fish and eggs are covered with a Cheddar and mustard béchamel sauce, which you can whip up while the oven preheats. Excellent with biscuits or toast.

        8 large hard-cooked eggs
        3 tablespoons unsalted butter
        3 tablespoons unbleached flour
        1½ cups milk
        2 teaspoons Dijon mustard
        ⅛ teaspoon cayenne pepper
        1½ cups grated extrasharp Cheddar cheese
        salt to taste
        ½ to ¾ pound cooked fish, flaked

If you haven't already, hard-cook the eggs, peel them, and refrigerate, covered. Preheat the oven to 375° and butter a 10-inch round or oval gratin dish.

Make the sauce: Melt the butter over medium-low heat in a small saucepan. Stir in the flour and cook, stirring, for 3 minutes. Gradually stir in the milk, increasing the heat slightly, and cook until the sauce has thickened to about the consistency of heavy cream, about 4 or 5 minutes. Stir in the mustard, cayenne, Cheddar, and salt. Cook for another minute and remove from the heat.

Cover the bottom of the gratin dish with a thin layer of the sauce. Quarter the eggs lengthwise and arrange them in a single layer over the sauce. Spread the flaked fish over the eggs and cover everything with the rest of the sauce. Bake for 30 to 35 minutes, until bubbly hot, then cool on a rack for 5 minutes before serving.

The Savory Side:
Vegetables, Chili,
and Hearty Breakfast Fare

HOW MANY TIMES HAS this happened to you? In the half-light of the morning you stumble across the kitchen and open the refrigerator door. There you stand, for several seconds or a minute, poking around by the light of the fridge but mainly just waiting: for inspiration, for ambition to strike, for the room service fairies to drop by with a four-course breakfast and a King Kong–size mug of joe. Your stomach lets out an impatient growl.

Then your eye glances over the remains of the day-before-yesterday's lasagne. Not quite what you had in mind, perhaps, but the commotion in your stomach tells you time is short. Quickly, you splash some water in a skillet and position the rigid cube of noodles and sauce in the center. Within seconds the intoxicating aroma sends a requisition to your brain's food center for garlic bread and salad. The bread warmed, salad dressed, lasagne now transformed to a bubbling, inviting mélange, you dig your fork into this feast and wonder: why don't I do this more often?

Call it the savory side of breakfast: hearty, often spicy or otherwise well-seasoned dishes that fall out of the breakfast mainstream. As with the leftover lasagne, savory breakfasts usually happen by default, but this option is worthy of more conscious decision making. The category includes vegetables, especially fresh and in season; meals based on beans, like the black bean chili that I love to serve over crunchy cornmeal biscuits; and warm, cheesy dishes like rarebit and polenta-stuffed peppers. These are often called brunch dishes—foods we might eat from midmorning to noon—but I think that term is too limiting; good food is good food, no matter what time of day you eat it. And you should eat it when the spirit moves you.

If you have a garden or simply love vegetables, you know there are times when a simple vegetable sauté or creamed corn on crisp toast points is the best of all breakfasts. Here in New Hampshire, and elsewhere in colder regions, preparing vegetables for breakfast effectively extends their season by doubling their duty. The potato is the hero of the breakfast plate. Everyone loves home fries, naturally, but we also slice and roast them with olive oil, bake them in gratins, make mashed potato patties. Our rule for mashed potatoes: always double the recipe so you have plenty left for patties. Most of the vegetable dishes pair up nicely with eggs, but all of them can stand alone too.

Melted cheese dishes—like rarebits and fondues—are comforting foods that chase away the cold and linger in our memory. They're quickly made and can easily be multiplied to serve a dozen or more. Fairly rich, they fit nicely into a weekend of invigorating outdoor activity, such as after mountain biking or before hitting the ski trails. Finish a hearty cheese breakfast with one of the lighter and refreshing fruit selections in Fruits Simple and Sublime.

Gratin of Potatoes and Bacon

Makes 4 servings

Here is a breakfast version of *gratin dauphinois,* the king of rich, creamy potato dishes. Back when most Americans lived on farms, folks ate dishes like this all the time; today we limit them to an occasional weekend splurge when nobody's looking or when we've just had enough with dietary temperance. Whereas most American-style potato gratins use flour between the layers to absorb the liquid (usually milk), this one does not. It is the relative thickness of the cream and the starch in the potatoes that allows this dish to thicken without added flour. Opinions vary, but I like a combination of half heavy cream and half light or half-and-half. But you can use half heavy cream and half milk if you prefer. Purists say that cheese only detracts from the flavor of the potatoes, and you can leave it out if you want. But I prefer the sprinkling of Parmesan on top.

6 to 8 slices of crisp-fried bacon
4 cups thinly sliced (no more than ⅛ inch thick)
   all-purpose potatoes
¾ cup heavy cream
¾ cup light cream, half-and-half, or milk
scant ½ teaspoon salt
1 garlic clove
unsalted butter for the pan
½ cup grated Parmesan cheese

If you haven't already, fry the bacon and blot it dry between layers of paper towels. Preheat the oven to 400°.

Put the potatoes in a large nonreactive saucepan. Add the creams and salt and gradually bring to a near boil over medium heat, stirring occasionally to keep from sticking. Remove from the heat, crumble the bacon and stir it into the potatoes. Rub a gratin dish with a bruised garlic clove, then lightly butter the dish.

Carefully pour the contents of the saucepan into the gratin dish and even it out with a fork. Sprinkle the cheese over the top, then bake for 1 hour, until the potatoes are tender and bubbly and the top is browned.

Three-Alarm Potatoes

Makes 4 servings

One of our favorite seaside New England towns is Rockport, Massachusetts, a place of expansive lawns that tumble down to the sea, fine art galleries, and parking tickets that will set you back the cost of a good bottle of wine. We like one restaurant in Rockport called the Greenery, where they serve a wonderful breakfast. One hot item on the breakfast menu is called *firehouse potatoes,* a hearty mélange of sautéed onions, potatoes, and tomatoes, mixed with hot peppers and sour cream. I was not too successful extracting the recipe from our waitress on the busy morning we ate there, but based on what she did tell me I was able to create a good facsimile. I like these with the added richness of the sour cream in the winter, but in the warmer months I just leave it out. Be sure to bake the potatoes a day or two ahead; leave them at room temperature the night before you bake the dish. Cold potatoes will cool the ingredients down and unnecessarily extend the baking time. These are hearty enough to serve alone, or they're great with eggs and bacon or ham.

3 tablespoons flavorless vegetable oil or olive oil
1 large onion, halved and sliced
½ teaspoon mild chili powder
1 large tomato, cut into bite-size chunks
¼ to ½ cup pickled jalapeño pepper slices, coarsely chopped
½ cup sour cream (optional)
4 medium-large baked potatoes, cut into bite-size pieces
salt to taste
1 tablespoon red wine vinegar
1 cup grated Monterey Jack or sharp Cheddar cheese

Preheat the oven to 425°. Heat the oil in a large, heavy ovenproof skillet. Add the onion and sauté over medium heat for 10 minutes, stirring often. Stir in the chili powder, cook for 30 seconds, then stir in the tomato. Cook the mixture for 2 to 3 minutes, stirring occasionally, until the tomato starts to soften and throw off some liquid.

Stir the jalapeño and sour cream—if you're using it—into the skillet. Add the potatoes and salt the dish to taste. Sprinkle the vinegar over the dish and stir.

Bake the dish for 10 minutes. Sprinkle the cheese over the top and bake for 5 minutes more, just until the cheese melts. Serve at once.

. . . .

Stovetop Potatoes Various Ways

Makes 4 to 5 servings

In their most basic form, these would be called *home fries*—good food, but I often hope for a bit more excitement from my breakfast potatoes. Home fries can be terribly good or just plain terrible, depending on how you approach the matter. The worst fate that can befall home fries is mushiness. It is also the most common sin against them. Leftover baked potatoes, skin and all, make some of the best home fries going; they have the firmness needed to hold up in the skillet without turning to mush. When you haven't had the forethought to bake extra potatoes, boiled red-skinned potatoes are just about as good. But it's very important not to overcook them in the preliminary boiling and to cool them down quickly under cold running water. If the rest of your breakfast is rich enough to your taste, serve the potatoes simply, without any adornments. Or choose one of the cheese variations if you're making a meal of the potatoes alone.

1½ pounds (about 6 or 7 medium) red-skinned potatoes or
    about 3 or 4 large leftover baked potatoes
2 to 3 tablespoons olive oil
1 small onion, chopped
salt and freshly ground pepper to taste
1 tablespoon unsalted butter

If you're using the red potatoes, scrub them under running water, then cut them into ¾-inch cubes and chunks. Put them into a pan of cold salted water and bring to a boil. Reduce the heat to a low boil and cook for about 5 minutes from the time they started boiling. When they are still firm, drain and run the potatoes under cold water for about 45 seconds to stop the cooking. Spread the potatoes on a cotton—not terry—kitchen towel and let cool. If you're using the baked potatoes, simply cut them into bite-size chunks and set aside.

    Heat enough olive oil to film the bottom of a large cast-iron skillet. Add the onion and sauté over medium heat for 1 minute, stirring. Add the potatoes, but don't disturb them for a couple of minutes so they form a crust. Salt and pepper the potatoes, then turn them with a spatula. Cut the butter into several pieces, letting it drop here and there in the skillet. Cook for 2 minutes more, undisturbed, then turn and cook for another minute. Serve as is or choose one of the following options.

Variations: *Stovetop Potatoes with Garlic:* Bruise a peeled garlic clove and stir it in the oil as it heats. Remove before adding the onion.

Stovetop Potatoes with Pesto and Parmesan Cheese: I love these in the summer when we have pesto. Omit the butter, tossing the potatoes with 2 tablespoons of pesto during the last 30 seconds. Sprinkle finely grated Parmesan cheese over the potatoes and serve.

Stovetop Potatoes with Sage and Cheddar Cheese: Mince a teaspoon of dried sage or several fresh leaves, minced, into the potatoes during the last minute. Grate extrasharp Cheddar cheese right over the potatoes and remove from the heat; the heat will melt the cheese. Fontina is also excellent.

Parmesan Potato Patties with Lovage

Makes 4 servings

A good mashed potato patty is a work of art and not something one encounters often today. They sound like a snap, but they're subject to a number of pitfalls: too much filler in the form of crumbs, too greasy, too bland. After years of fiddling, I now think grated Parmesan cheese is the best sort of filler you can use. Because it's slightly dry, it absorbs moisture and keeps the patties on the firm side. And it has a unique way of melting yet turning crisp at the same time, which enables the patties to become self-crusting as they fry. The best mashed potatoes for patties are the kind that haven't had too much liquid added to them; a bit of milk and butter is fine, but if the potatoes start out very loose, the patties will follow suit. So keep this in mind when you make your mashed potatoes. (We always make extra at dinner, so we can make patties the next day or two.) Herbs add a delicate flavorful touch to these. We like lovage and sorrel, but if they're unavailable you can use fresh parsley and celery seed. These are exquisite alongside any egg dish or—my favorite way—with a poached egg on top, garnished with more chopped fresh herbs.

2 cups cold leftover mashed potatoes
1¼ cups grated Parmesan cheese
1 small onion, minced
2 tablespoons minced fresh lovage or parsley or
   a combination
½ teaspoon celery seed (optional, but recommended
   especially if lovage is unavailable)
salt and freshly ground black pepper to taste
olive oil for frying
½ cup fine dry bread crumbs

Mix all the ingredients except the olive oil and crumbs in a bowl until evenly blended. Using about ⅓ cup per patty, form the mixture into 8 patties, each about ¾ inch thick. Place the patties on a small baking sheet lined with wax paper and freeze for 15 minutes.

Heat about 2 tablespoons olive oil in a medium-size cast-iron or other heavy skillet. You can use equal parts olive oil and unsalted butter if you prefer. When the oil is hot, gently rub a few crumbs on both sides of the patties and add 3 or 4 patties to the skillet; don't crowd them. Fry the patties over medium-high heat for 3 minutes. Don't disturb or move them with a spatula, so the crust can set properly. Flip and cook for 2 minutes on the second side. Serve right away or hold in a warm oven while you cook the remaining patties. You will need to add a little more olive oil/butter to the skillet for each batch.

Sage and Cheddar Potato Rösti

Makes about 10 patties, serving 5

Rösti, I have read, is the national potato dish of Switzerland, similar to our hash browns: cold boiled potatoes that are shredded and fried. So for advice on the subject I went to my Swiss friend Annie. Would the Swiss ever put sage in this dish? I asked her. Well, no. Cheddar? Never heard of it. Would they bake it as patties, instead of the traditional manner as one giant pancake? Here I was really holding out hope, because I've often had trouble getting it out of the pan in one piece to flip it. Not a chance. So what we have here is a less-than-authentic but still very fine rendition of rösti, or hash browns. One important point to remember is not to play with or poke them as they cook, or they'll fall apart before they've had a chance to set enough to be flippable. Serve these with almost any egg dish and breakfast meat.

> 6 medium-size red-skinned potatoes, peeled
> 1 teaspoon dried sage or slightly more fresh
> ¼ teaspoon salt
> 1 cup grated sharp Cheddar cheese
> 4 to 5 tablespoons flavorless vegetable oil
> 1 small onion, halved and thinly sliced
> 3 tablespoons unsalted butter, approximately

A day ahead, boil the potatoes in enough salted water to cover them by about an inch for 10 to 15 minutes. The potatoes should be tender enough to be pierced easily with a paring knife—though there should be a little resistance at the center. Drain and cool the potatoes, then cover and refrigerate overnight.

The next morning, grate the potatoes into a bowl using the large holes on a four-sided box grater. Toss and gently mix in the sage, salt, and cheese. Heat a tablespoon of the oil in a small skillet and sauté the onion over medium heat for about 7 minutes, until translucent. Mix the onion into the potato mixture.

Heat about a tablespoon or so of the oil in a large cast-iron skillet. Gently ball up about ½ cup of the potato mixture in your hand or loosely pack it into a ½-cup measure and put it in the skillet. Spread it out just a little, so it is about ½ inch thick, then press down not too firmly with a spatula to pack it. Put 3 or 4 patties into the skillet, as many as will fit without crowding. Flatten them all and pull in the edges with your spatula to round them up, but don't start trying to loosen them; they'll be much easier to flip once the cheese has melted and crisped. Cook the patties over medium heat for about 5 or 6 minutes, until nicely browned. Turn them, each time dropping a scant teaspoon of butter on the skillet where you flip the rösti. Cook for about 4 minutes more, until browned. Serve at once or hold them on a plate in a low oven. Repeat for the remaining mixture.

Olive Oil Roasted Potatoes

Makes 6 servings

This is a good breakfast recipe because the potatoes roast unattended while you go about your business. The prep time is minuscule: just slice the spuds, toss them in olive oil, and lay them in the pan. Rosemary gives them a lovely fragrance and flavor. If you would be so bold, add a clove or two of pressed garlic to the olive oil before you toss in the spuds; you might want to think twice if you're out the door to a heavy schedule of business meetings or the dentist. Serve with eggs, of course, and breakfast meats. We like to sprinkle them with red wine vinegar. Also very good with Bacon-Braised Kale (page 103). I prefer the cooked texture of a red-skinned potato, but I have used all-purpose potatoes, and they are fine too.

3 pounds medium-size red-skinned or
   all-purpose potatoes
3 tablespoons olive oil
2 teaspoons dried rosemary, crumbled, or 1 tablespoon
   chopped fresh
1 or 2 garlic cloves to taste, minced or pressed (optional)
salt and freshly ground pepper to taste

Lightly oil 1 or 2 large, shallow baking dishes; a jelly roll pan works well too. The potatoes should have enough room in the pan so they aren't overlapping; otherwise they won't crisp or brown nicely. Adjust the oven rack to the highest setting and preheat the oven to 450°.

Scrub the potatoes well and dry them thoroughly. Halve them lengthwise, then cut each half into 3 or 4 lengthwise wedges. Toss them in a large bowl with the olive oil, rosemary, and garlic if you're using it. Spread the potatoes in the pan so they aren't touching, then salt and pepper them. Bake for 30 to 35 minutes, until well browned; only the skin should offer any resistance when you pierce them with a paring knife. If they are browning too much, move the oven rack down one position. Don't turn or fiddle with them once they start cooking or they'll be more prone to stick to the pan. Serve right away.

Curried Vegetable Hash

Makes 4 to 6 servings

If you like waking up to big, bold flavors, here is a dish that will put some real punch on your plate. It's a visual feast as well, a medley of curry-tinted vegetables in shades of yellow, green, and winter-squash orange. In addition to the requisite potatoes, I add a generous portion of cubed winter squash to the hash. Not only does the flavor blend well with the curry, but the soft texture adds a bit of the mush I find desirable in hash; hash without a little mush just isn't hash. A poached egg, placed in the center of a serving, is just what you need to temper the curry. If you'd rather skip the egg, a dollop of plain yogurt is also good.

2½ tablespoons flavorless vegetable oil
1 large onion, finely chopped
1 bay leaf
1 garlic clove, minced (optional)
1 tablespoon curry powder

½ teaspoon hot red pepper flakes (optional)
2 cups peeled and diced winter squash in ½-inch cubes
2 cups peeled and diced all-purpose potatoes in ½-inch cubes
2 cups water
a large pinch of salt
1 small green bell pepper, chopped
2 cups small broccoli flowerets
½ cup frozen (thawed) or freshly scraped corn
¼ cup tomato puree or fresh or canned chopped tomatoes
chopped parsley for garnish

Heat 2 tablespoons of the oil in a large, heavy skillet. Add the onion and bay leaf and sauté over medium heat for 10 minutes, stirring often. Add the remaining ½ table-spoon oil to the pan, then stir in the garlic if you're using it, the curry powder, and the red pepper flakes if you're using them. Sauté for 30 seconds, stirring, then mix in the squash, potatoes, water, and salt. Bring the liquid to a boil, reduce the heat to a low boil, and cook, covered, for 8 minutes. Stir in the green pepper, broccoli, and corn. Cover and cook for another 6 minutes or so, until the broccoli is almost tender. Stir in the tomatoes and cook, uncovered, until all of the excess water has boiled off; the vegetables should still be quite moist, however. Serve hot, with a poached egg or yogurt, sprinkled with chopped parsley.

Bacon-Braised Kale with Poached Eggs

Makes 2 servings

Kale for breakfast? Sure. There's really nothing more far-fetched about the idea than creamed spinach with poached eggs; that's a pretty common dish. I've cut out the cream, however, which doesn't do much for kale anyway, and gleaned flavor from the bacon fat and a dash of tomato and vinegar. The kale soaks up the flavors like a sponge, and you end up with an incredibly tender and juicy mélange that can be put directly on the plate or served on top of thin slices of toasted French bread. The reserved bacon is then chopped with some lemon zest and parsley and scattered over the top. This is my idea of the perfect breakfast, along with a few spuds of one sort or another on the side; the Olive Oil Roasted Potatoes (page 100) would be my first choice.

1 medium-size (¾ pound) bunch of kale
3 slices of bacon
1 medium-size onion, finely chopped
¼ teaspoon salt
½ cup water
2 tablespoons canned crushed tomatoes in puree or
    chopped fresh tomatoes
up to ½ teaspoon balsamic or red wine vinegar
freshly ground pepper to taste
2 poached eggs (page 64)
8 to 10 parsley sprigs, stems removed
a little grated lemon zest

Strip the kale from the stems, discarding the stems. Fill a large bowl with cold water and agitate the kale leaves in it to wash them. Drain briefly in a colander, then chop the leaves coarsely and set them aside.

Heat a heavy nonreactive skillet with a lid and fry the bacon in it until quite crisp. Remove the bacon and cool on a plate lined with a paper towel. Pour off all but about 1½ to 2 tablespoons of the bacon fat. Add the onion to the bacon fat and sauté over medium heat for 4 to 5 minutes, stirring often. Stir in the kale, salt, and water. Cover and braise the kale for 10 to 12 minutes, until tender. Stir in the tomato and a few sprinkles of the vinegar, adding up to ½ teaspoon if you like the sharpness it adds. Pepper the kale to taste. If you haven't already, poach the eggs; reheat the kale to serve.

Mince the reserved bacon with the parsley and lemon zest. Put a pile of the kale on each plate and top with a poached egg. Sprinkle the bacon garnish over the top and serve piping hot.

Maple-Pecan Baked Squash

Makes 2 or 3 servings

I feel the same way about winter squash that most of the nuns in grammar school felt about me: has potential but needs to apply himself. Squash needs remedial help; it just doesn't turn me on without some special doctoring. This sweet treatment turns squash into serious breakfast material: a hearty, satisfying dish for chilly winter weekends. I can make a meal of this and biscuits or chilled stewed fruit. You can even throw together a quick fall fruit salad of pears, apples, and chopped dried figs or walnuts and put some in the cavity when you serve it. Or spoon in some cold applesauce or just plain cream.

> 1 medium-size (2-pound) butternut squash
> 1 tablespoon soft unsalted butter
> salt to taste
> 1 tablespoon maple syrup
> 1 cup shelled pecans
> ¼ cup packed light brown sugar
> 3 tablespoons cold unsalted butter, cut into ¼-inch pieces

Preheat the oven to 450°. Halve the squash lengthwise and scoop the seeds out of one half; save the other half for another use. Score the flat part of the exposed flesh with a paring knife several times, but keep the cuts back from the edge of the squash so the juices don't leak out as it bakes. Rub half of the soft butter over the flesh, then salt it lightly. Pour the tablespoon of maple syrup into the cavity and add the rest of the soft butter. Pour about ¼ inch of hot water into a shallow casserole large enough to hold the squash. Put the squash in the casserole flat side up and cover the casserole with foil.

Bake the squash for about 45 minutes, until the flesh is tender most of the way through; test it with a fork. Two or 3 times during the baking, baste the squash with the juices that accumulate in the cavity.

While the squash is baking, put the pecans and brown sugar in a food processor and process until the nuts are coarsely ground. Add the cold butter and continue to process until you have uniform crumbs. Refrigerate.

If all the water has not evaporated from the casserole, take the squash out with a couple of spatulas and pour off what remains. Put the squash back in the casserole and pat about half of the pecan crumbs onto the flat part of the squash. (Bag and freeze the rest of the crumbs for another squash or to use on muffins.) Lower the heat to 375° and bake, uncovered, for another 20 to 30 minutes, until the squash is tender throughout. Cut and serve; spoon any juices from the cavity into a small cup and use as sauce.

Avocado and Hard-Cooked Eggs with Gorgonzola

Makes 2 servings

My family and I love avocados, so when the price is right we think nothing of eating them for breakfast—on sandwiches, in omelets, you name it. Here's an idea I had one day when I put a pile of hard-cooked eggs next to some avocado halves and noticed how close in size the eggs and pits were. Normally, stuffed cuisine isn't part of my cooking lifestyle, but I couldn't resist tapering the pit cavity with a spoon and slipping half an egg right in there. Then I spooned on some Gorgonzola mixed with yogurt, topped it with chives, and enjoyed it immensely, thank you. Cook the eggs the night before, and this can be done in a flash.

> 1 ripe Haas avocado
> salt and freshly ground pepper to taste
> 1 lemon, halved
> 1 hard-cooked egg, peeled and halved lengthwise
> ¼ cup crumbled Gorgonzola or other blue cheese
> ¼ cup plain yogurt
> 1 tablespoon chopped fresh chives

Score the avocado lengthwise down to the pit, then give it a twist to separate the halves. Stick the point of a sturdy paring knife into the pit and carefully pry it out. Using a spoon, increase the size of the two pit cavities so they'll accept half an egg; this needn't be done with a machinist's precision unless you are feeling so obsessed. Salt and pepper the exposed surface of the avocado, then squeeze drops of lemon juice over it. Drop in the egg halves.

Mix the Gorgonzola and yogurt, spoon it over the avocado and egg, then garnish the top with chives. Serve with plain crackers or a toasted onion bagel. In season, some quartered cherry tomatoes go nicely on top of the Gorgonzola. Put the salt, pepper, lemon, and any extra Gorgonzola sauce on the table so you can add these as you eat.

Sage and Cornmeal Fried Green Tomatoes

Makes 4 servings

Everyone has green tomatoes in the fall, but we have more than our share here in New Hampshire. The resourceful cook looks on the bright side and tries to mine as many happy endings as possible out of this situation. I, for one, love fried green tomatoes, and this is my favorite way of doing them—in cornmeal and sage. The cornmeal leaves them crisp on the outside, and the muskiness of the sage balances the tartness of the tomatoes. I like to fry these in olive oil, but if you're cooking bacon you can leave a tablespoon or two of bacon fat in the pan and fry them in it. Serve hot out of the skillet to keep the exterior crisp. Excellent with all egg dishes.

> 2 medium-large green tomatoes
> salt to taste
> ⅓ cup yellow cornmeal, preferably stone-ground
> 2 tablespoons ground dried sage
> olive oil for frying

Cut the cores out of the tops of the tomatoes, then trim the top and bottom of each one, taking off a thin slice. Cut the tomatoes into ¼-inch slices. Salt each side of the slices very lightly, then set them aside on a plate for 5 minutes. Mix the cornmeal and sage on another plate and set it aside.

Heat a tablespoon or two of olive oil in a heavy skillet over medium-high heat. Press each side of the tomato slices into the cornmeal mixture and add them to the skillet when the oil is hot; keep the slices fairly close, but don't crowd them. Fry on each side for about 2 minutes, until golden brown, turning once. Serve right away. Wipe the skillet clean with bundled paper towels before frying successive batches in additional fresh oil.

Variation: Substitute 2 to 3 tablespoons finely grated Parmesan cheese for an equal amount of cornmeal.

Bacon, Egg, and Potato Pie

Makes 8 servings

This is a sort of one-dish breakfast, all the traditional breakfast courses within the walls of a short oatmeal pastry. It's an assembly job, with a number of steps, and therefore not something most of us would consider throwing together on the spur of the moment. Think of it as a weekend breakfast, something to serve with a simple fruit course. Cooked potatoes are layered with crisp bacon bits and fresh parsley and covered with a nutmeg-laced custard. Grated cheese is spread over the top, then the whole thing is baked to a turn. It can be served warm or made a day ahead and reheated the next day. If you prefer, use another prebaked pastry shell instead of the oatmeal.

> 1 9-inch pie shell, prebaked, made with Oatmeal Pastry
>   (page 183)
> 5 medium-size red-skinned potatoes, peeled
> 12 slices of crisp-fried bacon
> 3 large eggs
> 1 cup light cream or milk
> ¼ teaspoon salt
> a big pinch of ground nutmeg
> freshly ground black pepper to taste
> ¼ cup chopped parsley
> 1 cup grated smoked Cheddar, Gruyère, fontina, or other
>   good melting cheese

Cool the prebaked pastry thoroughly on a rack. Cut the potatoes into slices slightly thicker than ⅛ inch. Put them in a small pan and cover with salted water. Bring to a boil, then boil gently for 3 to 5 minutes, until *just* tender. Drain the water from the pan, then fill the pan with cold water to stop the potatoes from cooking further. Gently drain the potatoes, then spread them on several layers of paper toweling and blot dry. Transfer to a plate.

If you haven't already, crisp-fry the bacon and drain on paper towels. When it cools, break it into bits and set aside. Preheat the oven to 400°.

Make the custard by whisking together the eggs, cream, salt, nutmeg, and pepper just until uniform. Set aside.

Assemble the pie: Arrange a layer of potatoes on the bottom of the pie shell. Sprinkle with some of the bacon and parsley. Add layers of potatoes, bacon, and parsley until everything is used up. Slowly pour the custard over the potatoes, then top with the cheese. Bake for 30 minutes, reduce the heat to 375°, and bake for about another 30 minutes, until done. There should be no uncooked custard in the center; probe the pie with a fork to check.

Cool the pie on a rack for about 30 minutes before serving; these things taste better if you give them a rest first.

Garden Huevos

Makes 5 servings, 2 per serving

This recipe was generously donated by my friends Mike and Nancy Phillips, who own and run the Lost Nation Cider Mill in northern New Hampshire. Mike is an incredibly talented and hardworking farmer. What makes him really unique is that he's an organic farmer in a growing zone so inhospitable it has driven lesser men to pack it all in and take up aluminum siding or Stuff Envelopes at Home for Big Profits. Mike and Nancy's farm is a gorgeous sight in the summer—lush beds of basils, lemon thyme, lavender, and rosemary astride a profusion of vegetables and flowers. On our visits, Nancy's special ways with their organic produce have produced some memorable meals. This is one of my favorites: soft whole wheat tortillas wrapped around a sauté of corn, peppers, fresh herbs, cheese, and scrambled eggs. The Phillipses insist that homegrown sweet corn is essential, but don't hesitate to use somebody else's good sweet corn if you don't grow your own. In desperation I've even used frozen, and they turned out just fine. Serve with guacamole and corn chips. For a winter version, substitute ⅓ cup minced parsley for the chives and cilantro.

2 tablespoons olive oil or unsalted butter
1 large onion, finely chopped
1 large green bell pepper, finely chopped
1 garlic clove, minced
3 cups freshly scraped corn kernels
¼ cup minced fresh chives
2 tablespoons minced cilantro
salt and freshly ground pepper to taste
5 to 6 large eggs, lightly beaten
10 whole wheat flour tortillas
2½ cups grated sharp Cheddar or Monterey Jack cheese
lots of your favorite salsa
¾ cup sour cream, approximately

Preheat the oven to 350° and lightly butter a large shallow casserole or baking sheet. Heat the oil in a large skillet. Add the onion and pepper and sauté over medium heat for 5 minutes, stirring occasionally. Add the garlic and corn and continue to cook for 3 or 4 minutes, stirring now and then. Stir in the herbs, salt, and pepper. Reduce the heat to low and add the eggs. Stir, cooking the eggs just until they're set. Remove from the heat.

One at a time, heat the tortillas for a few seconds on a hot griddle, just long enough to make them pliable. Transfer the tortilla to a plate and spoon some of the corn and egg mixture down the center. Sprinkle about ¼ cup cheese over the filling, then dab salsa and sour cream over it. Fold one side of the tortilla over the filling, then roll it up like a carpet. Transfer the filled tortilla to the baking sheet, then prepare the rest in the same manner.

When they're all assembled, heat for 8 to 10 minutes in the oven. Serve with extra salsa and sour cream for garnish.

Polenta-Stuffed Peppers with Eggs and Chipotle Sauce

Makes 6 servings

This is a brunch dish with enough style and substance to serve for dinner. It involves several elements, but much of the work—cooking the peppers and making the sauce—can be done ahead. The peppers are blanched to tenderize them, then filled with polenta spiffed up with smoked Cheddar cheese and corn kernels. These are baked on a bed of tomato-based chipotle sauce. Chipotles are smoked jalapeños, and their deep flavor really gives the sauce a kick. An egg is added to the top of the pepper, covered with more cheese, and baked a few minutes longer. I like to put these in the middle of the plate, surrounded by a ring of shredded lettuce and avocado chunks dressed with lemon juice. Rich and spicy, this should be followed by a cool, light fruit compote.

> 3 large green bell peppers
> 1 recipe polenta (page 45)
> 1 cup freshly scraped or thawed frozen corn kernels
> 2 cups grated smoked Cheddar cheese
> 1 recipe Chipotle Sauce (page 228)
> 6 large eggs

Bring a large pot of water to a boil. As it heats, halve the peppers lengthwise, being careful not to cut out the stem end; it needs to stay intact to hold the egg in. Cut and pull out as much of the white ribs as you can and shake out the seeds. When the water comes to a boil, add the halved peppers and push them down into the water. Boil for about 4 minutes, until the peppers are just tender but not overly so. Transfer them to a colander with a slotted spoon and let cool.

Measure out 1½ cups of the prepared polenta and place in a bowl; pour the rest into a shallow baking dish and reserve for another use. Stir the corn kernels and not quite half of the smoked Cheddar into the polenta in the bowl. Set aside. Preheat the oven to 400°.

Spread the Chipotle Sauce in the bottom of a shallow casserole just large enough to hold the peppers. Spoon some of the polenta into each pepper; you should have enough to fill each one a little more than half full. Arrange the peppers close to one another in the dish and bake for 20 minutes.

Remove the casserole from the oven. Crack the eggs, one at a time, into a little cup or ramekin, then slide them into the top of each pepper. Sprinkle a little of the remaining cheese over each egg and bake for about another 10 minutes, until the whites are set; if you prefer, you can cook them longer, until the yolks are also set. Serve the peppers hot on a bed of the Chipotle Sauce.

Black Bean Chili

Makes about 3 quarts

This is the highly seasoned chili I use for a couple of eye-opening brunches—but don't let that stop you hard cores from diving into a plain bowl of this before scooting off to the office or out to ski. To my mind, the best chili is boldly seasoned; whether you use meat, tomatoes, or all those other things chili-heads fight over is secondary to a good flavorful base. Here I use generous portions of chili powder, cumin, coriander, and oregano. The flavor is also helped with a little cocoa powder, which you can't really taste but would miss if it were omitted. Besides serving this over Cornmeal Biscuits (page 149), try some alongside Creamy Scrambled Eggs (page 63) or in a bowl, topped with a poached egg (page 64) and grated cheese.

  1 pound dried black beans, picked over and rinsed
  3 tablespoons mild chili powder
  2 tablespoons ground cumin
  1 tablespoon ground coriander
  1 tablespoon dried oregano, crumbled
  ¼ to ½ teaspoon cayenne pepper or to taste
  1 tablespoon unsweetened cocoa powder

⅓ cup olive oil
2 large onions, chopped
1 large green bell pepper, chopped
2 to 3 garlic cloves to taste, minced
1 28-ounce can crushed tomatoes in puree
1¼ teaspoons salt
tomato juice if needed
¼ cup chopped cilantro or parsley plus a little extra for garnish

Put the beans into a large pot and cover with plenty of water. Bring to a boil, uncovered, then boil for 2 minutes. Turn the heat off, cover, and let sit for 1 hour. Drain the beans and put them back in the pot with a gallon of fresh hot water. Bring to a boil, then cook at a low boil, *partially* covered, for about 1 to 1½ hours, until tender. Remove from the heat, but don't drain. If you don't have a second large pot to make the chili in, transfer the beans and their liquid to a large bowl and wash out the pot.

Make the seasoning mixture by combining the chili powder, cumin, coriander, oregano, cayenne, and cocoa in a small bowl; set aside. Heat about half of the olive oil in a large pot. Stir in the onions and pepper and sauté over medium heat, stirring, for 7 minutes. Add the rest of the oil to the pot, then stir in the seasoning mixture and garlic. Lower the heat a little and stir the onion-spice mixture for 2 minutes; it may seem dry, but just keep stirring. When you add the liquid, it will loosen any particles stuck to the pot.

Add the beans and their liquid, the tomatoes, and the salt to the pot. Bring to a boil, then lower the heat to a bare simmer. Cook, covered, over very low heat for about 30 minutes, stirring every 5 minutes or so. If you like a thinner chili, loosen it up with tomato juice. Right before serving, stir in the cilantro or parsley.

. . . .

Cheddar Cheese Spoon Bread

Makes 6 servings

Spoon bread is something like a soufflé—only not quite so fussy—based on a cornmeal-thickened sauce known as a *rick*. It is baked in a shallow baking dish or gratin, puffs considerably, and then deflates after it has been out of the oven for a minute or so. Because of the cornmeal, the texture isn't as refined as that of a soufflé; it has a not unpleasant dryness to it, a texture like moist corn bread. The basic formula can be tinkered with by adding a little leftover or freshly scraped corn to the batter, bits of finely chopped ham, sausage, or what have you. We like this with homemade applesauce and/or a splash of Cranberry Orange Marmalade (page 222) on the side.

3 cups milk
1 cup yellow cornmeal, preferably stone-ground
½ teaspoon salt
⅛ teaspoon cayenne pepper
2 tablespoons unsalted butter, cut into ¼-inch pieces
1 teaspoon Dijon mustard
2 cups grated extrasharp Cheddar cheese
5 large eggs, separated

Preheat the oven to 375° and butter a large, shallow casserole or gratin dish.

Over medium heat, bring the milk to a near boil in a large, heavy saucepan. Gradually add the cornmeal as it heats, whisking almost continuously. When the mixture has thickened somewhat, lower the heat and stir in, one at a time, the salt, cayenne, butter, mustard, cheese, and egg yolks. The mixture should be smooth and thick. Remove from the heat.

Using an electric mixer, beat the egg whites until stiff. Fold them gently but thoroughly into the cornmeal mixture. Turn the batter into the prepared casserole and bake for about 40 minutes, until puffed and golden brown. Bring to the table at once and serve hot.

. . . .

Welsh Rarebit

Makes 4 servings

I've loved Welsh rarebit since I was a kid and my mom would throw a frozen block of it into the double boiler when she didn't feel like cooking on a Friday night, and the nine of us—come to think of it, it was probably two or three blocks—would smear it over toast and scarf it down. My interest in it waned during my navy years—navy chow will do that to a fellow—but it was rekindled as soon as I started making it from scratch; this time it was even better than I remembered. Welsh rarebit is one of the genuine breakfast comfort foods, a smooth, creamy savory whose intense aroma all but explodes in your face. The one essential is a good sharp Cheddar. Beyond that you can use porter, stout, regular beer, or milk as your liquid base, to regulate the pungency. A finish of minced parsley and onion adds a little color and cuts nicely through the richness of the rarebit. Serve on biscuits, toast points, or English muffins and don't miss it on the Rarebit Breakfast Reuben (page 124). Fresh sliced tomatoes are excellent on the side.

2 tablespoons unsalted butter
2 large egg yolks
¾ cup porter, stout, beer, or milk
1 tablespoon Dijon mustard
½ teaspoon Worcestershire sauce (optional)
pinch of cayenne pepper
¾ pound (about 4 cups loosely packed) sharp Cheddar
    cheese, grated
¼ cup loosely packed parsley leaves
½ small onion, chopped
toasted English muffins, warm biscuits, or toast

Melt the butter in the top of a double boiler set over, not in, simmering water. In a small bowl, whisk together the egg yolks, liquid, mustard, Worcestershire sauce, and cayenne and add it to the butter.

When the liquid is very hot, start adding the grated cheese about a quarter at a time, stirring well after each addition. As it melts, add the next batch of cheese, in each case stirring until it melts. Once all the cheese has melted, continue to stir and heat for 5 minutes more; the consistency will be like heavy cream. Mince the parsley and onion together and bring to the table in a small bowl. Serve the rarebit piping hot at the very last minute, over English muffins, toast, or biscuits. Let each person garnish his or her serving with the parsley and onion.

Blue Cheese Rarebit

Makes 4 servings

People either love or hate blue cheese, and you've got to love the stuff to like this. Think of your favorite blue cheese dressing, warmed, and you have some idea how this will taste. I put this on toast or biscuits, then garnish it with bits of ham or chopped toasted walnuts. You can control the intensity of the blue cheese by adding less aggressive flavors and building this into a more filling open-face sandwich. On top of the English muffin, for instance, you can put pieces of leftover chicken, steamed broccoli, or what have you, then sauce the top with the blue cheese. Serve with a little sweet something on the side, like a dollop of pear preserves or the Chunky Vanilla Pears on page 224.

½ cup milk or light cream
½ pound (about 2½ cups) blue cheese, crumbled
2 ounces cream cheese
toasted English muffins, 2 halves per person
chopped ham or chopped toasted walnuts (see note)
2 tablespoons minced parsley

In a small nonreactive saucepan, gently heat the milk. Add 1 cup of the crumbled blue cheese and whisk until the mixture is almost smooth. Add the cream cheese and whisk occasionally until the rarebit is smooth and heated through, about 2 to 3 minutes.

Stir the remaining blue cheese into the pan, cook for a second or two, and remove from the heat. Spoon the rarebit over toasted English muffins, garnishing with the ham or walnuts and the parsley. Serve at once.

Note: To toast walnuts, spread them on a baking sheet and toast for 10 minutes in a preheated 350° oven.

Karen's Spiced Scrambled Tofu

Makes 6 servings

Scrambled tofu dishes are often compared to scrambled eggs, more often—I suspect—by champions of tofu than by the folks at the egg trade associations. And though I can partly appreciate the comparison, I can't get excited about any tofu dish that doesn't stand on its own merits. I think this one does. Karen, my wife, has been making this for years, and perhaps because the kids were introduced to it at an early age it has always been one of their favorites. Tofu, of course, is pretty bland stuff and without the seasonings wouldn't pass muster at anybody's breakfast table. If you don't like too many spices in the morning, add half the recommended spices the first time you make this. Try it at breakfast or brunch, with Cornmeal Biscuits (page 149) and preserves; the preserves are a good counterpoint to the currylike seasoning.

3 tablespoons flavorless vegetable oil
1 large onion, finely chopped
1 medium-size bell pepper, finely chopped (optional)
2 teaspoons dried basil, crumbled
1 teaspoon mild chili powder
1 teaspoon turmeric
½ teaspoon ground ginger
2 1-pound cakes of firm tofu, drained and crumbled
⅓ cup canned crushed tomatoes in puree or chopped
    fresh tomatoes
salt to taste

Heat 2 tablespoons of the oil in a large skillet and add the onion and the pepper if you're using it. Sauté for 7 minutes over medium heat, stirring often. Turn down the heat, add the remaining oil, then stir in the spices and sauté for 1 minute, stirring constantly. Increase the heat slightly, add the crumbled tofu, and cook, stirring occasionally, for about 5 minutes. When most of the excess moisture has cooked off, stir in the tomatoes and salt to taste. Cook for another minute or two, then serve hot.

Chilaquiles for a Crowd

Makes 10 to 12 servings

Chilaquiles is one of our standards, a soft, fragrant casserole of corn tortillas, yogurt or sour cream, pinto beans, and a spicy sauce. A well-seasoned, tomato-based sauce is the key, and there needs to be plenty of it; not enough sauce or not enough seasoning and the casserole will taste bland or dry. This is a terrific brunch dish, so substantial that it needs only a big salad alongside.

You can make a regular family-size dish of this by halving all the ingredients. To speed this along, cook the beans—and perhaps make the sauce—the day before.

1 pound dried pinto beans

 SAUCE

¼ cup flavorless vegetable oil
2 tablespoons ground cumin
2 tablespoons ground coriander
1 teaspoon mild chili powder
1 29-ounce can tomato puree
2 cups crushed canned tomatoes in tomato puree
1 teaspoon salt

12 to 15 corn tortillas, 6 to 7 inches in diameter (see note)
1½ to 2 cups sour cream or plain yogurt, at room temperature
    (see note)
8 ounces Monterey Jack cheese, grated

Prepare the beans: Pick them over to remove any grit or dirt, then rinse them in a colander. Place them in a large pot with plenty of water and bring to a boil. Partially cover, then cook the beans at a low boil for 1 to 1½ hours, until tender. Salt the beans during the last 10 minutes—no sooner, or they'll take forever to cook. Drain the beans and set them aside. You will need 4 cups of beans for the casserole; reserve the rest for another use. Cover and refrigerate if you don't need them until the next day.

Next prepare the sauce: Heat the oil in a large, heavy saucepan. Add the spices and cook them, stirring, for 1 minute; they may clump a little, but that's fine. Add the tomato puree—carefully, because it may splatter—crushed tomatoes, and salt. Cover and simmer for 15 minutes, stirring occasionally. Remove from the heat.

To assemble: Preheat the oven to 400°. Lightly oil a large casserole, either a 10-by-14-inch or a deep 9-by-13-inch casserole. This can also be made in 2 smaller casseroles (and one can be frozen). Ladle about one-quarter of the sauce over the bottom of the casserole. Spoon one-third of the beans over the sauce. Stack the tortillas and cut them into 4 strips. Cover the beans with about one-third of the strips, then spread one-third of the sour cream or yogurt over the tortillas. Sprinkle one-third of the cheese over the creamy layer.

Continue the layering as before—sauce, beans, tortilla strips, sour cream or yogurt, and cheese—ending with a layer of sauce. Cover with foil and bake for 45 minutes, until hot throughout. Let stand for 10 minutes, covered, then serve.

Note: Some packaged tortillas tend to be thicker than others. If they're thickish—thus more absorbent—use the lesser number of tortillas. If they're thinner, use the greater number, overlapping the slices slightly.

We think this is plenty rich using plain yogurt, even low-fat. But if you prefer the richness of sour cream, use it instead; thin to a spreading consistency by stirring briskly with a spoon.

SANDWICHES TO
START THE DAY

I HAVE A SNEAKING suspicion that Americans eat sandwiches for breakfast far more often than you might imagine. Think about it: how many mornings have you started out with a plain piece of toast, only to cover it with bits and pieces from the vast landscape of your kitchen cabinets and fridge: cranberry sauce, a piece of sharp Cheddar, a slab of cold broiled chicken? Or, in summer, mayo, bacon, and a juicy slab of tomato? Avocado, chopped olives, and hard-cooked egg? I know I do it all the time. It's fast, creative, and personal; I've never made a breakfast sandwich I didn't love.

Here is a chapter devoted strictly to intentional breakfast sandwiches, designed to bring this habit out of the closet and into the early morning limelight. Breakfast sandwiches differ from lunch ones on some points, but they have common ground too. There's much less emphasis on meat, specifically cold cuts; they're primarily open-face and not meant for traveling. Bagels or English muffins are common foundations. And breakfast sandwiches are often warm and saucy, so assistance with a fork is sometimes required.

Once you've played around with some of the sandwiches in this chapter, you'll feel confident enough to strike out on your own. And you'll develop an eye for good breakfast sandwiches as you go about your daily cooking and shopping routines. I always find myself buying produce and pantry items with sandwiches in mind. I stock up on things like whole wheat English muffins, and if I'm in a new town I look for bakeries where I might find an interesting sourdough bread. When I make French bread, I set aside some slices for the morning; toasted and buttered, they're heavenly with nothing more than tomato slices and a dusting of Parmesan cheese.

Other stock items I keep on hand are small quantities of cheeses, pickles, relishes, and marinated vegetables. Jellies and preserves—like Cranberry Orange

Marmalade (page 222) and Cider Jelly (page 223)—add a sweet counterpoint to leftover ham, chicken, and turkey. Herb butters are simple to make and bring their own special flavors to morning sandwiches. Tomatoes are a staple in the summer. And avocados I love year-round.

If you're in a breakfast rut, try a sandwich. They might strike you as unusual at first, but once you've gotten in the habit you'll be hooked.

Paprikash Mushrooms on Toast

Makes 4 to 6 servings

This winter weekend dish features rich, creamy mushrooms in a white wine, sour cream, and paprika sauce. I like these on hearty whole grain toast points, with either a poached egg or herb scrambled eggs right in the center, but they're fine all by themselves too. If you have some leftover chicken in the fridge, cut it into bite-size pieces and add it to the mushrooms.

    3 tablespoons unsalted butter
    2 tablespoons minced shallots
    1½ pounds mushrooms, sliced
    ½ teaspoon salt
    1 cup dry white wine
    ½ cup sour cream
    2 teaspoons paprika
    freshly ground pepper to taste
    1 tablespoon chopped fresh dill or 1½ teaspoons dried
    4 thickish slices of whole grain or French bread, toasted
    chopped parsley for garnish (optional)

Melt the butter in a large nonreactive skillet over medium heat. Stir in the shallots and sauté for 30 seconds, stirring. Add the mushrooms and salt and stir to coat them with the butter. Cover and cook the mushrooms for a minute or so, until they've given off a good deal of liquid. Add the wine, cover, and simmer the mushrooms for about 2 minutes; there should still be a good amount of liquid in the pan. Remove the lid and boil the liquid down a little but not too much; you want these to be fairly saucy. Stir in the sour cream, paprika, pepper, and dill and simmer the sauce, covered, for 2 minutes more.

Rewarm the bread or toast it if you haven't already done so. Spoon the mushrooms over the bread and serve piping hot, garnished with parsley if you like.

English Muffins with Olive Cream Cheese and Tomatoes

Makes 2 servings

This simple but sophisticated open-face English muffin sandwich is one of my favorite fast summer breakfasts. I keep a crock of this spread—which can be multiplied easily—on hand in the fridge. Then breakfast can be on the table in just about the time it takes to toast the English muffins. Serve with cold tomato juice and some thin slices of cold ham.

¼ pound cream cheese, softened
6 or 7 good-quality large green olives, pitted and finely chopped
¼ teaspoon Dijon mustard
1 teaspoon hot red pepper flakes
pinch of salt
2 English muffins (4 halves), toasted
4 or 5 ripe cherry tomatoes, sliced into thirds
a little grated Parmesan cheese

In a small bowl, mix the cream cheese, olives, mustard, pepper flakes, and salt until evenly blended. Spread a not-too-thin layer of this mixture over each muffin half. Top with slices of tomato and a sprinkling of Parmesan cheese. Serve at once.

Open-Face Steak Sandwiches with Roquefort

Makes 2 sandwiches

Say you've just had the Mother of All Barbecues and you've got some great leftover steak begging for your inspired hand to transform it into something wonderful; this dish is for you. If you don't have any balsamic vinegar on hand, don't worry; it gives the steak just a touch of acidity to cut through the sharpness of the cheese, but the sandwich is really fine without it. You can, if you prefer, just crumble the Roquefort directly over the steak without mixing it with the milk, which in the heat of the oven makes a sauce that oozes over the whole sandwich. Otherwise the cheese just softens. Either way, this is wonderful. Serve with tomato juice.

> 2 tablespoons unsalted butter
> 1 medium onion, finely chopped
> 8 to 12 slices of leftover steak, a little less than ¼ inch thick
> 1 tablespoon balsamic vinegar
> 2 English muffins (4 halves) toasted, or 4 toasted slices of
>   French bread
> ½ cup Roquefort or other blue cheese
> 1 tablespoon milk

Preheat the broiler and get out a shallow baking dish.

Melt the butter in a skillet, add the onion, and sauté over medium heat for about 7 minutes, stirring often. Add the steak slices and heat for about 30 seconds on each side. Remove the pan from the heat and stir the vinegar into the skillet, mixing with a wooden spoon to coat the steak slices. Put the bread in the baking dish and lay 2 or 3 steak slices on each muffin half or piece of toast. Using a fork, mix the cheese and milk until evenly blended. Spoon a little of the thinned cheese over each sandwich and broil for just a minute or two, until the cheese is runny.

. . . .

Rarebit Breakfast Reuben

Makes up to 4 servings

Boy, is this a treat: toasted English muffins, thinly sliced corned beef, and sauerkraut draped with hot Welsh rarebit. If it sounds lengthy, you should know that the rarebit takes only 10 minutes to prepare, and then you're in business. The sharp flavors call for something mellow on the side—chilled apple or melon slices, perhaps with a squeeze of lime on them. The quantities here will make four servings, but they can be adjusted easily for fewer servings.

     1 recipe Welsh Rarebit (page 115)
     2 cups sauerkraut, drained
     ½ pound cooked corned beef, thinly sliced
     toasted English muffins (2 halves per person)
     minced parsley for garnish (optional)

Prepare the Welsh rarebit and hold it in the double boiler over low heat. Put the sauerkraut in a nonreactive skillet and cook over medium heat just long enough to heat it through and cook off most of the lingering liquid. Set aside in the pan. Stack the slices of corned beef and shred them with a sharp knife.

To assemble, put 2 toasted English muffin halves on each plate. Scatter some of the corned beef and sauerkraut over each half, then sauce the top with the rarebit. Serve at once, garnished with parsley if you like.

Variation: For a quick variation, substitute grated Cheddar for the rarebit. Broil to melt the cheese.

Asparagus and Scrambled Eggs on Toast

Makes 1 serving

This is an attractive egg dish, something special to do just for yourself or for several people; it can be multiplied easily. Simple too. Just scramble a couple of eggs, nestle blanched asparagus spears in them, and serve on toast with a little cheese melted over the top. That's the basic idea, but you can take that and play around with it as you please. You can vary the cheese; one of my favorites is thin rounds of goat cheese. Muenster is good too. If you like, first brush the toast with some pesto. And by all means use chopped fresh herbs on top when they are available. This is substantial enough to be your whole breakfast, perhaps with a simple fruit dish on the side.

> 6 medium-thick asparagus spears
> 1 large slice of French or Italian bread
> 2 large eggs
> 1 tablespoon cream (optional)
> salt to taste
> pinch of grated lemon zest
> ½ teaspoon dried dill or 1 teaspoon chopped fresh
> 1 tablespoon unsalted butter
> ½ cup grated Muenster or other mild cheese or
>   3 thin rounds of goat cheese
> 1 tablespoon chopped parsley or a combination of
>   parsley and fresh dill
> freshly ground pepper to taste

Bring about 1½ inches of salted water to a boil in a skillet. Break the tough lower end of the asparagus off each spear and drop the spears all at once into the water side by side. Boil for approximately 5 to 7 minutes, just until tender. Slip a spatula under them and transfer to a plate lined with a paper towel. Set aside.

Toast the bread, but keep it in the toaster so you can warm it at the last moment. Preheat your broiler if you don't have a toaster oven.

Lightly whisk the eggs, the cream if you're using it, a pinch of salt, the lemon zest, and the dill in a small bowl. Melt the butter in a medium-size nonstick skillet over medium-low heat, saving just a little of it to butter the toast. Add the egg mixture and scramble it with a fork, keeping the eggs moving so they don't set in big clumps. While the eggs are still a little loose, lay the asparagus spears side by side across the center of the eggs. Fold the edge of the eggs up over the asparagus on both sides. Turn off the heat and let them sit in the pan for 30 seconds.

Rewarm and butter the toast. Slide the eggs and asparagus out of the pan onto the toast in one piece. Top with the cheese and put it on an ovenproof plate. Heat under the broiler or in a toaster oven until the cheese is melted; goat cheese will soften but not ooze. Top with the herbs and some pepper and serve.

Variation: For an added splash of color, lightly sauté slices of red bell pepper in a bit of butter and scatter them over the asparagus spears.

Broccoli, Bacon, and Egg Croissant Sandwich

Makes 2 servings

A croissant sandwich may not be a novel idea, but the difference between your own and the flab-in-a-bag they crank out on the fast-food strip is the difference between night and day. I designed this recipe with the idea that most of us are likely to have the key elements on hand, making this a simple breakfast to pull off. Don't make a 10-mile trip to buy apple jelly if there's none in the cupboard; I wouldn't take it as an affront to my culinary genius if you had to do without it. The nicest thing about this sandwich is you get to invite your best friend over to share it with you (preferably one who you know has apple jelly on hand if you don't). Make the recipe work for you and consider your options. You can always leave out the eggs and increase the other ingredients or pad it with pieces of leftover chicken, olives, or what have you.

    2 cups broccoli flowerets
    4 slices of crisp-fried bacon
    1 recipe Creamy Scrambled Eggs (page 63)
    1 large croissant, halved and toasted
    a little soft unsalted butter
    Dijon mustard
    1 tablespoon apple jelly
    1 cup grated sharp Cheddar cheese

In a small saucepan, steam the broccoli so it still has a little bite left to it; it should be crisp-tender. Set aside. Break the bacon into bits and set it aside too. Before you actually scramble the eggs, assemble all the other ingredients and toast the croissant, preferably in a toaster oven; if you don't have a toaster oven, you may have to trim a hair off the bottom of the croissant before you cut it in half so it doesn't get stuck in the toaster. Preheat your oven broiler.

Butter both insides of the croissant lightly; spread with mustard and then apple jelly. Place the halves on a large ovenproof platter, flat sides up and points touching, to form a big croissant circle. Spoon the scrambled eggs into the center of the circle and scatter the broccoli over the eggs and bread. Sprinkle the bacon over the broccoli, then cover the whole thing with the grated cheese. Broil just until the cheese melts. Share the sandwich from the same plate or cut in half and serve.

Mushroom Scrambled Eggs and Brie Croissant Sandwich

Makes 1 serving

Gently scrambling eggs with mushrooms is a good trick for capturing the flavorful juices the mushrooms exude. Even alone they make a fine meal, but adding some softened Brie and a toasted croissant turns them into a refined breakfast sandwich for any day of the week. In summer, when we have fresh tarragon, I like to add a few finely chopped tarragon leaves to the scrambled eggs. Lacking that, you might sprinkle a touch of tarragon vinegar over the mushrooms just before you add the eggs to the skillet.

½ toasted croissant, lightly buttered
1 recipe Creamy Scrambled Eggs with Mushrooms (page 64)
a few fresh tarragon leaves, chopped (optional)
2 pieces of Brie, about 4 inches long and ⅛ inch thick
a sprinkle of hot red pepper flakes

Put the toasted croissant on an ovenproof plate and hold it in a 300° oven while you prepare the eggs. Scramble the eggs, adding a few finely chopped tarragon leaves if you like. Turn the eggs out into the crescent part of the croissant and lay the Brie over them; or cut it into chunks over the eggs. Put back in the oven just long enough to soften the Brie, about 2 minutes. Sprinkle the top with red pepper flakes to taste and serve right away.

Bagel with Smoked Cheddar, Eggs, Tomato, and Basil

Makes 2 open-face sandwiches

I can't think of much from the summer garden that doesn't lend itself to a breakfast sandwich; just begin with soft butter or fresh herb cream cheese and take it from there. Here is one idea I simply adore—eggs scrambled with smoked Cheddar cheese, then piled on a toasted bagel with tomato slices and a few snips of basil. The smoked Cheddar adds a deep, almost woodsy tone in contrast with the bright fresh flavor of the tomato and basil. Pull a couple of lawn chairs up to the edge of the garden and enjoy this in the morning sun with glasses of fresh lemonade.

> 1 bagel, halved
> soft unsalted butter
> Dijon mustard
> 1 recipe Creamy Scrambled Eggs with cheese (page 64),
>   using smoked Cheddar
> 4 thin fresh tomato slices
> salt and freshly ground pepper to taste
> a few fresh basil leaves

To assemble the sandwich, toast the bagel, butter the halves, and spread a little mustard on each half. Prepare the scrambled eggs as for Creamy Scrambled Eggs with Cheddar and Sage, using smoked Cheddar and omitting the sage, then spread half of the eggs over each bagel half. Top with tomato slices, salt and pepper them lightly, then tear the basil into shreds and sprinkle on top of the tomato.

. . . .

Bagel with the Works

Makes 2 open-face sandwiches

Here's a bagel with the right attitude, or—as we say nowadays—just plain *attitude*. It isn't for prissy eaters or those with clearly defined boundaries between breakfast and those other two meals of the day. While it has obvious Mediterranean leanings—tomatoes, basil, olives, feta—my objective was simply to create a signature version of the ultimate bagel rather than some theme sandwich. If you have access to good French or country bread, a slab of it would do well here in place of the bagel. This isn't at all necessary, but if you're planning ahead, marinate the feta cheese overnight in the basil and olive oil (the first step). In the summer, of course, you'd use the best sun-ripened tomatoes available; in off months, cherry tomatoes generally have more flavor and a better texture.

1 small piece of feta cheese (about ⅓ cup)
3 tablespoons olive oil
1 teaspoon dried basil, crumbled, or 1 tablespoon
   chopped fresh
1 bagel, halved
6 thin tomato slices
1 cup leftover chicken, preferably barbecued, cut into
   thin strips
½ ripe Haas avocado (the pebbly-skinned variety), peeled, pitted,
   and cut into chunks
5 or 6 good-quality green or black olives, pitted and sliced

At least a few minutes ahead but preferably the night before, crumble the feta cheese into a bowl, breaking it into not-too-small pieces. Drizzle it with the olive oil and gently toss with the basil. Set aside, covered if overnight.

When you're ready to assemble the sandwich, toast the bagel and put half on each serving plate. Drain the oil off the cheese, drizzling it onto the bagel halves. Set the cheese aside.

Cover each half with 3 tomato slices, followed by ½ cup of chicken. Scoop chunks of avocado over the chicken, then add the sliced olives and feta cheese and serve.

Olive Cream Cheese, Egg, and Avocado on Toast

Makes 2 open-face sandwiches

This sandwich has a base of cream cheese blended with chopped olives and parsley. The sharpness of the olives is tempered but nicely enhanced by the hard-cooked egg and avocado. A slice or two of tomato, if they're in season, is excellent. If you have cumin seeds in the spice cabinet, toast a few and sprinkle them over the top. You'll save time in the morning if you cook the eggs the night before.

    2 hard-cooked eggs
    3 ounces cream cheese, slightly softened
    3 tablespoons chopped parsley
    6 good-quality black or green olives, pitted and finely chopped
    freshly ground pepper to taste
    2 slices of whole grain bread or bagel halves, toasted
    1 ripe Haas avocado
    salt to taste
    ½ lemon
    olive oil

If you haven't done so the night before, hard-cook the eggs, letting them cool for 5 minutes in their shells in ice water. Peel and slice.

In a small bowl, mix the cream cheese with the parsley, olives, and a few grinds of pepper. Spread the cream cheese mixture over each piece of toast; there will be some left over. Cover with sliced eggs. Cut the avocado in half and remove the pit. Spoon the flesh out onto the sandwich, mashing it slightly with a fork. Salt and pepper the top to taste, then squeeze lemon juice over the avocado. Drizzle a bit of olive oil over the top and serve.

Pear and Feta Cheese Baguette

Makes 1 serving

Sweet pears, salty cheese, good bread—amazing how that's about all it takes to make a memorable breakfast sandwich. In summer I sprinkle fresh herbs from the garden over the top: chopped basil, parsley, perhaps some lemon thyme or lemon balm. It's important that the pears be ripe and juicy, not dry or underripe.

½ tablespoon unsalted butter, softened
1 6- to 8-inch section of baguette, halved lengthwise
1 ripe, juicy pear
½ lemon
¼ cup feta cheese
freshly ground black pepper to taste
a sprinkle of fresh herbs (optional)

Spread the butter over half of the baguette; you won't need the other half unless you make two sandwiches. Heat a heavy skillet, then put the bread in the pan buttered side down. Let the bread brown for a couple of minutes, then place it browned side up on a plate.

Peel, core, and slice the pear, lining the slices up on the bread in a thick, overlapping row. Squeeze a little lemon here and there over the pears, then crumble feta cheese over them. Give the top of the sandwich a dusting of pepper and sprinkle with herbs if you have some on hand. Serve.

Smoked Salmon and Herb Cream Cheese Sandwiches

Makes 16 to 20 little sandwiches

These inviting little sandwiches are made on biscuits; I like buckwheat biscuits myself, but most any plain, cornmeal, or Cheddar cheese biscuit will work well too. Once the biscuits have cooled, they're spread with an herb and mustard cream cheese and topped with a small slice of smoked salmon. These are especially nice at a seaside retreat, for a small gathering of friends. If you want to double the number of servings with almost no extra work, simply make these as open-face sandwiches. Roll out the biscuit dough rather than patting it—so you end up with a flat top—then use both the bottom and top of the split biscuit to build your sandwiches. You'll also need to double the cream cheese filling and buy extra salmon.

1 recipe Buckwheat Buttermilk Biscuits (page 147) or
    other biscuits
¼ pound cream cheese
1 teaspoon Dijon mustard
2 to 3 tablespoons finely chopped mixed herbs such as parsley,
        basil, lovage, a little oregano, or others
1 teaspoon fresh lemon juice
freshly ground pepper to taste
¼ pound smoked salmon, thinly sliced

Prepare the biscuits as directed, cutting them into rounds with a 2- or 2¼-inch biscuit cutter. Bake according to the instructions. Cool the biscuits thoroughly on a rack.

While the biscuits cool, blend the cream cheese, mustard, herbs, lemon juice, and pepper. Cut the biscuits in half, spreading the bottom with a little of the herb cream cheese. Lay a small piece of smoked salmon over the filling and cover with the top of the biscuit. Arrange the sandwiches on a platter and serve.

ALL THINGS WARM AND SWEET: QUICK BREADS, COFFEE CAKES, AND MORE BREAKFAST BAKING

PERHAPS MORE THAN ANY other part of the morning meal, quick breads, coffee cakes, and other fresh baked goods are universally adored. Usually sweet and filling, their aroma alone is enough to jump-start even chronic early morning laggards. Around here no one dares linger in bed when the smell of cinnamon and spice, berry muffins, or toasted almond coffee cake starts swirling up the stairs: everyone knows by now there's slim pickings left for latecomers.

With few exceptions the quick breads here take about 30 minutes from start to finish—and only a few minutes of that is actual preparation time. So there is no reason to think of biscuits, muffins, and scones as strictly weekend fare. Light eaters can enjoy muffins or biscuits with butter and preserves, or—if you're on a tight schedule—you can add variety to the menu with convenience items like yogurt, applesauce, juice, and coffee. The quick (baking powder and soda) coffee cakes take longer to prepare and bake, but even they're approachable on a weekday if you allow yourself a little extra time. Yeast coffee cakes and breads are generally weekend items, when there's no rush to get out of the house. All of these recipes make ample quantities, so you can freeze any leftovers in individual serving portions, then pop them in the toaster oven and enjoy them throughout the week.

Organization—of your thoughts and materials—is the key to baking. Morning baking will ultimately become a frustration if you can't decide what to bake or figure out where the muffin pan disappeared to. Know thyself. If the morning tends to leave you in a fog, decide the night before what sounds enticing. Track down ingredients and put them on your work surface. You can even mix the dry ingredients in advance and leave them right on the counter.

Many cooks aren't too confident about baking, but there's nothing to be afraid of. It takes a little practice to master yeast breads, but even if you have no desire to try them, a repertoire of good quick breads will serve you nicely. Confidence comes with experience and enjoyment. A lot of people catch the baking bug with quick breads first, then move on to yeast breads. Remember that recipes are valuable, especially in baking, but there is no substitute for personal experience and observation. Think of baking recipes as broad strokes and yourself as the arbiter of personal details. It is often what appears to be the small things—like the amount of spice in the muffins, the right blend of flours, soaking your dried fruit if it's too dry—that makes the difference between a recipe that's merely good and a great one that has your signature on it.

· ·

THE WELL-STOCKED BAKER

How many times have you decided on some great-sounding scone or coffee cake, only to find your larder's missing at least one key ingredient? You can avoid this frustrating situation by checking your supply of baking staples every week or so, before you head for the grocery. Here are some key items:

• *Flours and grains*. Store unbleached flour in an easily accessible airtight container in a cool place. Whole grain flours, cornmeal, bran, and wheat germ should be double-bagged and stored in the freezer. Store rolled oats and whole millet at room temperature.

• *Spices*. Buy small quantities of cinnamon, nutmeg, cloves, ginger, cardamom and replenish supplies often to keep them fresh.

• *Unsalted butter*. Keep an extra pound in the freezer.

• *Unflavored vegetable oil*

• *Eggs*

• *Sweeteners*. Sugar, light and dark brown sugars, confectioners' sugar, honey, molasses, and maple syrup.

• *Extracts*. Pure vanilla and lemon are essential; almond is nice to have around too.

• *Lemons*. The zest goes into muffins, scones, coffee cakes, etc.

• *Dried fruits*. Raisins, cranberries, cherries, currants, dates, figs.

• *Nuts and seeds*. Walnuts, almonds, pecans, poppy, sesame, and sunflower seeds. Freeze them.

• *Leavenings*. Keep yeast in the freezer. Baking powder and baking soda are fine at room temperature, tightly covered.

Millet Corn Muffins

Makes 12 muffins

As a rule I don't like a hodgepodge of grains in my baked goods; I think mixing one or two with a background of unbleached flour allows you to savor the ones that are there without diminishing their individual charms. Such is the case with this millet muffin. You can appreciate millet's natural sweetness and crunch in this muffin. Softening the grain in hot water makes the millet slightly softer, but it still manages to retain its texture. There is a little cornmeal too, for the golden hue and slight roughness the millet seems to invite. These are good with, among other things, Strawberry Rhubarb Compote (page 210).

½ cup millet
1⅔ cups unbleached flour
⅓ cup yellow cornmeal, preferably stone-ground
2 teaspoons baking powder
½ teaspoon baking soda
½ teaspoon salt
1 large egg
1 cup milk
½ cup sour cream
¼ cup packed light brown sugar
½ teaspoon vanilla extract
⅓ cup flavorless vegetable oil
granulated sugar for sprinkling on top (optional)

Put the millet in a small mixing bowl and add enough hot tap water to cover. Set aside. Preheat the oven to 400° and lightly butter 12 muffin cups.

In a large mixing bowl, toss together the flour, cornmeal, baking powder, baking soda, and salt. In a separate bowl, whisk the egg until frothy, then blend in the milk, sour cream, brown sugar, vanilla, and oil. Set aside.

Heat a large, heavy skillet. Drain the millet, then add it to the skillet. Toast the millet, stirring over medium-high heat, until the water evaporates and the grain starts to pop; you may hear some popping sounds or just see the grains start popping or both. Either way, once the grain has popped for 30 seconds, remove it from the heat and scrape it onto a plate and cool for 5 minutes.

Add the millet to the dry mixture. Make a well in the dry mixture, then add the liquid and stir the batter until blended evenly. Let the batter sit for 2 minutes, stir it again several times, then divide the batter evenly among the buttered cups. Sprinkle the top of each muffin with a big pinch of sugar if you like, then bake for 20 minutes. Cool the muffins in the pan for 2 minutes, then remove them and serve hot.

Pecan Maple Oat Muffins

Makes 10 muffins

Neither pecans nor maple syrup is getting any less expensive these days, but don't wait for the price to go down to try these. They're wonderful. The pecan topping sort of caramelizes over the top and edges of the muffins; you end up with a crunchy crust that's so good you'll be scraping off the muffin tins. The muffin itself is light textured but still nubby and grainy with the bits of whole wheat flour and oats; I think a few oats are always welcome in muffins.

 **TOPPING**

1 cup shelled pecans
⅓ cup packed light brown sugar
2 tablespoons unbleached flour
¼ cup unsalted butter, cut into ¼-inch pieces

 MUFFINS

1½ cups unbleached flour
½ cup whole wheat flour
⅓ cup rolled oats (*not* instant)
1 tablespoon baking powder
½ teaspoon salt
½ teaspoon ground cinnamon
1 large egg, lightly beaten
1 cup milk
⅓ cup maple syrup
¼ cup flavorless vegetable oil
½ teaspoon vanilla extract

Preheat the oven to 400° and butter 10 muffin cups. Set aside. Make the topping: Put the pecans, brown sugar, and flour in a food processor. Process briefly, until the nuts are coarsely chopped. Add the butter, then process again until you have fine, uniform crumbs. Set aside.

Mix the flours, oats, baking powder, salt, and cinnamon in a large bowl. Whisk the egg in a separate bowl, then blend in the milk, maple syrup, oil, and vanilla. Make a well in the dry ingredients and add the liquid. Stir just until the batter is blended evenly.

Spoon the batter into the muffin cups, then spread about a tablespoon of the nut topping over each muffin; if there's any topping left, just bag and freeze it for another batch of muffins. Bake the muffins for 22 minutes. Cool them in the pan on a rack for 5 minutes, then pop the muffins out and serve them hot.

Cranberry Poppy Seed Corn Muffins

Makes 12 muffins

Some people think I work for the Cranberry Council of America because I use so much of this fruit. Cranberries are great in baking; I go through at least 25 pounds in a year, not only in baked goods but also in sauces, pancakes, and more—if it can be cranberried, I've probably tried it. Here's a particularly good cranberry muffin recipe, a sweet jumble of contrasting colors, textures, and flavors. There's the rich red of cranberries against the pale yellow crumb of the muffin. The poppy seeds add yet another note, and the crumb topping makes them downright irresistible. A good fall muffin.

1½ cups unbleached flour
1 cup yellow cornmeal, preferably stone-ground
1 tablespoon baking powder
¾ teaspoon salt
1 teaspoon ground cinnamon
3 tablespoons poppy seeds
1 large egg
1 large egg yolk
½ cup packed light brown sugar
1¼ cups milk
finely grated zest of 1 lemon
¼ cup unsalted butter, melted and cooled
1½ cups fresh cranberries
1½ cups Oat and Brown Sugar Crumb Topping (page 171)

Preheat the oven to 400° and butter 12 muffin cups. Mix the flour, cornmeal, baking powder, salt, cinnamon, and poppy seeds in a large bowl. In a second bowl, whisk the egg, egg yolk, and brown sugar until smooth. Whisk in the milk and lemon zest.

Make a well in the dry ingredients, add the liquid, and stir. While there are still traces of dry, fold in the melted butter and cranberries; stir just until the batter is blended.

Divide the batter evenly among the muffin cups and top each one with some of the crumb topping. Bake for 22 minutes. Cool the muffins in the pan on a rack for 2 or 3 minutes, then pop them out of the pan and serve hot.

Apple Walnut Crumb Muffins

Makes 12 muffins

Wheat germ gives these moist, plump muffins a grainy touch without weighing them down. I like to grate the apple, the way I've done it here, but you can cut it into little chunks instead. Cover the muffins thickly with the crumb topping because some of it always rolls off as the muffins rise in the oven.

½ cup toasted wheat germ plus a little for dusting
    the muffin cups
2 cups unbleached flour
1 tablespoon baking powder
2 teaspoons ground cinnamon
½ teaspoon salt
1 large egg
½ cup lightly packed dark brown sugar
1¼ cups milk
¼ cup unsalted butter, melted, or flavorless vegetable oil
1 large apple, peeled, cored, and grated
1 cup chopped walnuts
1½ cups Oat and Brown Sugar Crumb Topping (page 171)

ENTERTAINING BREAKFASTS

Few of us think of the morning as prime time for throwing a party, but there's a lot to recommend the idea if, like me, you're a morning person (i.e, one whose energy, charm, and wit are in full flower from dawn until noon). The benevolent nature of breakfast takes all the pressure off the cook to replicate the latest trendy meal or create five incredible courses; breakfast can be much simpler and lighter. Everyone's guard is down in the morning, so the atmosphere tends to be lively but relaxed. And since there's usually no alcohol involved, you don't have to worry about send-ing everyone home safely or spending a big chunk of cash on potables.

Since the whole idea is to stay casual, a breakfast party should include only as many friends or family members as you feel comfortable with at one time. In the summer, being outdoors increases the potential guest list; people can spill over into the patio or backyard without pushing the carrying capacity of your house. Indeed these outdoor areas should be set up with chairs and tables—dressed up with vases of flowers and glasses of fresh orange and grapefruit juices—so the invitation to sit and linger is obvious.

The menu can be as elaborate or as simple as you like, but it should be appropriate to the season, and there should be plenty to go around. Befitting the occasion, I like to do something a little unexpected, make a meal you couldn't get at the local diner. One of my favorite simple starting dishes is slices of homemade pound cake served with fresh sliced fruit—or poached fruit—in its own juice. Depending on the rest of the menu, I may or may not include freshly whipped cream. Another nice cake beginning, perfect with the first mugs of coffee, is a double batch of Sam's Hot Chocolate Dunkers, a type of biscotti (page 185). I

also like to serve yeasted coffee cake (page 160) because it's just a little more special than muffins or biscuits.

For something more substantial, it's hard to beat a good homemade hash, one of those good dishes nobody makes anymore. Poached eggs are the traditional accompaniment, but for a party consider baked eggs (page 71) also.

It's thoughtful to offer both fresh regular and decaf coffees as well as a variety of teas. On hot summer days iced coffee or a pitcher of fresh iced herb tea would be just the ticket. Don't forget to plan some games for after the meal, like badminton or horseshoes. Or just take a leisurely stroll or a morning dip in the lake.

Butter 12 muffin cups and sprinkle a little wheat germ into each one. Tap the muffin pan on all sides to spread the wheat germ around. Preheat the oven to 400°.

In a large bowl, combine the flour, wheat germ, baking powder, cinnamon, and salt. Whisk the egg and brown sugar in a separate bowl. Whisk in the milk. Make a well in the dry ingredients, add the liquid—including the melted butter—and stir to blend. When a few streaks of dry are still visible, fold in the grated apple and walnuts.

Divide the batter evenly among the muffin cups. Scatter a good amount of crumb topping over each muffin and bake for 22 minutes. Cool the muffins in the pan on a rack for 3 minutes, then pop them out and serve hot.

Banana Walnut Muffins

Makes 12 muffins

Moist, light, and soft, these are a favorite of my daughter Alison, who likes the way they're so "banana-y." Alison *really* likes these with a crumb topping (page 171); add some if you have it in the freezer or have a second pair of hands available to make it while you mix up the batter. The banana keeps these moister longer than most muffins, so they're a good choice for packing into lunches or taking on a hike. I love them spread with peanut butter and honey.

1 large egg
⅓ cup packed light brown sugar
2 large very ripe bananas, mashed (1 cup)
¾ cup milk
¼ cup flavorless vegetable oil
1½ cups unbleached flour
1 cup whole wheat pastry flour
1 teaspoon baking soda
1 teaspoon baking powder

½ teaspoon ground nutmeg
½ teaspoon ground cinnamon
½ teaspoon salt
¾ cup finely chopped walnuts

Preheat the oven to 400° and butter 12 muffin cups. In a bowl, whisk the egg, brown sugar, bananas, milk, and oil. In a separate bowl, mix the remaining ingredients. Make a well in the dry mixture, add the liquid, and stir just until evenly blended. Divide the mixture equally among the muffin cups and bake for 20 to 22 minutes; when done, the centers should not yield easily or feel squishy under gentle finger pressure. Cool in the pan on a rack for a couple of minutes, then remove them from the pan and serve at once. Store leftovers in a sealed plastic bag.

If you plan to keep these for more than 24 hours—say you want to have them for the whole week—slice them and freeze in a double plastic bag. Then pop them right into the toaster oven for a few minutes.

Blueberry Lemon Scones

Makes 10 scones

I see more and more scones showing up in bakeries and gourmet food stores across the country, so Americans are clearly becoming enamored of them. That's no surprise; scones are delicious, especially your own. Scones are sweet biscuits, and they come in every stripe—those made with oats and other grains; with dried or fresh fruit; some cooked on a griddle, but most baked. Unlike regular biscuits, scones stay fresher a little longer because the higher proportion of fat and sugar helps to preserve them. That means you can make a batch for breakfast, send some off to school with the kids, and still enjoy a few the next morning. This is a sour cream scone. Sour cream tenderizes baked goods and loosens the structure, so these tend to spread a bit rather than rise too high. Still, they're wicked good tasting, especially in the summer, when fresh berries are available. You can also use frozen berries right out of the freezer with excellent results.

2 cups unbleached flour
⅓ cup sugar plus extra for sprinkling on top
3 tablespoons toasted wheat germ
1 teaspoon baking soda
1 teaspoon baking powder
½ teaspoon salt
¼ teaspoon ground nutmeg
6 tablespoons cold unsalted butter, cut into ¼-inch pieces
scant cup sour cream
1 large egg
1 teaspoon lemon extract
½ teaspoon vanilla extract
finely grated zest of 1 lemon
1½ cups fresh or frozen blueberries
2 to 3 tablespoons milk as needed

Preheat the oven to 400° and lightly butter a large baking sheet.

In a large bowl, mix the flour, ⅓ cup sugar, wheat germ, baking soda, baking powder, salt, and nutmeg. Add the butter and cut it in until it is broken into very fine pieces. In a separate bowl, whisk together the sour cream, egg, extracts, and lemon zest. Make a well in the dry ingredients, add the liquid, and quickly mix into a shaggy, cohesive mass, folding in the blueberries a few strokes before the dough is blended entirely. Don't be too rough at this stage—especially if the berries are fresh—because you'll turn them to mush.

Divide the dough in half. Keeping in mind that you want 5 scones from each half, use a large spoon to scoop enough dough into your floured hands to make one scone. Round it gently with your palms and lay it on the prepared sheet. Repeat for the remaining scones, leaving a little room between them for spreading.

Brush each scone with a little of the milk, then sprinkle them with sugar. Bake for 20 minutes, until golden brown and crusty. Transfer to a rack and cool for several minutes before serving. These are good warm or at room temperature or anywhere in between.

· · · · · · · · · · · ·

Buckwheat Buttermilk Biscuits

Makes 12 to 16 biscuits

These have a mild buckwheat flavor that goes as well with butter and honey as it does with cheeses; these biscuits and a selection of fall fruits and Cheddars make a fine breakfast. I also like these under Welsh rarebit and with thin slices of ham tucked inside. You can increase the amount of buckwheat flour up to half of the total amount (1 cup buckwheat, 1 cup unbleached) but start with the lesser amount in the original recipe and work up from there. Most people aren't aware just how assertive buckwheat can be. These are the biscuits I like to use with smoked salmon and herb cream cheese for little breakfast sandwiches (page 133).

> 1½ cups unbleached flour
> ½ cup buckwheat flour
> 1 tablespoon baking powder
> ½ teaspoon salt
> 5 tablespoons cold unsalted butter, cut into ¼-inch pieces
> 1 cup buttermilk, or ¾ cup sour cream thinned with
>   ¼ cup water or milk

Preheat the oven to 450° and lightly butter a large baking sheet. In a large bowl, combine the flours, baking powder, and salt. Add the butter and cut or rub it in until the mixture resembles coarse rolled oats. Make a well in the dry mixture and add the buttermilk all at once. Stir vigorously, just until the dough coheres in a solid mass.

Let the dough rest for 1 minute, then turn it out onto a lightly floured surface and knead 2 or 3 times. Pat or roll the dough out to a thickness of about ¾ inch. Cut the dough into rounds, placing the rounds on the prepared sheet with a little room between them. Bake for 12 to 15 minutes, until crusty and browned. Serve at once.

Sour Cream Bran Biscuits

Makes 12 to 16 biscuits

It is incredibly rare to find a good biscuit outside one's own home, at least here in New England; down South is a different story, of course, but I'm happy living where I am. The key is hot, just-from-the-oven freshness. Good biscuits are like butterflies: here one minute and gone the next. They don't even reheat that well because reheating dries the interior out. I've learned from experience that a *slightly* damp dough is better than one that you have to keep adding liquid to; you can always deal with a dampish dough by using a little extra flour on your hands and counter, but when you keep adding liquid to a dry dough you overwork it, and that makes a tough biscuit. So do add all your liquid at once and stir it in briskly right away. Here is a favorite sour cream biscuit of mine, one with a ration of bran for a little nub and color. They're high risers and blessed with that perfect blend of textures I was talking about. Great with soup for dinner too.

2 cups unbleached flour
¼ cup wheat bran (*not* bran cereal)
1 teaspoon baking soda
1 teaspoon baking powder
¾ teaspoon salt
5 tablespoons cold unsalted butter, cut into ¼-inch pieces
1 cup sour cream
¼ cup water

Preheat the oven to 425° and lightly butter a large baking sheet.

In a mixing bowl, toss together the flour, bran, baking soda, baking powder, and salt. Add the butter and rub it into the dry ingredients until you have small, flat flakes; it will look something like rolled oats. Measure the sour cream into a glass measuring cup and stir the water into it. Make a well in the dry ingredients and pour in the liquid all at once. Quickly stir the dough into a shaggy, cohesive mass. Turn the dough out onto a floured surface and knead 2 or 3 times with floured hands.

Pat the dough out to a thickness of not quite 1 inch. Cut into rounds using a small- or medium-size (1½- or 2-inch) cutter and place them on the sheet, leaving at least 1½ inches between them. Bake for 12 to 14 minutes, until golden brown and crusty. Serve at once.

Cornmeal Biscuits

Makes about 12 biscuits

Here's a simple, light biscuit with a crunchy exterior and an attractive pale golden hue. I like to roll them thin—slightly less than ½ inch—for an extracrisp biscuit when I serve these as the base for Black Bean Chili (page 112), leftover stews, or creamed chicken.

1½ cups unbleached flour
½ cup yellow cornmeal, preferably stone-ground
1 tablespoon baking powder
½ teaspoon salt
¼ cup cold unsalted butter, cut into ¼-inch pieces
¾ cup milk

Preheat the oven to 425° and lightly butter a large baking sheet. In a large bowl, mix the flour, cornmeal, baking powder, and salt. Add the butter and cut it in until the mixture resembles coarse crumbs. Make a well in the dry ingredients, add the milk, and stir until the dough coheres. Let it sit for 2 minutes. Scrape the dough out onto a floured surface and knead 2 or 3 times with floured hands. Pat or roll the dough ½ to ¾ inch thick—a thicker biscuit will give you softer insides—and place on the sheet. Bake for 12 to 15 minutes, until golden brown. Place in a cloth-lined basket and serve hot.

Banana Wheat Germ Soda Bread

Makes 2 loaves

I have been spinning variations of soda bread for as long as I can remember. I particularly like it for breakfast because, unlike yeast bread, you can have a delicious slicing loaf out of the oven within an hour of the word go. This one uses bananas for part of the liquid base. It has a light texture, with an earthy golden cast from the wheat germ and the small amount of whole wheat flour. And nobody has to tell you how well walnuts work with the bananas. Think of this as an all-purpose breakfast bread but one that's good enough to be the focal point of the meal: I'm content to serve this alone, with soft butter or a crock of lightly sweetened cream cheese and lots of freshly brewed coffee.

3 cups unbleached flour
½ cup whole wheat flour
½ cup toasted wheat germ
2 teaspoons salt
1 teaspoon baking soda
1 teaspoon baking powder
2 tablespoons unsalted butter at room temperature
1 cup plain yogurt
1 large very ripe banana, well mashed (½ cup)
⅓ cup milk
⅓ cup packed light brown sugar
1 cup chopped walnuts

Preheat the oven to 400° and lightly butter a large baking sheet. In a large bowl, toss together the flours, wheat germ, salt, baking soda, and baking powder. Cut the butter into small pieces, dropping them into the dry ingredients. Rub the butter into the dry ingredients until it is reduced to fine pieces.

In another bowl, whisk the yogurt, banana, milk, and brown sugar together. Make a well in the dry ingredients, then add the liquid and the walnuts. Stir vigorously until the dough pulls together in a dense, cohesive ball.

Flour your work counter, then scrape the dough out onto it. Cut the dough in half, then knead each half into a ball with floured hands. Place the balls on the baking sheet and make a single incision, about ½ inch deep, across the center of each one with a sharp serrated knife.

Bake the loaves for 35 to 40 minutes, until golden brown and crusty. The bottoms should sound hollow when tapped with a finger. Cool on a rack for about 15 minutes before slicing.

Lost Nation Apple Coffee Cake

Makes 12 servings

This is a recipe from my friends Mike and Nancy Phillips. Nancy prepares and sells this coffee cake to customers who visit their Lost Nation Cider Mill in northern New Hampshire during apple season; it always sells out quickly, says Nancy, and visitors often buy several extra pieces to take home with them. It may seem as if there are too many apples in this batter as you stir it, but just keep mixing until the batter coats all of the slices. Excellent with coffee or hot cider.

 TOPPING

½ cup unbleached flour
⅓ cup packed light brown sugar
½ teaspoon ground cinnamon
pinch of salt
¼ cup cold unsalted butter, cut into ¼-inch pieces
½ cup finely chopped walnuts or pecans

 ## CAKE

½ cup (1 stick) unsalted butter, softened
1 cup sugar
2 large eggs at room temperature
1 teaspoon vanilla extract
1 cup unbleached flour
½ cup whole wheat flour
1 teaspoon baking soda
½ teaspoon salt
1 teaspoon ground cinnamon
¼ teaspoon ground nutmeg
3 cups peeled and thinly sliced apples

Make the topping: Mix the flour, brown sugar, cinnamon, and salt in a large bowl. Add the butter and cut or rub it in until the butter is broken into small pieces. Add the nuts and continue to rub until the mixture is uniformly clumpy. Cover and refrigerate. Butter a 7- by 11-inch or 9-inch square baking pan and preheat the oven to 350°.

Using an electric mixer, cream the butter, gradually adding the sugar. Beat in the eggs, one at a time, beating for about 30 seconds after each addition. Blend in the vanilla. In a separate bowl, sift together the flours, baking soda, salt, and spices. Fold the dry mixture into the creamed mixture in 2 additions, then fold the apples into the batter until the batter coats all of the apples.

Scrape the batter into the prepared pan and even out the top with a fork. Sprinkle with the topping and bake for approximately 35 to 40 minutes, until a tester inserted in the center of the cake comes out clean. Cool the cake in the pan on a rack for 1 hour before slicing. Covered and refrigerated, this cake will keep for 2 days.

Apricot Almond Coffee Cake

Makes 12 servings

Besides buying lottery tickets, my other big character flaw in this lifetime is a weakness for coffee cakes. But whereas your chances of winning the lottery are substantially lower than those that you'll fall into a cistern and drown, it's almost a sure bet that you'll fall for this soft, wheaty coffee cake covered with apricot preserves and slivered almonds. As I often do, I've included a good measure of whole wheat flour because I like the extra texture and character it imparts, not to mention the clear edge it offers in the nutrition department. Try another kind of preserves if you like; peach is also quite good. Incidentally, this was adapted from an American Spoon Foods recipe—they're the good people who make just-plain-heavenly fruit spreads and preserves, among other things (see Sources).

1 cup unbleached flour
1 cup whole wheat pastry flour
1 teaspoon baking powder
½ teaspoon baking soda
¼ teaspoon salt
¼ teaspoon ground nutmeg
½ cup (1 stick) unsalted butter, softened
½ pound cream cheese, softened
¾ cup sugar
2 large eggs at room temperature
1 teaspoon vanilla extract
finely grated zest of 1 lemon
½ cup milk
1 9- or 10-ounce jar apricot preserves
1 cup slivered almonds

Preheat the oven to 350° and butter a 9- by 13-inch baking pan. Sift the flours, baking powder, baking soda, salt, and nutmeg into a bowl. If any pieces of bran don't go through the sifter, just dump them into the bowl. Using an electric mixer, cream the butter and cream cheese together in a separate bowl, gradually adding the sugar. Beat in the eggs, one at a time, beating until smooth after each addition. Blend in the vanilla and lemon zest.

Mix half of the dry ingredients into the creamed mixture until smooth. Blend in the milk, then add the rest of the dry ingredients, mixing just until the batter is smooth. Turn the batter into the prepared pan and level the top with a spoon.

If the preserves are thick, empty them into a bowl and thin slightly with a little water. In any case, stir them up and spoon the preserves here and there over the top of the batter; use the entire jar. Spread the preserves with a spoon so they cover the surface, then sprinkle the almonds evenly over the top. Bake for 30 to 35 minutes, until a tester inserted in the center of the cake comes out clean. Cool in the pan on a rack for 1 hour before serving—*if* you can wait that long.

Blueberry Cream Cake

Makes 10 servings

Sometimes I want to make a cake, but I don't want the bother or required foresight to soften butter, drag out mixers, and all that business. So I came up with this, an easy-to-mix summer cake for times when we need to unload a bunch of blueberries, which is often because we have them coming out of our ears by August; not only do we grow our own, but our neighbor Elzey lets us pick from his dozen or so bushes. *And* they grow wild along the trail to our beach spot here at Stinson Lake. (Do you know how *long* it takes to walk a quarter of a mile with four kids when there are pockets of blueberries at every turn?) The requisite richness here is delivered by the heavy cream; no butter is required. I use yellow cornmeal in the batter to give the cake a pretty golden cast, so the color scheme is gorgeous—yellow cake speckled with blueberries and dusted with confectioners' sugar. Serve with tall glasses of lemonade.

1½ cups unbleached flour
½ cup yellow cornmeal, preferably stone-ground
2½ teaspoons baking powder
½ teaspoon salt
¼ teaspoon ground nutmeg
2 large eggs
1⅓ cups heavy or light cream at room temperature
⅓ cup sugar
1 teaspoon lemon extract or the finely grated zest of 1 lemon
1 teaspoon vanilla extract
1½ to 2 cups fresh blueberries
confectioners' sugar for the top

Preheat the oven to 350° and butter a 10-inch springform pan or a 9-inch square pan. Flour the pan, tapping out the excess.

Into a large bowl, sift the flour, cornmeal, baking powder, salt, and nutmeg. In a separate bowl, whisk the eggs just until frothy, then blend in the cream and sugar. Stir in the extracts. Make a well in the dry ingredients, add the liquid, and stir gently. When just a few streaks of dry are left, fold in the berries.

Scrape the batter into the prepared pan and bake for 40 minutes. When done, a tester inserted in the center of the cake will come out clean; also, the top should feel firm under gentle finger pressure. Cool the cake in the pan for 10 minutes, then remove the sides of the springform pan. With the square pan, just cool the cake right in the pan.

When the cake cools, sift confectioners' sugar generously over the top. Slice and serve.

Tess's Strawberry Celebration Cake

Makes one 9-inch cake, serving 8

I named this cake after my daughter Tess, because she loves strawberries and celebrations and cakes, especially when she gets to decorate them. Here is a cake Tess is fond of making, one she likes to decorate with fresh flowers from the garden. The layers are made of sponge cake, doused with warm strawberry jelly, then stacked with plenty of whipped cream and fresh strawberries. (I always buy extra because Tess has a habit of nibbling while she works.) It needn't look like a masterpiece when you're done. And in fact half the fun is piling so much between the layers that the filling oozes out all over the place. If you have kids, be sure to have them help you too. Serve this right away or hold it in the refrigerator, loosely covered with plastic wrap, for an hour or two.

    1 quart fresh strawberries
    ¾ cup strawberry jelly
    1 tablespoon water
    2 cups cold whipping cream
    ⅓ cup confectioners' sugar
    ½ teaspoon lemon extract
    1 recipe Basic Sponge Cake (recipe follows)

Chill a bowl and beaters for beating the whipped cream. If the strawberries are small, hull but leave them whole. If they're on the large side, hull them and cut into ¼-inch slices from stem end to tip. Put the strawberry jelly in a small saucepan with the water. Heat it gently to thin it out, mashing it with a fork to facilitate the process. Remove from the heat.

Using the chilled bowl and beaters, beat the cream until it holds soft peaks. Add the confectioners' sugar and lemon extract and continue to beat for a few more seconds, until the texture is a little stiffer. Cover and refrigerate until you need it.

To assemble, cut the cake in half horizontally, making 2 layers. Place one of the halves on a serving plate, cut side facing up. Reheat the strawberry jelly just to thin it, then spoon half of it over the bottom layer and spread it evenly. Spread whipped cream thickly on the cake and cover the cream with a layer of small whole strawberries or slices. Put the second layer on the first, cut side up, and repeat the layering: jelly, cream, and berries, arranging the latter in a pretty pattern on top. If you have any whipped cream left, ice the side of the cake if you like. Serve right away or cover loosely with plastic wrap and refrigerate.

Basic Sponge Cake and Variations

Makes one 9-inch cake

With this one simple cake and the variations suggested you can make quite an assortment of breakfast dishes. These include several breakfast trifles—combinations of cake, fruit, and a creamy element like custard sauce or yogurt—and the preceding Strawberry Celebration Cake. Even though this is no more difficult to prepare than your average quick bread, you can save time in the morning by making the cake the day or night before; the quality of the cake will not suffer for sitting around for a few hours, and if anything the slight extra dryness will help the cake absorb the sweet sauces that generally accompany it. Be sure to have all ingredients and equipment ready and waiting so you can proceed through the recipe without delay.

5 large eggs at room temperature
⅔ cup sugar
pinch of salt
1 teaspoon vanilla extract
1 cup sifted unbleached flour
2 tablespoons unsalted butter, melted and cooled to lukewarm

Butter a 9-inch cake or springform pan. Line the bottom with a circle of wax paper and butter it too. Preheat the oven to 350°.

Put the eggs in a bowl of hot water for 1 minute, to warm them slightly, then break them into the bowl of your electric mixer or a mixing bowl. Begin beating the eggs on medium-high speed, gradually adding the sugar and salt with the mixer going. Beat the eggs and sugar on medium-high speed for about 5 minutes (with a freestanding mixer; this will take longer with a handheld mixer), until the mixture is thick enough to fall from the beaters in a thick ribbon. Add the vanilla and beat for a few more seconds.

Sift the flour over the beaten eggs about one-third at a time, gently folding it in with a large rubber spatula after each addition. When there are no more visible streaks of flour, gently but quickly fold in the melted butter. Scrape the batter into the pan and bake for approximately 30 to 35 minutes; when done, a tester inserted in the center of the cake should come out clean. Cool the cake in the pan on a rack for 5 minutes. Invert it onto a wire rack, peel off the wax paper, and cool completely before proceeding. If you're not using the cake right away, wrap it in plastic wrap and refrigerate overnight.

Variations: *Whole Wheat Sponge Cake:* Substitute 1 cup sifted whole wheat pastry flour for the unbleached flour. This will make a denser cake with a wheaty flavor.

Nut Sponge Cake: Toast about 1¼ cups almonds or hazelnuts in a preheated 350° oven for 8 to 10 minutes. Cool thoroughly, then process to a fine meal in the food processor. Measure out 1 cup of the meal and substitute for the flour. This is more compact than the basic recipe, best used for single-layer cakes.

Whole Wheat Poppy Seed Pound Cake

Makes 2 loaves

Readers of my previous books know I'm partial to whole grains in baking, but I honestly don't have any whole grain axes to grind. I just think whole grains offer home cooks rich possibilities, with an unexpectedly fine flavor payoff. This pound cake is a perfect example; I swear it's the best pound cake of any persuasion I have ever tasted, bar none—and it's made with all whole wheat flour. Heavy? Forget it. This is light, moist, and tender due to the high proportion of whole wheat *pastry* flour, the whole wheat equivalent of regular cake flour. The cake has a creamy, off-white interior, flecked with poppy seeds for just a bit of crunch. We love this out of hand for a quick breakfast snack or draped with a warm fruit compote, several of which you can find in the Fruits Simple and Sublime chapter.

2½ cups whole wheat pastry flour
1 teaspoon baking powder
½ teaspoon salt
½ teaspoon ground nutmeg
¼ cup poppy seeds
1 cup (2 sticks) unsalted butter at room temperature
1 cup packed light brown sugar
½ cup granulated sugar
5 large eggs at room temperature
1½ teaspoons lemon extract
1 teaspoon vanilla extract
⅓ cup milk

Preheat the oven to 325° and butter two 3¾- by 8-inch loaf pans. (You can find this precise size in the grocery store, the rigid foil kind sold in the baking section. They work particularly well here.) Cut 2 pieces of wax paper 8 inches wide to line the sides and bottoms of the pans, extending a little above the sides. (Don't worry about the ends.) Butter the paper and tuck it into the pans, buttered side up.

Sift the whole wheat pastry flour with the baking powder, salt, and nutmeg. Stir in the poppy seeds and set aside. Using an electric mixer, beat the butter until soft and creamy, then add the brown sugar ½ cup at a time, beating for about 30 seconds after each addition. Add the granulated sugar and beat for about 30 seconds more. Beat in the eggs one at a time, beating briefly after each one. Mix in the extracts.

Stir (or blend on the lowest speed) half of the dry ingredients into the creamed mixture. When almost incorporated, blend in the milk, followed by the rest of the dry ingredients. Mix just until the batter is uniformly blended, then divide it evenly between the pans. Bake for approximately 60 minutes, until a tester inserted in the center of the cake comes out clean. Cool the cakes in their pans on a rack for 25 minutes. Turn them out of the pans and cool on the rack for another 30 minutes with the paper on. Peel off the paper and cool to room temperature. Slice when cooled, storing leftovers in sealed plastic bags. The cake will keep at room temperature for 3 days, refrigerated for about 7.

Holiday Spiral Coffee Cake

Makes 2 cakes, each about 8 servings

This cake isn't too much for looks—short and stubby, and the top usually cracks—but it tastes so good it should almost be illegal. I call it a holiday cake because it's the sort of indulgent thing I figure others might eat only at Christmas or New Year's, but in fact I make it year-round, even during mud season, when there's nothing much at all to celebrate. The dough is yeasted, but fear not since there is very little kneading and no rising—only a short respite in the fridge to firm it up before rolling. The filling is the real clincher: walnuts, dates, brown sugar, cinnamon, raspberry jam, and *chocolate*—tastes like something made in heaven. Wait about 1 hour before slicing this. Wrap the second one up for a friend or freeze it for later. Or freeze the dough for later—thaw it in the fridge overnight—and make up only half the filling.

1¼-ounce envelope active dry yeast
⅓ cup lukewarm water
3 cups unbleached flour plus a little more for kneading
⅓ cup sugar
½ teaspoon salt
9 tablespoons cold unsalted butter, cut into ¼-inch pieces
2 large eggs, lightly beaten
2 tablespoons milk
1 teaspoon vanilla extract

 FILLING

1½ cups shelled walnuts
1½ cups pitted dates
½ cup packed light brown sugar
1 teaspoon ground cinnamon
1 12-ounce jar raspberry preserves
1 tablespoon water
¼ pound semisweet chocolate, finely chopped
a little granulated sugar for the top

First make the dough: In a small bowl, sprinkle the yeast over the water and set aside to dissolve. In a large bowl, mix the flour, sugar, and salt. Add the butter and cut it in with your hands or a pastry blender until the mixture resembles fine crumbs. Make a well in the dry ingredients, then add the dissolved yeast, beaten eggs, milk, and vanilla. Stir the liquids to blend them, then mix the dough with a wooden spoon until it coheres in a shaggy mass. Sprinkle a little flour on the dough and let it sit for 2 minutes.

Turn the dough out onto a lightly floured surface and knead for 2 minutes, using as little extra flour as possible to keep it from sticking. Let the dough rest for a minute, then roll it into a rectangle—just a little longer than wide—about ¾ inch thick. Slide it onto a baking sheet, cover with plastic wrap, and refrigerate for 30 minutes while you make the filling.

Combine the walnuts, dates, brown sugar, and cinnamon in the food processor and chop it up until you have small but not too fine bits. Empty the preserves into a small bowl, add the water, and stir to smooth it out. Butter two 4½- by 8½-inch loaf pans, not dark ones.

To assemble: On a lightly floured surface, roll the dough into a 20- by 12-inch rectangle. Spread the entire surface evenly with the raspberry preserves, leaving a 1-inch border on the long edge farthest from you. Sprinkle the date-nut mixture evenly over the jam, then do the same with the chocolate. Moisten the 1-inch border with a pastry brush.

Starting at the other long edge, roll the dough up, keeping it snug but not overly taut. Roll it right onto the border; it will seal itself. Cut the roll in half and place half in each pan. Set the loaves aside and preheat the oven to 350°.

After 10 minutes, sprinkle the top of each cake with a little sugar and bake for 50 minutes. Let the cakes cool for 15 minutes in the pans, then gently remove them from the pans and cool on a rack. Cool for 1 hour before slicing. This is best eaten the same day. Wrap leftovers well as soon as the cake is cooled.

Currant Walnut Cinnamon Bread

Makes 2 large loaves

Here is an oatmeal loaf jam-packed with currants and chopped walnuts, hearty enough that a couple of toasted and buttered slices and a cup of coffee or tea will tide you over nicely. The crumb of this loaf is on the coarse side because of the water. I like it that way for toasting purposes, but if you want a slightly more refined texture, use all or part lukewarm milk (except for the water you dissolve the yeast in). It takes a bit of patience to mix and knead this dough because the large quantity of currants, walnuts, and oats makes it somewhat lumpy and dense. Just take your time and knead the dough directly in a big bowl if you have one; I like my big stainless-steel "everything" bowl for this. If you like a grainy slice of French toast, this would be an excellent choice.

2¾ cups lukewarm water
1¼-ounce envelope (about 2¼ teaspoons) active dry yeast
1 cup rolled oats (*not* instant)
1 cup whole wheat flour
4½ cups unbleached flour, approximately
2 tablespoons honey, warmed slightly
2 teaspoons salt
¼ cup flavorless vegetable oil
1½ cups dried currants
1½ cups chopped walnuts
1 tablespoon ground cinnamon
1 tablespoon sugar plus a little extra for the top

Measure ¼ cup of the water into a glass measuring cup or bowl and sprinkle the yeast over it. Stir with a fork and set aside to dissolve. Meanwhile, pour the rest of the water into a large mixing bowl and add the oats. Once the yeast has dissolved, stir it into the oat water. Using a wooden spoon, stir the whole wheat flour and 1½ cups of the unbleached flour into the liquid. Cover the bowl with plastic wrap and set this sponge aside in a warm, draft-free spot for 30 minutes.

After 30 minutes, stir the honey, salt, and oil into the sponge. Add the currants and walnuts. Stir in the remaining unbleached flour, about ½ cup at a time, until you have a kneadable dough. Knead the dough for 5 minutes, adding flour to the bowl or to your work counter to keep the dough from sticking; don't knead too vigorously at first, or the dough will be very sticky. After 5 minutes of kneading, cover the dough with plastic wrap and let rest for 10 minutes, then knead for 5 minutes more. Place the dough in an oiled bowl, turning to coat the entire surface. Put the dough in a warm, draft-free spot and let rise until doubled in bulk; it may take up to 2 hours. Butter two 4½- by 8½-inch loaf pans and set them aside.

Once the dough has doubled, punch it down, turn it out onto a floured work surface, and divide in half. Knead each half into a ball and let the balls rest, covered, for 5 minutes. Working with one piece of dough at a time, roll the dough into an oblong about 14 inches long and 8 inches wide at the center. Spray or brush the dough lightly with water using a plant mister or brush. Mix the cinnamon and 1 tablespoon sugar and sprinkle half of it over the dough. Starting at a narrow end, roll up the dough as you would a carpet. Pinch together at the seam and place the dough seam down in one of the buttered pans. Repeat for the other piece of dough. Cover the loaves with lightly oiled plastic wrap and set them aside in a warm, draft-free spot until doubled in bulk. About 15 minutes before they're fully doubled, preheat the oven to 375°.

Just before baking, sprinkle several big pinches of sugar over each loaf. Bake the loaves for approximately 50 minutes. When done, the bottoms of the loaves will give a hollow retort. Cool the loaves on a rack for at least 30 minutes before slicing. Store in sealed plastic bags. It is best to freeze a loaf if the first one will take you more than 2 days to finish.

Crumb Buns

Makes 10 buns

I grew up in Plainfield, New Jersey, something I'd just as soon you didn't spread around because it could blow big holes in my reputation as a country cook. We had a great bakery on Park Avenue in Plainfield called Stires. My mom was a regular customer there, and my own giant sweet tooth can surely be traced to Stires's big black and white cookies, brownies, cakes, and other goodies. Sundays we would swing by on the way home from church and pick up a coffee cake or two and a dozen of the incredible sugar-dusted crumb buns. (There were always the free cookies too, but in retrospect I think these were a sort of ongoing bribe to get the nine of us out of the bakery as quickly as possible to make room for other customers.) Stires is gone now, but I've re-created its crumb buns as best I can remember. There's really nothing secret about the recipe, just a good sweet dough, crumb topping, and a dusting of confectioners' sugar. Serve with steaming hot coffee and the Sunday *New York Times*.

¼ cup lukewarm water
1¼-ounce envelope (about 2¼ teaspoons) active dry yeast
1 cup milk
⅓ cup sugar

3 tablespoons unsalted butter, cut into ¼-inch pieces
2 teaspoons vanilla extract
finely grated zest of 1 lemon
1 large egg at room temperature, lightly beaten
1½ teaspoons salt
1 cup whole wheat flour
2¾ cups unbleached flour, approximately

 CRUMB TOPPING

¾ cup unbleached flour
¾ cup packed light brown sugar
6 tablespoons cold unsalted butter, cut into ¼-inch pieces
confectioners' sugar for the top

Pour the water into a measuring cup and sprinkle the yeast over it. Stir with a fork, then set aside to dissolve. Meanwhile, heat the milk and sugar in a small saucepan until the sugar dissolves. Pour the liquid into a large mixing bowl and add the butter. When the liquid cools to about body temperature, stir in the dissolved yeast, vanilla, lemon zest, egg, and salt.

Using a wooden spoon, stir the whole wheat flour and 1 cup of the unbleached flour into the liquid. Beat in as much of the remaining unbleached flour, about ½ cup at a time, to make a soft, kneadable dough. Turn the dough out onto a floured surface and knead the dough for 5 to 6 minutes—until smooth and elastic—using only enough of the remaining flour to keep the dough from sticking. Place the dough in a lightly oiled bowl, turning to coat the entire surface. Cover with plastic wrap and place in a warm, draft-free spot until doubled in bulk, about 1½ hours.

Butter a 7½- by 11½-inch shallow casserole or baking pan. When the dough has doubled, punch it down and turn it out onto a lightly floured surface. Divide the dough in half, then cut each half into 5 equal pieces. Cover the pieces with plastic wrap and let rest for 5 minutes. After 5 minutes, shape each piece of dough into a ball. Roll each ball under your palm, stretching it out into a sort of fat hot dog 3½ inches long. Place the pieces side by side in the pan, evenly spaced in 2 rows of 5 each. Lightly oil a piece of plastic wrap and place it over the buns, oiled side down.

Wait 5 minutes, press down lightly on the buns to flatten them *slightly,* then cover again. Place the buns in a warm, draft-free spot until almost doubled in bulk, about 35 to 45 minutes. About 15 minutes before that point, preheat the oven to 350°.

While the buns are rising, make the topping: Mix the flour and brown sugar in a bowl. Add the butter and cut or rub it into the dry ingredients until you have fine, uniform crumbs. Set aside.

When the buns have doubled, sprinkle the crumbs evenly over the top of them. Bake for 40 minutes, until the tops of the buns—not the topping part—are golden brown. Invert the buns out of the pan, then reinvert them onto a rack to cool. Cool for about 15 minutes, then sieve confectioners' sugar over the top. Serve warm or at room temperature, cooling thoroughly on the rack. Store leftovers in a sealed plastic bag.

Apple Rhubarb Crisp

Makes 6 servings

Apple and rhubarb are on opposite ends of the harvest, but they sure work well together in this crisp. Since most domestic storage apples tend to be pretty tired by the spring, watch for the better-quality New Zealand apples, like Granny Smith, Gala, or Royal Gala. To eliminate the sometimes troublesome stringiness of larger rhubarb stalks, I like to peel rhubarb as you would a piece of celery: just get your paring knife under the red skin and peel it back. If that doesn't work, just slide the knife under the skin and peel the length of it. Since the color is in the skin, I will sometimes add some red to this by including ½ cup frozen cranberries. I like this with sour cream or yogurt cheese (page 230), sweetened with a little maple syrup or honey.

TOPPING

1 cup unbleached flour
⅓ cup granulated sugar
⅓ cup packed light brown sugar
½ teaspoon ground cinnamon
¼ teaspoon salt
½ cup (1 stick) unsalted butter, cut into ¼-inch pieces

 FILLING

3 cups peeled and sliced (¼ inch thick) rhubarb
½ cup sugar
finely grated zest of 1 lemon
3 large apples
½ cup cranberries (optional)
1 tablespoon unbleached flour

Make the topping: Mix the flour, sugars, cinnamon, and salt in a large bowl. Add the butter and cut or rub it in until the mixture is uniformly clumpy. Cover and refrigerate. Preheat the oven to 350° and lightly butter a 10- or 11-inch round baking dish or oval gratin of roughly the same size.

Put the rhubarb in a large bowl and toss with the sugar and lemon zest. Peel, core, and slice the apples, then mix them in with the rhubarb. Add the cranberries if you're using them and the flour. Turn the mixture into the prepared baking dish. Crumble the topping over the fruit, then bake for approximately 40 minutes, until the fruit is soft and the dish is bubbling hot around the edges. Cool the dish on a rack for about 15 minutes before serving.

. . . .

Apple Apricot Crunch

Makes 6 servings

This crunch is a kissing cousin to a crisp, crunchier because it uses a lot of oats and brown sugar in the topping. I make a number of variations of this for my friend Steve's restaurant right here in little old Rumney, New Hampshire, and it outsells all the other desserts by a mile (except maybe the chocolate truffle cheesecake I also make for him, but it's not for breakfast). Instead of fresh apricots—good ones being hard to find in the north country—this uses apricot preserves. The preserves and topping add just enough sweetness that no additional sugar is necessary. Start with a good tart apple for the best results. This is great plain or with a little light cream or plain yogurt poured over the top. If you have individual baking dishes, use them so there's no fighting over what's left in the casserole.

> 6 cups (about 5 or 6 large) peeled, cored, and sliced tart apples,
>   such as Granny Smith
> ¾ cup good-quality apricot preserves (1 10-ounce jar is enough)
> 1 tablespoon fresh lemon juice
> finely grated zest of 1 lemon

 ## CRUNCH TOPPING

> 1 cup rolled oats (*not* instant)
> 1 cup unbleached or whole wheat flour
> ⅔ cup packed light brown sugar
> ½ teaspoon ground cinnamon
> ¼ teaspoon salt
> ½ cup (1 stick) cold unsalted butter, cut into ¼-inch pieces

Preheat the oven to 375° and butter 6 1½-cup individual baking dishes or a 10-inch round casserole or ceramic pie plate. In a large bowl, mix the apples, apricot preserves, lemon juice, and zest. Divide the mixture evenly among the individual baking dishes or scrape it into the larger dish. Place the dish or dishes on a large baking sheet and bake for 20 minutes on the lowest oven rack.

While the apples bake, mix the oats, flour, brown sugar, cinnamon, and salt in a bowl. Add the butter and rub it in with your fingers until the mixture turns into uniformly damp crumbs. After 20 minutes, slide the oven rack out and spread the topping evenly over the apples. Bake for another 25 minutes, until the juices bubble madly and the top is a shade or two darker. Transfer the baking dish(es) to a rack and cool for at least 10 minutes before serving. Serve warm or at room temperature. Leftovers can be covered with foil, refrigerated, and reheated within two days.

Note: If you're lucky enough to find good fresh apricots, substitute 1 cup sliced, peeled apricots for the apricot preserves; thicken the fruit with 1 tablespoon flour.

Cherry Almond Crumble

Makes 4 servings

A crumble is different from a crisp in that the topping generally has oats, nuts, and/or other large bits in addition to the flour. This is one of the first and finest cherry dishes I serve when the cherries start finding their way to market in the summer. If cherry pie is a bit complicated and decadent for breakfast, this is perfectly acceptable: cherries and a bit of apple, doused with Amaretto and finished with a crumble of brown sugar, almonds, and oats. And butter of course—you can't make a crumble or a crisp without butter. Serve this alone or with a little lightly sweetened whipped cream.

> 1 pound Bing cherries, pitted
> 2 large crisp apples, preferably Granny Smith, peeled, cored, and
>   coarsely chopped
> 2 tablespoons sugar
> 2 teaspoons Amaretto (optional)
> 1 tablespoon unbleached flour

TOPPING

½ cup unbleached or whole wheat flour
¼ cup rolled oats, instant or old-fashioned
⅓ cup packed light brown sugar
¼ teaspoon ground nutmeg
¼ teaspoon ground cinnamon
¼ cup cold unsalted butter, cut into ¼-inch pieces
¼ cup sliced almonds, coarsely chopped

Butter 4 individual ovenproof dessert dishes or one 9-inch pie plate and set aside. Preheat the oven to 375°.

Mix the cherries, apples, sugar, Amaretto, and flour in a bowl. Divide the mixture evenly among the individual bowls or pour all of it into the pie plate. Bake for 20 minutes. Put the individual dishes on one sheet for easy handling.

Meanwhile, make the topping: Combine the flour, oats, brown sugar, and spices. Add the butter and cut or rub it in until the mixture is crumbly. Mix in the almonds. Scatter the topping evenly over the fruit and bake on the top shelf of the oven for 20 minutes more, until the fruit is bubbling hot. Cool the crumble on a rack for at least 15 minutes before serving.

OAT AND BROWN SUGAR CRUMB TOPPING

Makes about 2½ cups

We keep a bag of this in the freezer virtually all the time (the recipe multiplies easily and keeps forever when frozen). It is *the* crumb topping to use on muffins, for throwing together a quick fruit crisp, or to use in place of streusel on coffee cakes. There's room here for a few personal touches. I often use whole wheat flour instead of unbleached. And I like to substitute up to ½ cup toasted wheat germ for an equal amount of the flour.

1 cup unbleached or whole wheat flour
¾ cup rolled oats (*not* instant)
⅔ cup packed light brown sugar
1 teaspoon ground cinnamon
pinch of salt
½ cup (1 stick) cold unsalted butter, cut into
    ¼-inch pieces

Mix the flour, oats, brown sugar, cinnamon, and salt in a large bowl. Add the butter and rub it into the dry ingredients until you have uniform, dampish crumbs. If it seems overly clumpy, rub in a tablespoon or two more flour. Store whatever you aren't using right away in a sealed plastic bag in the freezer.

Blueberry Peach Cobbler

Makes 8 servings

Cobbler is one of those dishes that remind people of the good old days. It puts people at ease, which is why cobbler is such a nice idea for breakfast; breakfast should never be a stressful part of your day. That's why the idea of the power breakfast—an oxymoron if there ever was one—never lasted: it gave people indigestion. There's a small frame of opportunity every summer to enjoy blueberry peach cobbler, and that's when you should go for this. If the fruit is good, it will need only a bit of sugar and lemon. For the topping I like this cornmeal biscuit-cake, enriched with a little bit of wheat germ. The corn and wheat germ add a certain wholesome flavor and style to the cake without weighing it down. Serve as is, with whipped cream or Vanilla Custard Sauce (page 227).

2 pounds (about 6 medium) ripe peaches, peeled
1 pint blueberries
finely grated zest of 1 lemon
⅓ cup sugar
1½ tablespoons unbleached flour

 TOPPING

1½ cups unbleached flour
½ cup yellow cornmeal, preferably stone-ground
¼ cup toasted wheat germ
¼ cup sugar plus a little more for sprinkling on top
½ teaspoon baking soda
¼ teaspoon salt
5 tablespoons cold unsalted butter, cut into ¼-inch pieces
1 large egg
¾ cup milk
½ cup sour cream
1 teaspoon vanilla extract

Preheat the oven to 400° and butter a 9- by 13-inch baking dish. Slice the peaches into a large bowl, discarding the pits. Add the blueberries and lemon zest. Mix the sugar and flour in a small bowl, then add it to the fruit and mix well. Turn the fruit into the buttered baking dish and place it in the oven while you prepare the topping.

For the topping, sift the flour, cornmeal, wheat germ, ¼ cup sugar, baking soda, and salt into a large bowl; if anything doesn't pass through the sifter, just dump it into the bowl. Add the butter and cut it into the flour mixture until it is broken into small bits. In a separate bowl, beat the egg until frothy, then blend in the milk, sour cream, and vanilla. Make a well in the dry ingredients, add the liquid, and stir just until uniformly blended.

Take the fruit out of the oven and spoon the topping here and there over it. Sprinkle a little sugar over the top and bake for 30 minutes, until the fruit is bubbly around the edges. Cool on a rack for 10 to 15 minutes before serving.

Trifles, Tarts, and More
Elegant Breakfast Fare

BREAKFAST HAS ITS MOODS, according to the company, season, and such, and the mood in this chapter is decidedly elegant. What's elegant? Out of the ordinary, for one. Delicate and fetching. Not meant to be downed he-man style, as you might a big plate of hash and poached eggs. These are dishes to be served on your fine china and savored slowly, in the company of intimate friends and soothing music.

I include here trifles, a category that encompasses a variety of cakes layered with fruit or fruit preserves and finished with a custard sauce. For the cake I like to use either homemade sponge cake, store-bought ladyfingers, or homemade pound cake. And to reduce the calories and preparation time, plain yogurt might replace the custard sauce. Try some of the following recipes, then use the same basic ingredients and principles to invent your own versions of trifle.

Breakfast tarts certainly aren't everyday fare, but those who enjoy working with pastry should not rule out the possibility. Why not? The couple I've included in this chapter are easier than a pie to make—they have only a single crust—and they can be made up to several hours ahead if you like, then gently reheated. Everybody seems to love a good, rich cup of coffee today, and a wedge of something special like a breakfast tart is just the right companion. Coffee or hot chocolate is about all you need with the walnut biscotti (Sam's Hot Chocolate Dunkers) or with a slice of the sugar-dusted blueberry strudel I prepare with packaged phyllo dough.

Shortcakes are right up there on everybody's list of special breakfasts. I've paired the traditional strawberries with a not-so-traditional lemon-and-cornmeal shortcake. And for fall there's a sweet hazelnut shortcake served with a compote of pears and dried cherries, topped with a coffee mascarpone.

Then there are two bread puddings and a handful of delicate custards to round out this section. The former are here not so much because they are elegant—though they're certainly excellent—but because their custardy cousins are here. The custards, on the other hand, are right at home here among the fancier breakfast dishes. These are rich custards—I've never had a lightened version that didn't disappoint me—flavored with real maple syrup, vanilla beans, and coffee. There's also a lemon one with fresh caramelized raspberries. Some swear by warm custard, but I think the flavor and texture are vastly improved when the custard is served cold.

Strawberry Pound Cake Trifle

Makes 4 servings

Here's a special weekend breakfast you'll want to make as soon as the first really good local strawberries show up in your neighborhood. I get goose bumps just *thinking* about how wonderful this is: homemade pound cake covered with sliced ripe strawberries and served with a pool of cool Vanilla Custard Sauce. Such a transcendent breakfast experience doesn't just happen without a little forethought, naturally: you will need to make both the pound cake and the custard sauce a day ahead. Invite your best friend over on Sunday morning. Put a clean tablecloth on the picnic table and add a vase of freshly picked flowers. Then linger over breakfast and rediscover the simple pleasures in life.

    1 pint ripe strawberries, hulled
    a little sugar and fresh lemon juice if needed
    4 slices Whole Wheat Poppy Seed Pound Cake (page 159)
    1 recipe Vanilla Custard Sauce (page 227), chilled
    fresh mint leaves for garnish (optional)

If the strawberries are on the large side, slice them into bite-size pieces; small strawberries can be left whole. If the berries are a little underripe, toss them with a teaspoon or two of sugar and a squeeze of fresh lemon juice.

Lay the slices of pound cake in individual shallow serving bowls. Cover with strawberries, then ladle custard sauce over the whole thing. Garnish with a sprig of fresh mint leaves if you like.

. . . .

Raspberry Yogurt Trifle

Makes 4 servings

A lovely summer breakfast for family or friends, this dish brings together tart, sweet, soft, and colorful elements in a striking presentation. While there is no doubt this is best with fresh summer raspberries, I also make it with frozen berries in the winter, and it's almost as good. The first order of business here is to make the simple sponge cake and then a raspberry sauce. The cake is sliced into wedges, then served on a bed of the sauce. The top is finished with more sauce, a dollop of yogurt, and a few fresh raspberries are scattered here and there. For an even more fetching look, use some blueberries too.

> 1 quart fresh or frozen raspberries
> ¼ cup water
> ⅓ cup sugar
> 1 tablespoon fresh lemon juice
> 1 recipe Basic Sponge Cake (page 157)
> 1 cup plain yogurt
> fresh mint leaves for garnish (optional)

In a large nonreactive saucepan, combine 3 cups of the raspberries, the water, and the sugar. (If the berries are frozen, thaw the remaining ones at room temperature.) Cover and bring to a boil over medium heat. Reduce the heat to a low boil and cook the berries for 5 minutes. Remove from the heat and cool for 5 minutes. Transfer the berries to a food processor and process to a smooth puree. (If you want a seedless puree, pour it through a sieve at this point.) Pour into a bowl, stir in the lemon juice, and cool. Cover and refrigerate until needed.

To assemble the trifle, pour about 3 tablespoons of the raspberry sauce onto 4 large dessert plates. Cut 4 wedges of sponge cake, then cut the wedges in half. Put the halves side by side on the plate with the ends of each half pointing in opposite directions. Spoon another 2 or 3 tablespoons of sauce neatly over the cake and put a generous dollop of yogurt in the center of it. Scatter some of the remaining raspberries over each serving. Garnish with mint leaves if desired.

. . . .

Banana Coffee Trifle

Makes 5 servings

This could just as easily be called a tiramisù as a trifle. Like a tiramisù—the Italian dessert that gained such fame over the last few years—the ladyfingers are dampened with brewed coffee. A blanket of Kahlúa-flavored mascarpone cheese is spooned over the cake, then covered with sliced bananas. If you're using store-bought ladyfingers, this is a simple but snazzy breakfast course you can throw together in no time at all. This should follow something light and not too rich—maybe thin slices of the Leftover Pasta and Artichoke Heart Frittata on page 75 or corn fritters. Or serve it alone, with a pot of freshly brewed coffee.

½ pound mascarpone cheese
2 tablespoons sugar
2 tablespoons Kahlúa
2 or 3 tablespoons plain yogurt (optional)
10 ladyfingers
¾ cup cold freshly brewed strong coffee; espresso is best
3 ripe bananas

In a small bowl, stir the mascarpone, sugar, and Kahlúa vigorously with a wooden spoon until the sugar is dissolved. If you would prefer to lighten the texture somewhat, stir in the yogurt a tablespoon at a time to reach the desired consistency. You may have to add a little more sugar if you use the yogurt. Set aside.

Arrange 2 split ladyfingers in the bottom of each individual serving dish, flat sides up. Moisten them with about 2 tablespoons of coffee. Spread some of the mascarpone over each set of ladyfingers. If you're not serving right away, cover and refrigerate at this point. Otherwise, top with sliced peeled bananas and serve.

. . . .

Lemon Cornmeal Shortcakes with Strawberries and Cream

Makes 6 large servings

Local is the operative word when it comes to the very best strawberry short-cake: you really do need local berries, cream from a local farm (if you live anywhere near farm country), and shortcakes from your own oven. Nonlocal strawberry shortcake can still be a fine experience, but there's always a measure of compromise involved. My feeling is since this is sort of rich, better to wait and splurge on the real thing a couple of times during berry season. This lemon cornmeal shortcake does justice to the waiting. It's a light, crusty biscuit, soft on the inside, with a golden hue that serves as a gorgeous backdrop for the berries. Slightly sweet, it has lemon and orange zest as well as lemon extract, a triple hit of citrus that really brings out the best in the berries. If your berries are less than perfect, remember that a tablespoon each of sugar and lemon juice will do them a big favor.

1⅔ cups unbleached flour
⅓ cup yellow cornmeal, preferably stone-ground
¼ cup sugar plus a little more for the shortcakes and up to
    ¼ cup for the cream (optional)
2 teaspoons baking powder
½ teaspoon baking soda
¼ teaspoon salt
6 tablespoons cold unsalted butter, cut into ¼-inch pieces
1 large egg
½ cup milk
¼ cup sour cream
1½ teaspoons lemon extract
1 teaspoon vanilla extract
finely grated zest of 1 lemon
finely grated zest of 1 orange
2 cups heavy cream, well chilled
1 quart strawberries, cut or sliced into bite-size pieces

Before you begin, refrigerate the bowl and beaters you'll use to whip the cream. Lightly butter a large baking sheet and preheat the oven to 425°.

Sift the flour, cornmeal, sugar, baking powder, baking soda, and salt into a large bowl. Add the butter and cut or rub it into the dry ingredients until the mixture resembles coarse crumbs. Whisk the egg in a separate bowl, then whisk in the milk, sour cream, extracts, and zests. Make a well in the dry ingredients, then stir in the liquid all at once, just until the dough gathers into a ball.

Using a spoon, divide the dough into roughly 6 equal gobs, right in the bowl. Spoon them into your floured hands, one at a time, rounding them gently in your palms. Drop the balls onto the sheet, leaving some room between them for spreading.

Using a tablespoon or so of the heavy cream, brush the surface of each ball with a little of it. Sprinkle the top of each one with a pinch of sugar, then bake for 15 minutes, until browned and crusty. Transfer the shortcakes to a cooling rack.

Pour the remaining cream into the chilled bowl and whip it until it holds soft peaks. If the berries are sweet, you may not want to sweeten the cream at all; if they aren't perfect, or you prefer sweetened cream, beat in up to ¼ cup of sugar toward the end of the beating.

Split the shortcakes and pile strawberries on the bottom half. Spoon on the whipped cream and top with the other half of the biscuit.

Hazelnut Shortcakes with Stewed Figs and Coffee Mascarpone

Makes 6 or more servings

What the vibrant bright red of strawberry shortcake is to spring, the earthy tones of this shortcake are to fall and winter. Buttery, delicately flavored hazelnut shortcakes are split and covered with a winter compote of figs cooked in port and fennel seeds; since the compote is made ahead, this is not a difficult morning dish to make, especially if you toast the hazelnuts the night before to save another step.

Instead of the usual whipped cream—which you could use if you prefer—I like the way the coffee mascarpone adds yet another deep accenting flavor. Because it is fairly rich, and because the compote juices provide a good deal of moisture, you need only a tablespoon or so of the mascarpone with each serving. This can serve 6 as a main breakfast course, but you could make up to 12 smaller shortcakes and serve this as part of a larger meal.

1 recipe Stewed Figs with Fennel Seed (page 213)
½ cup hazelnuts
¼ cup sugar plus more for the tops
2 cups unbleached flour
1½ teaspoons baking powder
½ teaspoon baking soda
½ teaspoon salt
6 tablespoons cold unsalted butter, cut into ¼-inch pieces
1 large egg
½ cup plus 2 tablespoons milk
¼ cup sour cream

 COFFEE MASCARPONE

1 tablespoon instant coffee powder
2 tablespoons Kahlúa
7 ounces (1 scant cup) mascarpone cheese
⅓ cup confectioners' sugar

If you haven't already, prepare the fruit compote and refrigerate overnight. To toast the hazelnuts, spread them out on a baking sheet and place in a preheated 350° oven for about 12 minutes, until they're fragrant. Transfer them to a clean kitchen towel, fold it over, and rub off the skins; it isn't necessary to rub off every last bit of skin if some adheres. Set aside to cool. Increase the heat to 425° and lightly butter a large baking sheet.

When the nuts have cooled, combine them in a food processor with the sugar. Process to a fine meal, then mix in a bowl with the flour, baking powder, baking soda, and salt. Add the butter and cut it in with your hands or a pastry blender until the mixture resembles fine, uniform crumbs.

In a separate bowl, whisk the egg until frothy, then whisk in the ½ cup milk and the sour cream. Make a well in the dry mixture, add the liquid, and stir just until the dough is uniform and no dry streaks remain. Shake a little flour over the dough and let it sit for a minute.

Using a large spoon, scoop up one-sixth of the dough into your floured hands. Round the dough gently in your palms, then place the dough on the sheet. Repeat for the remaining dough, making 6 shortcakes. Brush each shortcake with milk, then sprinkle a big pinch of sugar over each one. Bake on the middle rack of the oven for about 20 minutes, until the tops are golden brown; the tops should not yield to gentle finger pressure. Transfer the shortcakes to a rack and cool for 5 minutes.

Make the coffee mascarpone: Put the instant coffee in a small cup. Gently heat the Kahlúa in a small saucepan, and when it shimmers pour it over the coffee; stir to dissolve. Combine the coffee liquid, mascarpone, and confectioners' sugar in a bowl and stir briskly with a spoon until uniform. Cover and refrigerate until needed.

To assemble, split the shortcakes in half, placing the bottoms on individual serving plates. Spoon some of the fruit compote over each bottom biscuit, then put a small scoop of the coffee mascarpone off to one side of the fruit. Top with the other half of the shortcake, placed off center so you don't hide everything.

Apple and Pear Tarte Tatin with Oatmeal Crust

Makes 6 large servings

There are occasions when you want to pull out all the stops at breakfast—a special anniversary, a wedding morning, the first day of summer—and really strut your baking stuff; here's what you serve. Tarte tatin is a traditional French dessert, a sort of sublime cobbler with a pastry crust. I use a combination of apples and pears work, I like this oatmeal one; it can be mixed easily in the food processor, and the oats give the pastry the rough texture of a country landscape and a wholesome flavor besides. And for those who need an excuse to serve this in the morning, the oats offer the necessary link to breakfast respectability. Start making the pastry when you put the fruit on the stove to cook; it will be ready just about when the fruit is finished cooking.

> 3 large ripe but firm pears (Bartletts are good)
> 5 large Granny Smith or Golden Delicious apples
> ¾ cup sugar
> juice of ½ lemon
> ¼ cup unsalted butter
> 1 recipe Oatmeal Pastry (recipe follows)
> whipped cream

Peel, halve, and core the pears and apples. Slice each of the halves into quarters and toss them gently in a bowl with ¼ cup of the sugar and the lemon juice. Set aside for 15 minutes, then drain off and discard the juice. Preheat the oven to 425°.

Make the caramel: Melt the butter in a heavy 9- or 10-inch skillet, preferably cast iron. Stir in the rest of the sugar and cook, stirring, over medium-low heat, for about 4 minutes; it will turn into a caramel of a medium amber shade. Don't let it get too dark. Remove from the heat. Arrange the apples and pears in the skillet, rounded side down, with the narrow end of the slices pointing toward the center of the pan. Alternate slices of apples and pears in any reasonable arrangement; keep the slices close together. You will probably have at least enough slices for 2 concentric circles and some for the center. Arrange them any way you like in the center, but keep them rounded side down. Take any remaining fruit sections and cut them into chunks right over the fruit that's already in place, leveling it out when all the fruit is cut.

Put the pan back over medium-high heat and cook, covered, for 10 minutes. Use a bulb baster to occasionally baste the fruit with the juices that accumulate in the pan. Uncover and cook for about another 8 to 10 minutes, until most of the excess liquid has cooked off, leaving only a thick syrup in the pan. (Tilt the pan to check it.)

Roll the pastry out on a sheet of lightly floured wax paper into a circle just slightly larger than your pan. Invert it over the fruit, remove the paper, then tuck the pastry down the side of the pan with a butter knife. Poke several steam vents in the pastry with a paring knife, twisting it to open the holes. Bake for 25 minutes.

As soon as it comes out of the oven, carefully place a plate right on top of the pastry and invert the tarte onto it; be very careful of hot dripping juice from the pan. (Wear long sleeves and an oven mitt.) Cool for 5 to 10 minutes, then slice and serve with whipped cream.

Oatmeal Pastry

Makes one 9-inch pie shell

I frankly think an oatmeal pastry is far more interesting than a straight unbleached flour one: it has a nubby texture and a discernible if subtle oatmeal flavor. And because oats are pretty much synonymous with breakfast, a crust like this is perfectly appropriate for breakfast and brunch dishes. Here is an oatmeal crust I make entirely in the food processor, first adding the oatmeal and sugar to chop up the oats—otherwise it would be too tricky to handle. Unlike most crusts, it becomes *more* difficult to handle once you chill it because the combination of coldness and oat pieces tends to make it crumbly. So roll the pastry right after you mix it, *then* refrigerate it until you need it. Prebaked, this is an excellent crust for all fruit pies.

½ cup rolled oats (*not* instant)
2 tablespoons sugar (omit for a savory crust)
1 cup unbleached flour
¼ teaspoon salt
7 tablespoons cold unsalted butter, cut into ¼-inch pieces
1 large egg yolk
1 to 2 tablespoons ice-cold water

Put the oats and sugar in a food processor and process for 10 to 15 seconds, until the oats are chopped into a mix of fine flour and small oat pieces. Add the flour and salt and process for a few more seconds. Add the butter, then process just long enough to chop it into fine bits. Mix the egg yolk and 1 tablespoon of the water together. With the machine running, add the liquid. Process briefly, then check the consistency of the pastry: press it together with your fingertips and see if it sticks together. It should, but if it seems slightly dry, don't hesitate to add the last tablespoon of water, because the oats will soak it right up.

Dump the pastry onto your work surface and press it into a ball, kneading it once or twice. Roll the dough out onto a sheet of lightly floured wax paper, then slide the paper and pastry onto a baking sheet. Cover tightly with plastic wrap and refrigerate up until about 5 to 10 minutes before you need it. This brief rest at room temperature will relax the dough and make it more manageable.

· · · · · · · · · · · · · · ·

Raspberry Peach Free-Form Tart

Makes 6 servings

A free-form tart is one in which the sides are just folded up over the filling rather than studiously pushed and coaxed into the side of a tart pan. There is a casualness about such a tart that corresponds quite well to the tone of a summer breakfast or brunch, when this would be a really fine pastry choice. A little sweetened whipped cream and freshly brewed coffee would do nicely for the occasion. Any favorite piecrust recipe can be used here; mine is Oatmeal Pastry.

> 1½ cups fresh raspberries
> 3 medium-size ripe peaches, peeled, pitted, and sliced
> ⅓ cup sugar
> 1 tablespoon fresh lemon juice
> 1 tablespoon cornstarch
> 1 recipe Oatmeal Pastry (preceding recipe) or any other pie pastry

Combine the raspberries, peaches, sugar, and lemon juice in a bowl. Toss gently to mix, then let sit for 15 minutes. Stir in the cornstarch and set aside. Preheat the oven to 425°.

Prepare and roll your choice of pastry into a 12-inch circle, transferring it to a lightly buttered 10-inch pie pan; let the edges hang over the sides. Scrape the filling into the center of the tart and spread it around. Fold the sides of the pastry over the filling and bake for 30 minutes. Lower the heat to 375° and bake for another 30 minutes, until the filling is bubbling. Cool the tart in the pan on a rack for at least 30 minutes before slicing and serving.

· · · · · · · · · · · · ·

Sam's Hot Chocolate Dunkers (aka Scottioes)

Makes about 2 dozen

Since our neighbor Elzey built himself a pond, our kids have essentially wintered over at his place to get in as much skating as possible. They often head over to Elzey's even before breakfast, so we try to bring them an early snack of hot chocolate and something to nibble on before it gets too late. These dunkers really fit the bill. They have a dry, crunchy texture like the biscotti they were patterned after (*scottioes* is what our four-year-old Sam calls biscotti). Because they're dry and sturdy, they hold up well in hot chocolate, coffee, or milk; we've enjoyed a number of memorable breakfasts sitting around the table drinking tea and coffee and munching on these. As part of a larger breakfast, you might want to serve these with yogurt, applesauce, or a fruit compote; the cinnamon and slight sweetness of these go well with all kinds of fruit. Pack leftovers into lunches. These keep for at least 10 days.

     2 cups shelled walnuts
     1 cup whole wheat flour
     ¾ cup unbleached flour
     ½ teaspoon baking powder
     ½ teaspoon salt
     ⅔ cup packed light brown sugar
     1 teaspoon ground cinnamon
     ¼ cup cold unsalted butter, cut into small pieces
     2 large eggs
     2 tablespoons cold water
     1 teaspoon vanilla extract
     1 teaspoon sugar for the top

Spread the walnuts on a baking sheet and place them in a preheated 350° oven for 10 minutes. Dump them off the sheet onto a plate and set aside to cool. Chop coarsely when cooled.

Mix the flours, baking powder, salt, brown sugar, and cinnamon in a large bowl. Add the butter and cut it in with a pastry blender until the mixture resembles a coarse meal. (You can also do this in a food processor: process the dry ingredients, add the butter, and process again.) Mix in the chopped nuts.

In another bowl, lightly whisk the eggs, water, and vanilla and pour it over the dry ingredients. Stir together with a fork, then use your hands to blend and pack the dough into a cohesive mass; it will feel something like pie pastry, though slightly damper. Divide the dough in half and shape each half into a ball. Dust your work surface and the dough lightly with flour. Roll each piece under your palms into a log about 1½ inches in diameter. Place the log on a lightly buttered baking sheet and flatten it out so the center is about ¾ inch high and the sides are rounded off. Repeat for the other half of the dough, placing it on the sheet as well. Refrigerate the dough for 15 minutes while you preheat the oven to 350°.

When the 15 minutes are up, sprinkle the top of each piece of dough with some of the sugar. Bake for 25 minutes. Using 2 spatulas, transfer each piece to a rack and cool for 15 minutes.

Slide the pieces onto a cutting board. Using a sharp serrated knife, cut each piece of dough diagonally into ¾-inch-wide slices. Place them back on the sheet, cut surface down, and bake for another 15 minutes. Transfer to a rack and cool. Leave them on the rack for up to several hours to dry even further before storing in a sealed tin or jar.

Blueberry Strudel

Makes 6 servings

Homemade strudel dough is beyond the scope of this book, but that doesn't preclude homemade strudels made from packaged phyllo dough. Though most any fruit lends itself to this treatment, this is one of my favorites—just straight blueberries, a little sugar, and lemon. The finished strudel is dusted with confectioners' sugar, and the deep blue interior against the pure white coating is gorgeous. For a pretty presentation, put individual slices on a plate surrounded by an assortment of fresh summer berries. Or—this is really deluxe—make the raspberry sauce for the trifle on page 176, pour a pool of it onto individual serving dishes, and put the slices on top. Then scatter a few extra berries around in the sauce.

2 cups fresh or frozen blueberries
¼ cup confectioners' sugar plus extra for the top
1 tablespoon unbleached flour
finely grated zest of 1 lemon
6 tablespoons unsalted butter, melted
6 full sheets (14 by 18 inches) packaged phyllo dough, thawed

Preheat the oven to 350° and lightly butter a large baking sheet. In a bowl, mix together the blueberries, sugar, flour, and lemon zest. Set aside. Melt the butter and turn off the heat, but keep it in a warm place so it stays loose.

Remove the phyllo dough from the package and lay the sheets on top of one another on the counter in front of you; keep the pile covered with 2 sheets of overlapping plastic wrap. (Immediately put the unused phyllo back in its wrapper and into the box.)

Take the top sheet of phyllo off the stack and place it on your work surface, short edge facing you. Brush the surface thoroughly with melted butter. Place a second sheet on top of the first, butter it thoroughly, then repeat until all 6 pieces are buttered and stacked in front of you.

About 4 inches up from the short edge closest to you, scrape the blueberry filling onto the phyllo, leaving a margin of about 3 inches on each side; the filling should cover an area roughly 8 inches long and 3½ to 4 inches wide. Fold the bottom 4 inches of phyllo up over the filling, butter it, then fold in the sides and butter them. Fold the filled section of dough up the length of the dough, buttering the new exposed portion of phyllo with each fold. Place the strudel on the baking sheet, seam down. Butter the top.

Using a sharp paring knife, make 3 or 4 small incisions through the top layers of dough into the filling; twist the knife a little to widen the incisions. Bake for 40 to 45 minutes, until golden brown. Cool on the baking sheet for 15 to 20 minutes, then cut into slices with a sharp serrated knife. Sieve confectioners' sugar generously over each slice and serve.

Variation: Substitute 1 cup raspberries or halved pitted sweet cherries for an equal amount of blueberries.

. . . .

Cranberry Orange Bread Pudding

Makes 6 servings

People often ask me how I come up with my recipes, to which I respond that there are many different ways. This one, for example, was inspired by a restaurant review I read in a magazine that claimed such-and-such restaurant served *the* best bread pudding in the world, a cranberry-orange one. There was no recipe, but the flavor combination sounded like a real winner, so I got right to work on my own version. To pack a lot of cranberry flavor into this I've used dried sweetened cranberries, which you can find in most health food stores nowadays (or through American Spoon Foods; see Sources). I've lightened this pudding by separating the eggs, beating the whites, and folding them in near the end. The brown sugar on top gives the pudding a crunchy exterior that contrasts beautifully with the soft, creamy interior. Note that you will have to let the bread soak in the liquid mixture for 2 hours or overnight, so plan accordingly.

1 cup dried sweetened cranberries
¼ cup water
6 cups 2- or 3-day-old white bread, cut into ¾-inch cubes
finely grated zest of 1 orange
2½ cups light cream or milk
4 large eggs, separated
½ cup plus 2 tablespoons granulated sugar
1 teaspoon vanilla extract
¼ cup packed light brown sugar

Put the cranberries in a saucepan with the water, bring to a boil, and cover. Remove from the heat and let stand until cooled. Pour the contents of the pan into a bowl, cover, and set aside.

Put the bread in a large ceramic bowl and grate the orange right over it. In a separate bowl, whisk together the light cream, egg yolks, ½ cup granulated sugar, and vanilla. Pour the liquid over the bread and toss gently to coat well. Cover and refrigerate for at least 2 hours, tossing gently every 30 minutes or so. (If you let this sit overnight, of course you don't have to get up every 30 minutes to do this.)

About 10 minutes before baking, put a kettle of water on to boil. Get out a 10-inch round ceramic or glass casserole or a gratin dish of roughly the same capacity and butter it well. Get out a second casserole large enough to hold the first one and preheat the oven to 350°.

Beat the egg whites and remaining 2 tablespoons of sugar with an electric mixer until they hold stiff peaks. Fold the egg whites into the bread mixture, folding in the plumped cranberries on the last few turns. Scrape the pudding into the buttered casserole and even it out. Sprinkle the brown sugar over the pudding and place the smaller casserole inside the larger one. Pour enough of the boiling water into the large casserole to come about halfway up the sides of the smaller one, then bake for 50 minutes. Serve hot or warm, alone or with a splash of milk or light cream.

Maple Bread Pudding

Makes 6 servings

Good bread pudding should be light, not overly sweet, and, above all else, fresh; like most egg dishes, it doesn't hold up or rewarm without losing most of its original ethereal charm and soft texture. Our favorite version is sweetened with—what else?—maple syrup, though you can make a fine version with honey or brown sugar. (If you do use honey, warm it before adding to the milk, because it doesn't dissolve in cold milk.) The raisins are traditional, but if your family likes them, use chopped pitted dates or even figs; there's lots of room here for personal touches. The top may also be sprinkled with chopped walnuts in addition to the cinnamon sugar. I top the dish with a simple dusting of cinnamon sugar, which gives it a very thin, crisp, sweet coating. Serve warm, with light cream, preserves, or a warm fruit compote on the side.

5 cups 2- or 3-day-old white or light whole wheat bread
1 teaspoon ground cinnamon
3 tablespoons unsalted butter, melted
3 large eggs
2 large egg yolks
2 cups milk
½ cup maple syrup, warm honey, or brown sugar
1 teaspoon vanilla extract
1 cup raisins
2 tablespoons sugar

Butter a 10-inch round casserole or an oval gratin dish of similar proportions. Get out another casserole, large enough to hold the first one, and put a pot of water on to boil.

In a large pottery or stainless-steel bowl, toss the bread with ½ teaspoon of the cinnamon and the butter. In a separate bowl, whisk the eggs and egg yolks until frothy. Blend in the milk, maple syrup, and vanilla. Pour the liquid mixture over the bread and refrigerate for 1 hour or as long as overnight, occasionally tossing everything gently with a rubber spatula to redistribute the liquid. When you're about ready to bake it, fold in the raisins. Preheat the oven to 350°.

Turn the pudding into the buttered dish. Mix the sugar with the remaining ½ teaspoon cinnamon and sprinkle it over the top. Pour about 1 inch of the boiling water into the large casserole and place it in the oven with the rack pulled out slightly. Put the pudding casserole into the water bath and bake for 50 minutes. Remove the pudding from the water bath and cool for at least 10 minutes, but preferably no more than an hour before serving.

Lemon Custards with Caramelized Raspberries

Makes 6 servings

Lemon custard is wonderful; topped with sugared raspberries and run under the broiler, it almost defies description. The sugar hardens, the raspberries soften, then they glisten like sweet red jewels atop the creamy custard. Use only fresh, dry raspberries; if they're wet, they'll inhibit the sugar from caramelizing properly. In-season berries are best, but I've cheated and used imported ones so I could serve this to Karen, my wife, for an Easter Sunday breakfast in bed. Start this early in the morning for brunch or the night before so it has plenty of time to chill.

> 2 cups light cream
> 1 cup heavy cream
> finely grated zest of 2 lemons
> 8 large egg yolks
> ½ cup plus 2 tablespoons sugar (see note)
> 1½ teaspoons lemon extract
> ½ teaspoon vanilla extract

Combine the creams in a medium-size nonreactive saucepan. Add the grated lemon zest and warm over medium heat for about 5 minutes, until hot to the touch. Cover, remove from the heat, and let steep for 10 minutes. Preheat the oven to 325° and put a kettle of water on to boil.

Meanwhile, stir—don't whisk—the egg yolks with the sugar until blended. Once the cream has steeped, gradually stir it into the egg yolks until blended. Put a wire strainer over a 4-cup measure or other heatproof pitcher and strain the custard. Stir the extracts into the liquid.

Pour the custard into 6 custard cups, leaving about ¾ inch headroom in each; skim off any surface foam with a spoon. Put a large shallow casserole on top of the stove. Place the custard cups in the casserole and pour enough of the boiling water into the casserole to come about halfway up the sides of the cups; if it is a little short of the mark, don't worry.

Carefully put the casserole in the oven and cover loosely with a foil tent; if you lay the foil flat across the cups, you may conduct too much heat to the surface of the cups and overcook the tops. Bake for approximately 40 to 50 minutes; the centers may seem a little wobbly when done, but the edges will be firmer. To check, stick a teaspoon into the center of one and pull it up; if loose liquid drips off the spoon instead of coating it, give the custards 5 to 7 more minutes.

Take the custards out of the casserole and transfer them to a rack. Let them cool to room temperature. When they're thoroughly cooled, cover them individually and refrigerate for at least 4 hours or overnight.

CARAMELIZED BERRIES

1 pint raspberries
¼ cup sugar

The easiest way to caramelize these is with a propane torch; just fire it up and zap the sugar, adjusting the distance of the flame so you don't cremate the berries. Otherwise, preheat the broiler. Put the cold custards right next to one another on a baking sheet just large enough to hold them or on the broiler tray if you can remove it easily.

Arrange the berries closely, domed side up, on top of each custard; cover the entire surface of each custard, but don't cram them so close that they burst. Once all the custards are covered, sprinkle 2 teaspoons sugar over each one, then slide the custards under the broiler about 5 to 6 inches from the heat. Leave them in just long enough to caramelize the topping; this may take as little as 2 minutes. If in doubt, slide the tray out and poke one with a fork; the sugar should have hardened. It may be light amber in color, but the coating won't be the dark caramel shade you may have seen on a brown sugar crème brûlée. Serve within 5 minutes if possible.

Note: To make an even more intense lemon flavor, add the grated zest of an additional lemon to the sugar and process it in the food processor for 30 seconds before blending it with the yolks.

Maple Custard

Makes 6 servings

Custard is an excellent medium for enjoying the pure flavor of maple syrup because—in this version at least—there are no other competing flavors, save for a bit of vanilla to round out the taste. I make this custard in varying degrees of richness for different occasions. Use the recipe as is if you want to stay on the light side. Or you could reverse the proportion of creams and go even richer. For special days I make a maple crème brûlée using all heavy cream, caramelizing a tablespoon of brown sugar over the top of each cup right before serving. Any way you mix it, you can't miss with this. It really needs no adornment, but a few toasted chopped walnuts or hazelnuts on top are very good if you like.

    2 cups light cream
    1 cup heavy cream
    ½ cup maple syrup
    8 large egg yolks
    1 teaspoon vanilla extract

Put a kettle of water on to boil and get out 6 custard cups. Preheat the oven to 325° and adjust the oven rack to the lowest setting.

In a medium-size nonreactive saucepan, bring the creams and maple syrup to a near boil, stirring occasionally. While that heats, stir the egg yolks with a wooden spoon in a large mixing bowl until blended evenly. Stir—don't whisk—the cream mixture into the egg yolks about 1 cup at a time. Strain the mixture through a sieve into a 4-cup measure or large pitcher—anything you can pour from easily. Stir in the vanilla.

Pour the custard evenly into the cups and place them in a large shallow casserole, leaving room between them. Pour enough of the boiling water into the casserole to come halfway up the sides of the cups. Carefully place the casserole in the oven, then cover the casserole and custard cups with a slightly tented piece of foil. It needn't be tucked snugly around the rim of the pan, so long as it covers the cups. Bake for approximately 40 to 50 minutes. When done, the custards will be just a tad wiggly and loose in the center but not actually liquidy; gently shake one to see. If you're still in doubt, cut about 1 inch down into it with a small spoon; if it does not cut, it should at least coat the spoon very thickly. If loose liquid runs in to fill the cut, give it 10 more minutes.

Transfer the custard cups to a rack. Cool for at least 20 minutes before serving. The texture is creamiest if you cool and then chill this for at least a couple of hours before eating; I prefer it chilled overnight. But if you like warm custard, just dig in.

Variation: *Maple Crème Brûlée:* The custard must first be chilled overnight. Spread 1 tablespoon light brown sugar over the top of each custard. Place the custards on a small baking sheet and position them about 6 inches from the broiler. Broil until the brown sugar caramelizes, which should take only a minute or a little longer. An easier and more controllable method is to caramelize the sugar with a propane torch if you happen to have one.

Dark Coffee Custard

Makes 6 servings

Here is a coffee custard made in an unusual fashion, with finely ground fresh coffee beans. The result is a custard as robust as a cup of dark roasted coffee, with little flecks of coffee throughout. There are ways you can regulate this to make it more or less strong, depending on your preference. Obviously you can use the lesser amount of coffee. And you can strain the mixture through cheesecloth to remove much of the fine grit. These small particles leave the custard ever so slightly gritty—I don't mind it at all—but you may prefer to remove what you can of them. (Note: This can also be made with instant coffee for an easier-to-make version.) Serve this as a straight custard, with a touch of milk or light cream on top. Or do it up as Coffee Crème Brûlée for a special breakfast; instructions follow.

> 1½ cups heavy cream
> 1½ cups light cream
> 1½ to 2 level tablespoons whole roasted coffee beans or 2
>   tablespoons instant coffee powder
> ½ cup plus 3 tablespoons sugar
> 8 large egg yolks
> ½ teaspoon vanilla extract

Put a kettle of water on to boil and get out 6 custard cups or ramekins. Also get out a shallow casserole large enough to hold the cups without crowding them. Preheat the oven to 325°.

In a heavy saucepan, begin to heat the creams over medium-low heat. Meanwhile, put the coffee and 3 tablespoons of the sugar into a coffee grinder or blender and pulverize them as finely as possible; it will come out feeling like confectioners' sugar. Whisk the grounds into the heating creams. (If you're using instant coffee, simply whisk it into the cream as it heats.)

Using a wooden spoon, stir the egg yolks, vanilla, and remaining ½ cup sugar together in a large bowl. When the cream is almost boiling, gradually stir it into the egg yolk mixture until evenly blended. Strain the custard through a sieve into a second bowl, lining the sieve with several layers of cheesecloth if you want to remove some of the coffee particles. Divide the custard evenly among the custard cups and place them in the casserole, leaving some room between them. Pour in enough hot water from the kettle to come almost halfway up the sides of the cups. Cover the top of the custards with a large sheet of foil, slightly tented up in the center.

Bake for approximately 50 to 60 minutes. When done, the centers will still be a little wobbly but not liquidy. Transfer the cups to a rack to cool, then refrigerate, covered, for several hours or overnight before serving.

Variation: *Coffee Crème Brûlée:* Sieve 1 tablespoon of packed light brown sugar over each cup. Put the cups in a shallow casserole and surround them with ice. Run them under the broiler, several inches from the heat, just long enough for the brown sugar to caramelize.

Vanilla Bean Custard

Makes 6 servings

Vanilla beans give custard a lovely, full flavor that's not quite attainable with vanilla extract—though I have nothing against pure vanilla extract; don't get me wrong. In fact, if you'd just as soon skip the extra expense and little bother of messing with the vanilla beans, fine—this will still come out beautifully. There's just something special, particularly when you have company, about using the real thing. My family is a house divided on custard: some of us like it warm, others well chilled. Either way, you can make a simple but elegant light breakfast of nothing more than chilled custard with a bowl of exquisitely ripe fresh berries or sliced soft fruit; peaches are a favorite. One of the smartest things I ever did was teach my 12-year-old son, Ben, to make this. Now we eat it about twice as often as we used to. This recipe is adapted from a Joël Robuchon recipe, from his *Simply French* cookbook (Morrow, 1991).

2⅓ cups light cream
2 plump vanilla beans, slit in half lengthwise, or
    ½ teaspoon vanilla extract
6 large egg yolks
½ cup plus 2 tablespoons sugar

Get out a large shallow casserole and set it near the oven. Place 6 custard cups in it, leaving space between them. Preheat the oven to 325° and put a kettle of water on to boil.

Pour the cream into a large saucepan and scrape the seeds from the vanilla beans into it. Bring almost to a boil, then turn off the heat and let the mixture steep for 15 minutes. (If you're using vanilla extract, just heat the cream and proceed, adding the vanilla when you take the cream off the heat.) Meanwhile, in a separate bowl beat the egg yolks and sugar with an electric mixer until thick and lemon colored, about 3 minutes. After the cream has steeped, slowly pour the cream into the egg yolks and sugar, whisking as you pour. Strain the mixture through a sieve, then divide the custard evenly among the cups.

Carefully, so you don't splash, pour enough of the boiling water into the casserole to come about halfway up the sides of the cups. Cover the cups loosely with one large sheet of foil, slightly tented, and bake for about 50 minutes. When done, the custards will be firm near the edge but still a little wobbly in the center; they should not be puffing up. Take the cups out of the pan and cool them to room temperature on a rack. Chill for up to 24 hours before serving. Or serve warm, after they've been out of the oven for 30 minutes.

Ricotta Coffee Cream

Makes 6 servings

This coffee-flavored ricotta pudding was inspired by a Marcella Hazan recipe. Technically it isn't a pudding, because it has no eggs and isn't cooked, but it has the texture of a light pudding or mousse. The coffee flavoring makes it right for breakfast, especially if you want a fast dish to make the night before to serve guests the following morning. It could be the prelude for something more substantial, like waffles or pancakes, but my first choice would be stewed figs (page 213) and this served together, with berry muffins on the side.

1 pound ricotta cheese
½ cup sugar
⅓ cup plus 1 tablespoon brewed strong coffee, cooled
1 tablespoon Kahlúa or other coffee liqueur
½ teaspoon vanilla extract
¼ cup heavy cream

Put the ricotta and sugar in a food processor and process to a smooth puree. With the machine running, add the coffee in a stream, then the Kahlúa, and vanilla. Scrape down the sides of the bowl, then turn the machine on again and add the cream. Process for 10 more seconds. Divide the mixture among 6 ramekins or custard cups. Cover and chill for several hours or overnight before serving.

Fruits Simple and Sublime

"All millionaires," wrote the British novelist Ronald Firbank, "love a baked apple"—a sentiment even those of us of lesser means can appreciate. Wealthy indeed is the breakfast cook who realizes the glory of not just the apple but all manner of seasonal fruits. For people who like to begin the day on a light, refreshing note, fruit is the perfect choice. Sliced sweet cherries in mint, a compote of summer berries, baked peaches with a crunchy topping—what could be simpler, so alive with color, or more evocative of the season?

A good cook should be aware of the seasonal progressions of fresh fruit, the ebb and flow into the market, and be prepared to seize the moment of peak enjoyment. Storage facilities and express transportation have extended the season of some fruits and completely eliminated availability problems in other cases. But the savvy cook will always try to distinguish between what is, as cookbook author Perla Meyers puts it, merely fresh and what is fresh and in season. One needn't be embarrassed to use a storage apple in March or fresh raspberries in December; all of us have gotten used to this sort of cross-seasonal eating. Market knowledge and quality, however, will help you determine when a fruit can stand nicely on its own, when it needs some flavor enhancement, and when poaching is your best solution.

Here you will find preparations for both fresh and dried fruits, for all the seasons. The emphasis is, for the most part, on the straightforward, simple approach—with things, as the great gourmet Curnonsky once explained the meaning of *cuisine,* that taste like themselves.

Few of these fruit dishes take much time to prepare. Some, like the poached dishes, should be made a day ahead, but these will last, and a doubled recipe could see you through the week. Others need just a few moments and demand to be eaten right away. A lot of these could be made over a weekend and enjoyed in no particular hurry.

Don't forget that fruit is naturally low in calories and fat, and most of the following recipes—excluding some of the obviously richer ones—are good news for calorie watchers.

Sparkling Strawberries and Grapefruit

Makes 6 servings

This is not an everyday fruit dish; the sparkling white wine suggests that this is more fitting for a little romantic patio breakfast or a Fourth of July brunch for several couples. You can't fudge on the quality of the berries here; they must be absolutely fresh and ripe. Later in the season you could try substituting a few raspberries for some of the strawberries. Serve this in your prettiest glass dishes, champagne glasses, or snifters.

1 quart strawberries
2 ruby red grapefruits
3 or 4 oranges as needed
½ cup sparkling white wine
fresh mint sprigs for garnish (optional)

Wash the berries and slice them in half or into quarters if they are very large. Place them in a bowl. Halve the grapefruits and section them. Scoop out the sections into the bowl with the berries, but don't squeeze in the grapefruit juice; you can do that on the side and drink it if you like. Toss the fruit, then divide it evenly among the serving dishes.

Squeeze the oranges and strain the juice. Measure out ¾ cup of it. Mix in the sparkling wine, then pour it evenly into the serving dishes, just covering the fruit. Refrigerate the dishes if you're not serving them right away. Serve within an hour, garnished with the fresh mint if you like.

. . . .

Cantaloupe Boats

Makes 2 servings

This is a handsome and generous presentation for a fruit salad, served in hollowed cantaloupe halves. You can use a melon baller to clean out the melon, or if you'd rather you can cut the melon into chunks; either way looks nice. As with any fruit salad, everything depends on the quality of the fruit. Rather than follow this recipe to the letter using less than wonderful fruit, be adaptable to the season and market. Later in the summer, for instance, you would be better off substituting blueberries for the strawberries. I've included grapes because they're generally available year-round, but peeled, sliced kiwifruit also works well.

1 ripe cantaloupe
1 pint perfect strawberries
2 cups green grapes, halved
3 tablespoons lime juice or part lime and part lemon juice
3 tablespoons honey
1 tablespoon minced fresh mint or 1 teaspoon lemon thyme,
   if available

Halve the cantaloupe and scoop out the seeds. Take a small slice out of the rounded end of each half so the melon vessel will stand upright. Using a melon baller, scoop the flesh out of each half and into a bowl. Or make cuts into the flesh from the center toward the rind with a paring knife, taking care not to puncture the rind. Run your knife around the outside of the cuts and the chunks will pop right out. In either case, use a spoon to clean up the halves, scraping out any bits and pieces of remaining flesh. Eat it as you clean if you wish, but don't add these odds and ends to the rest of the fruit.

Halve the strawberries—or quarter them if very large—and add them to the bowl along with the grapes. Warm the lime juice and honey in a small saucepan, pour it over the fruit, and stir. Toss in the mint or lemon thyme.

· · · · · · · · · · · ·

Let the fruit macerate in the juice for up to an hour in the refrigerator to mellow. Scoop the fruit and its juice into the melon halves. Garnish with leaves of fresh mint or lemon thyme and serve cold.

Rose-Macerated Oranges

Makes 4 servings

It might be sexist, or just plain foolish, to ascribe gender preference to certain dishes, but this is indeed a ladies' pleasure. At least the lady in my life adores them, and I love making them for her. And yes, I think they're wonderful too. Soaking oranges in a rose water bath infuses them with a delicate, sensual perfume that sets the mood for a casual breakfast (in the garden? bed?), accompanied by fresh berry muffins or Blueberry Lemon Scones (page 145). Serve the oranges in ramekins on saucers, surrounded by rose petals and a sprig of mint if there's some around. A fresh pot of herbal tea would round out the meal nicely.

    5 navel oranges
    4 teaspoons sugar
    1 lemon
    ½ teaspoon rose water
    ½ vanilla bean (optional)

Prepare the oranges: Place one orange on a cutting board and cut a ¼-inch slice off the top and bottom. Using a sharp paring or fillet knife, slice the rind and white pith off the orange while you stand the orange on one of its cut ends. Lay the orange on its side and cut into ¼-inch-thick rounds using a serrated knife.

As you slice each orange, lay them flat in a deep, narrow bowl; after you layer in each orange, sprinkle a teaspoon of sugar on top of the slices. Prepare 4 of the oranges in this manner.

Juice the last orange and the lemon and strain the juice into a bowl. Stir in the rose water and pour over the oranges. If you're using the vanilla bean, slice it lengthwise. Hold each half over the bowl and loosen the seeds with a paring knife, then submerge each half in the liquid. Cover and chill for at least 2 hours before serving, gently stirring the slices at least once.

Compote of Grapefruit, Oranges, and Pineapple

Makes 4 servings

This uncooked compote is almost like a soup with a thick "broth" of pineapple pureed with grapefruit juice. It was inspired by, though it has fewer of the refinements of, a Perla Meyers recipe in her *Art of Seasonal Cooking* (Simon & Schuster, 1991), one of the best cookbooks out there, to my mind. Because it's sometimes tricky to find a good, ripe pineapple in supermarkets, I've used the more reliable canned crushed pineapple. Perla uses whole peppercorns in the poaching liquid for her version; I simply give each portion a few turns of the pepper grinder. (Pepper with citrus fruit is one of those odd-sounding combinations that required a leap of faith for me to try originally; once I did, I couldn't—and still don't—believe how well it works.)

> 2 large pink or red grapefruits
> 1½ cups unsweetened crushed pineapple
> 2 tablespoons sugar
> 4 large navel oranges
> freshly ground black pepper to taste

Halve the grapefruits and section them. Using a paring knife, coax the sections out into a large strainer set over a mixing bowl. Set aside.

Put the crushed pineapple and sugar into a food processor. Pour the grapefruit juice in with the pineapple, transferring the grapefruit sections to the mixing bowl, and process to a fine puree. Pour the puree over the grapefruit sections.

Using a sharp paring knife, peel the oranges, removing all the rind and white pith. Holding the oranges above the mixing bowl, cut the flesh between the membranes into segments, letting the segments fall into the compote. Stir the compote and, if there is time, cover and refrigerate before serving.

To serve, spoon the compote into bowls and grind a little fresh pepper over each serving.

Citrus and Kiwifruit Compote with Vanilla Sugar

Makes 4 to 5 servings

Sometimes the addition of a single, subtle flavor can mean the difference between a good dish and one you'll be sure to make again. That's the case with this easy compote. Grapefruit, clementines, and kiwifruit are fine alone, but layering them with vanilla sugar reveals an unexpected harmony of flavors. This can be assembled ahead in goblets or attractive glasses. If you have the time, it's best to let this sit in the fridge, covered, for about an hour before serving so the vanilla has time to bloom and permeate the fruit and juice.

½ vanilla bean
2 tablespoons sugar
4 kiwifruit
8 clementines
3 large red grapefruits

Slit the vanilla bean lengthwise and scrape the seeds from it into a small bowl with the sugar. Set aside. Peel the kiwifruit and cut it into slices about ⅛ inch thick. Divide it evenly among attractive glasses and sprinkle about ½ teaspoon of the vanilla sugar over the slices. Peel the clementines, pull any stringy pith off the fruit, and separate the sections. Cover the kiwifruit with sections of clementines and sprinkle with more vanilla sugar. Halve the grapefruits and section them. Divide the sections among the glasses and sprinkle with the rest of the vanilla sugar. Cover and refrigerate.

Stewed Dried Pears and Apricots

Makes 4 to 5 servings

Dried fruits pack an intense amount of flavor into every bite, but wrestling with a bowlful of leathery fruit is not my idea of a relaxed breakfast. To enjoy the full flavor of dried fruits without the aerobic jaw workout, stew them. Stewing apricots and pears in water not only softens them but also allows you to infuse the fruit with another layer of flavor, in this case vanilla, which highlights the sweetness of the fruit. This takes only a few minutes to prepare in the evening, and it is ready to eat the following morning. It's good alone, with warmed light cream, or served on the side with waffles or pancakes. Try on top of hot cereal too.

½ pound dried pears, cut in half
½ pound dried apricots, cut into thirds
2¼ cups water
¼ cup sugar
½ vanilla bean, halved lengthwise

Combine the pears, apricots, water, and sugar in a small saucepan. Holding the vanilla bean over the pan, loosen the seeds with the tip of a paring knife, then drop the bean into the liquid. Bring to a boil, lower the heat, then simmer the fruit for 15 minutes, occasionally stirring the fruit up from the bottom. Remove from the heat, then transfer the contents of the pan to a bowl. Cool to room temperature, cover, then refrigerate until serving time.

Cherries with Mint-Lemon Sugar

Makes 4 servings

Here's a tasty way to prepare cherries when you want an easy fruit course for breakfast. This is especially good if the cherries available aren't at their peak of ripeness; the lemon and mint can't completely atone for their underripeness, but they certainly make the best of the available flavor. I've tried these with heavy and light cream, but ultimately I think they taste best alone; the richness of the cream seems to detract from and gloss over the flavor peaks. If you grow your own mint, experiment with the different varieties, such as lemon and orange mints, which will add another interesting element. These are delicious alongside slices of Whole Wheat Poppy Seed Pound Cake (page 159).

1 pound Bing cherries
⅓ cup loosely packed fresh mint leaves
2 tablespoons sugar
finely grated zest of 1 lemon
½ vanilla bean (optional but highly recommended)
fresh mint leaves for garnish

Pit and halve the cherries and set them aside in a mixing bowl. Pile the mint leaves, sugar, and lemon zest on a cutting board; if you're using the vanilla, halve it lengthwise and scrape the seeds into the pile also. Using a chef's knife, mince the mixture quite finely. Toss half of the sugar mixture with the cherries and, if you have the time, cover and set it aside for 30 minutes. If not—or when the 30 minutes is up—divide the cherries evenly among four pretty serving bowls. Sprinkle a little more of the sugar mixture over each bowl of cherries, garnish with a few mint leaves, and serve.

Variation: For a midday brunch, consider adding a splash of kirsch to the cherries.

Pineapple and Mango with Honey Curry Sauce

Makes 4 servings

This exotic little tropical fruit salad is wonderful for those who don't mind a little spice in the morning. One of the difficulties of pulling this off successfully is finding good, ripe fruit—often a chancy proposition in our modern supermarkets. Fully ripe mangoes will be almost as tender as a ripe avocado, with tight, not shriveled, skin. The fruit should have a pleasant, if faint, aroma at the stem end. Pineapples can be hard to judge too. Ripe ones tend to be relatively soft, heavy with juice, and light in color rather than a deep green. In any case, you simply cut up the fruit and lay it on pretty plates with some lime wedges and serve the sauce on the side. You can use other cut-up fruit if you like, such as grapes or even thin apple slices—whatever you like. Unsweetened shredded coconut is available at health food stores.

1 ripe mango
1 ripe pineapple
1 lime
1⅓ cups plain yogurt
1 teaspoon curry powder
2 to 3 tablespoons honey
½ cup sweetened flaked coconut or unsweetened shredded coconut

Prepare the mango: Hold the fruit in front of you stem up, narrow side facing you. Starting about ½ inch to either side of the stem, make a vertical cut all the way through the mango. Do the same on the other side of the stem. Peel the skin from around the center section, then cut the flesh down to the seed at about ¾-inch intervals. Run a paring knife around the seed to free the sections. Peel and slice the outer sections into bite-size pieces. Divide the pieces among 4 serving plates.

Cut the top and bottom off the pineapple. Lay it on its side and cut it in half. Lay each half on a cutting board on a cut end then cut the skin off using a large knife. Slice the pineapple into ¾-inch rounds, cut out the cores, and cut each ring into 5 or 6 pieces. Divide the pieces evenly among the plates and set them aside. You may need only about half the pineapple.

Cut the lime into lengthwise quarters, then slice each quarter in half again, leaving you with 8 thin wedges. Put 2 wedges on each plate.

Make the sauce by whisking together the yogurt, curry powder, and honey. Let each person squeeze lime juice directly on his or her fruit and serve the sauce and coconut on the side.

Grapefruit, Avocado, and Feta Cheese

Makes 2 servings

Grapefruit, avocado, and feta cheese might sound like odd bedfellows, but they're actually surprisingly compatible, a breakfast song sung in tasty three-part harmony. Such simplicity requires top-notch ingredients: a ripe but not overripe California Haas avocado (not the bigger, less interesting kind from Florida); sweet and juicy (heavy in proportion to its size) grapefruit; and not-too-salty feta cheese (if it tastes too salty, rinse it under cold running water). You can have this on your plate in about the time it takes to toast an English muffin.

1 large red grapefruit
1 just-ripe Haas avocado
1 small piece (perhaps ¼ cup) feta cheese
freshly ground pepper to taste

Halve the grapefruit and section it, popping the pieces out into a sieve placed over a bowl. Halve the avocado, remove the pit, then slice each half into 6 or 8 equal lengthwise slices. To serve, arrange half of the avocado slices on each plate like the spokes of a wheel. Put a pile of drained grapefruit sections in the center of each plate, then crumble some of the feta cheese over everything. Give each serving 2 or 3 turns of fresh pepper and serve. You can spoon a little of the grapefruit juice over each avocado slice or just drink it with your meal.

Strawberry Apricot Croustade with Vanilla Sauce

Makes 4 servings

A croustade refers to a casing made from pastry, bread, potatoes, or pasta. In this recipe I use puff pastry shells. (Pepperidge Farm makes a pretty good frozen puff pastry shell; just pop them in the oven for 25 minutes.) The shells are filled with slices of strawberries and apricots—or the first good peaches, which usually trail into market when strawberries are at their peak. Since the shells aren't overly capacious, I like to pile extra fruit around the shell and have it come tumbling out of the casing as well. Then vanilla sauce is spooned over the whole shebang. It looks pretty enough for a company breakfast, but try it for any family weekend breakfast or brunch; just make the sauce a day ahead.

4 puff pastry shells
1 pint strawberries
4 perfectly ripe apricots or 2 medium-size peaches, peeled
sugar and ½ lemon if needed
1 recipe Vanilla Custard Sauce (page 227), chilled
fresh mint leaves for garnish (optional)

Bake the frozen puff pastry shells as directed and set aside on a rack to cool. Clean and hull the strawberries, cutting them into bite-size pieces. Pit and slice the apricots or peaches and mix them with the strawberries. If all of the fruit is not perfectly ripe, toss with a little bit of sugar and a squeeze of fresh lemon juice and set aside for 10 minutes.

To serve, place the shells on serving plates. Pile the fruit in and around the shells, then cover generously with the custard sauce. Garnish with fresh mint leaves if you have some handy.

Cold Pineapple Slices with Warm Maple Caramel Sauce

Makes 4 servings

This might be one of the best-kept secrets to come out of New England in a while, our native maple syrup teamed up with pineapple. To fully appreciate the individual flavors I first chill the pineapple, then apply the sauce while it's still hot. The sauce starts to set when it comes in contact with the bowl and fruit and soon turns into a thickish warm glaze. The top is then sprinkled with a few chopped nuts or granola for texture and served right away. This makes a good starter course for a breakfast with friends or just a nice quick something to get you out the door. (If you're in a hurry, you don't have to chill the pineapple, but even if you have only five extra minutes you can stick it in the freezer.) Find a good fresh pineapple if you can, but canned slices will do if that's all you have.

8 pineapple slices, about ½ inch thick
½ cup maple syrup
½ cup heavy cream
a few pinches of ground nutmeg
½ cup chopped walnuts, pecans, or granola

Arrange 2 overlapping slices of pineapple in each of 4 serving bowls. Cover with plastic wrap and refrigerate for 30 minutes.

When you're almost ready to serve, bring the maple syrup to a boil in a medium-size nonreactive saucepan. When the entire surface has reached the boiling point, boil for 2 minutes. Immediately stir in the cream, return to a boil, and boil for another 15 seconds. Divide the hot sauce evenly over the pineapple, dust each serving with a tiny pinch of nutmeg, and sprinkle with nuts or granola. Serve at once.

Strawberry Rhubarb Compote

Makes 4 to 6 servings

Rhubarb can be wonderful if it's given the careful treatment it deserves, something less if not. Typical is the experience of a friend who won't touch the stuff because his mom used to cover it with unholy amounts of sugar and cook it half the day into a sort of rhubarb sludge. Here, the method of poaching the rhubarb allows you to regulate its progress easily: as soon as it approaches the point of tenderness, you snatch it off the heat and cool it down. The poaching syrup is then reduced, cooled, and poured over the rhubarb and sliced fresh strawberries. It's wonderful all alone, for a celebratory spring breakfast, or used in place of plain strawberries for shortcake. Folded into whipped cream, it also makes a lovely strawberry-rhubarb fool.

You can make this the night before, but don't add the strawberries until 30 to 60 minutes before you plan to serve it.

¾ pound rhubarb
2 cups water
⅓ cup sugar
1 wide strip of lemon zest
juice of ½ lemon
4 whole cloves
2 teaspoons minced candied ginger
1 pint fresh strawberries, hulled

Put a shallow baking dish or casserole in the freezer before you begin.

Trim the rhubarb, discarding the leaves and any bruised or tough ends. Peel the rhubarb as you would celery, to remove the strings: get a sharp paring knife just under the surface and peel the stringy covering off the stalks. Put the peelings into a nonreactive saucepan with the water, sugar, lemon zest, lemon juice, and cloves. Bring to a boil, lower the heat slightly, then cover and boil gently for 5 minutes. Drain the mixture, pouring the liquid back into the original saucepan.

Cut the peeled rhubarb into approximately ½-inch pieces; if the stalks are quite wide, you'll have to slice them lengthwise first. Bring the poaching liquid to a simmer and add the rhubarb. Simmer gently, partially covered, for 3 to 5 minutes; at the first sign of tenderness (pierce a piece with a paring knife), transfer the rhubarb from the liquid with a slotted spoon to the chilled casserole. Spread the rhubarb out in the casserole, then refrigerate, uncovered.

While the rhubarb cools, bring the poaching liquid to a boil and reduce to about ½ cup. Pour it into a serving bowl and add the minced ginger. Cool to room temperature.

If the strawberries are large, slice them into bite-size pieces; if they're small, just halve them. Add the strawberries and rhubarb to the poaching liquid. Toss gently, then refrigerate for 30 to 60 minutes before serving.

. . . .

Quince and Sour Cherry Compote

Makes 5 to 6 servings

The quince is an odd, seldom eaten fruit, once preferred by New Englanders but now even here much neglected. What's odd about it is that the quince's resemblance to both apples and certain pears doesn't square, at least in its fresh state, with its flavor: raw, almost everyone agrees it's too sour, mealy, tough, and generally unappetizing. This has not always been the case, because in ancient times it was eaten raw. Today we almost always eat quinces cooked with sugar, which renders their flesh sweet and somewhat grainy, with at least a faint resemblance to cooked apples. If you run across quinces in the marketplace, this compote is a good way to acquaint yourself with them. The slices are gently simmered in water, sugar, vanilla, and other flavorings. As they cook, the quinces turn an appetizing pink; the addition of a few dried sour cherries enhances the color and plays well with both the vanilla and the quinces. Serve small portions of this with a little cold light cream.

    4 quinces
    5 cups water
    ⅔ cup sugar
    ½ vanilla bean, slit lengthwise
    1 cinnamon stick
    1 large strip each of lemon and orange zest
    ⅓ cup dried sour cherries

Cut the quinces into quarters, then cut each quarter into 3 slices. Peel each slice, then cut out the cores. Put the cores and peels into a nonreactive saucepan with the water and bring to a boil. Lower the heat and simmer, covered, for 20 minutes. Drain off and save the water; discard the peels and cores.

Pour the water back into the saucepan and add the sugar, vanilla bean, cinnamon stick, and citrus zest. Stir in the quince slices and bring back to a boil. Lower the heat, cover, and simmer the fruit for approximately 1½ to 2 hours, until the quince slices are tender and have turned pinkish.

Put the sour cherries in a heatproof storage bowl or serving dish and pour the contents of the saucepan over them. Cool to room temperature, stirring occasionally, then cover and refrigerate. Chill well before serving.

Stewed Figs with Fennel Seed

Makes 4 to 5 servings

Somewhere along the way, figs got a bum rap; *Webster's* defines a fig as a worthless trifle, a distinction one can only imagine traceable to the fruit's sheer preponderance and widespread familiarity. Historian Waverley Root tells us the recorded use of figs goes back at least as far as 3000 B.C., when the Assyrians used fig syrup as a sweetener. Apicius fed figs to his pigs to improve their flavor, and other breeders fattened their hogs on figs and honey to plump the livers, from which they made pork foie gras. Never tried that one myself, but I do like to make a simple poaching liquid of honey, port, and water to plump my dried figs. Dried figs can be leathery, so this is a suitable tactic for morning figs; it leaves them with an agreeably soft texture and a flavorful syrup to spoon over them. Use this technique for any variety of dried figs. It even works for the large Turkish figs, which often have tough skins. These are excellent alone, with light cream, or—for a special treat—with the Ricotta Coffee Cream on page 197. They must sit at least overnight before you can eat them.

2 cups water
⅓ cup honey
¼ cup ruby port
¾ pound dried figs
1 long, wide strip of lemon zest
½ teaspoon fennel seed, crushed, plus a few whole seeds for garnish

Heat the water, honey, and port in a medium-size nonreactive saucepan. Remove the stems from the figs. Cut the figs in half lengthwise, then stir them into the liquid along with the lemon zest and fennel seed. Bring to a boil over medium heat, then lower the heat and simmer for about 20 minutes, partially covered. Stir them occasionally, but do it gently so you don't push the soft seedy centers out of the figs; this is unavoidable to some extent, but you don't want to overdo it.

Remove the figs from the heat, then transfer the contents of the pan to a bowl. Cool to room temperature, cover, and refrigerate overnight before serving. Serve individual portions with a few additional whole fennel seeds sprinkled over the top.

Warm Compote of Pears and Cranberries

Makes 4 to 6 servings

I don't know if anything can satisfy like a warm fruit compote on a chilly winter morning. We get a lot of chilly mornings here in New Hampshire, so we tend to eat a lot of warm compotes, and this is typical of one we might enjoy in winter. I'm a cranberry hoarder by nature—all those pies and muffins and such—so there are usually plenty in the freezer waiting to be composted. (Cranberries freeze very well, by the way; buy a case in the fall and stash them.) Compotes are easy to improvise, and they live by no hard and fast rules other than that they shouldn't be too sweet and the fruit shouldn't cook so long that it turns to mush. Here I use a minimum of sugar (or honey) so you don't miss the cranberry tartness, then simmer the mixture just until the pears are tender; pears overcook easily, so watch the timing. Serve this alone, with muffins, as a pancake topper, with plain yogurt, or as the filling for a winter shortcake. Also excellent served over a slice of Whole Wheat Poppy Seed Pound Cake (page 159).

½ cup apple cider or water
⅓ cup sugar or honey
1 cup cranberries
1 tablespoon fresh lemon juice
4 large ripe pears, peeled, cored, and each cut into 8 equal slices
¼ cup raisins

In a medium-size nonreactive saucepan, bring the cider, sugar, and cranberries to a boil over medium heat. Cover and cook for 2 or 3 minutes, until the cranberries soften. Add the lemon juice, pears, and raisins and mix gently with a rubber spatula so you don't cut or gouge the pears. Reduce the heat, cover, and simmer the mixture for 5 minutes, stirring once or twice. Remove the cover and simmer for another 2 to 6 minutes, stirring occasionally, until the pears are just tender. Transfer the compote to a bowl and serve. Cover and refrigerate any leftovers, which can be reheated the next day.

Poached Dried Figs and Pears

Makes 4 servings

Serving poached fruit isn't quite as simple as serving fresh, but it isn't a whole lot more difficult either. Think of poaching as adding a new layer of flavor, an added dimension. In the case of dried figs—which tend to be pretty chewy—poaching can do an awful lot to improve the texture too. I love figs, but it is virtually impossible to find fresh figs here in New Hampshire. My solution is poaching Black Mission figs in red wine. They have smaller and fewer seeds than the more common Turkish figs, and they poach up to a lustrous mahogany color that's quite pretty against the ruby-red pears. Be sure to choose pears that are not quite—but almost—ripe. These must be made a day before serving. Serve alone or with a touch of whipped cream.

2 cups dry red wine
1 cup sugar
1 cinnamon stick
10 Black Mission figs, halved and stemmed
2 large not-quite-ripe pears, peeled, halved, and cored

In a large enameled or stainless-steel saucepan, bring the red wine, sugar, and cinnamon stick to a boil. Add the figs and pears. Bring back to a boil, then lower the heat and simmer for about 30 minutes, carefully turning the pears with a slotted spoon every 10 minutes. Remove the pan from the heat when the pears are tender and cool to room temperature. Transfer to a bowl and refrigerate overnight before serving.

Maple Bananas Foster with Custard Sauce

Makes 4 servings

My friends and family have accused me of trying to reinvent an American cuisine based on New Hampshire–made maple syrup. That's unfair. I can think of at least three or four things I haven't added maple syrup to over the years. Anyway, maple really *does* go well with bananas in this New England version of the classic bananas Foster. This is one of those extremely easy dishes that's just as easy to blow if you (a) don't use good firm bananas or you (b) keep the bananas on the heat too long, either of which will result in bananas Foster mush—fine for babies but not quite what we had in mind. So have everything right at hand, including your eaters, before you begin. Wonderful—and traditional—with vanilla ice cream, but the way I like it best is with cool custard sauce. Make the custard sauce the night before so it has a chance to chill. Be sure to select short bananas so they're easy to turn in the pan.

4 firm, barely ripe bananas
2 tablespoons unsalted butter
¼ cup pure maple syrup
3 tablespoons light or dark rum
1 recipe Vanilla Custard Sauce, chilled (page 227)
ground nutmeg for dusting
½ cup toasted hazelnuts (page 46), finely chopped (optional)

Peel the bananas and carefully cut them in half lengthwise; set aside. Melt the butter in a large skillet over medium heat. Stir in the maple syrup, then immediately add the bananas. Cook for 15 seconds on one side, flip them with a spatula to coat the other side, and cook for 15 seconds more. Pour in the rum, heat for a few seconds, then ignite the liquid with a long match, keeping your face and all other burnables back from the pan until the flames subside (be careful because the flames can be difficult to see in the light of day). Cook for another few seconds, basting the bananas with the pan juices. Serve 2 slices of banana in each of 4 shallow serving bowls. Spoon some of the pan sauces over each helping, followed by a couple of tablespoons of custard sauce. Dust with nutmeg and serve right away. Garnish with the chopped hazelnuts if you're using them.

Baked Stuffed Apples with Red Currant Glaze

Makes 6 servings

I've never much cared for baked apples without a lot of extras and fanfare, because you can eat only so much warm apple plain. That being the case, here is a baked apple in full regalia, stuffed with dates, nuts, brown sugar, and cinnamon and glazed with red currant jelly. The jelly is spooned into the crater on top of the apple, and as it heats it essentially self-bastes the apple from within and without. Finally the pan juices are spooned over the apples, and they're served with just a plop of sour cream or yogurt. An altogether satisfying way to eat a baked apple.

> 6 large Golden Delicious apples
> ½ cup pitted dates
> ½ cup shelled walnuts
> ¼ cup packed light brown sugar
> 1 tablespoon unsalted butter
> ¼ teaspoon ground cinnamon
> 1 cup plus 2 tablespoons red currant jelly
> 1 tablespoon fresh lemon juice or brandy
> ½ cup plus 1 tablespoon hot water

Preheat the oven to 375° and butter a shallow casserole large enough to hold the apples without crowding them. Core the apples and peel the upper third of each one. Using your paring knife, score each apple ¼ inch deep around the perimeter where the flesh and remaining skin meet; this score will give the apple a place to expand without bursting somewhere else. Again using your paring knife, fashion the top of the apple into a crater about 1½ inches wide. Take a very narrow slice off the bottom of each apple so they'll stand up without wobbling and set the apples aside.

Put the dates, walnuts, brown sugar, butter, and cinnamon into a food processor and chop them very finely. Put the apples in the baking dish, packing some of this mixture down into each one. In a small bowl, whisk 1 cup currant jelly with the tablespoon of lemon juice and the tablespoon of hot water. Spoon the jelly mixture evenly into the craters on top of each apple, spreading a little of it around the peeled section.

Bake the apples for 45 minutes, then pour the remaining ½ cup hot water into the baking dish and bake for another 20 minutes or so, until a paring knife inserted at the thickest point meets only gentle resistance toward the center. During the last 15 minutes of baking, baste the apples with the pan juices every 5 minutes.

Put an apple into each serving dish and scrape the pan juice into a small bowl. Whisk in the remaining 2 tablespoons jelly, then sauce the top of each apple with the liquid. Serve at any temperature, with a dollop of sour cream or yogurt, lightly sweetened or not.

Baked Skillet Peaches

Makes 6 servings

This dish is something like a crisp, only made with peach halves instead of slices. The peaches start out in a skillet on top of the stove and end up in the oven, soft-baked and covered with a crunchy almond and coconut topping. Serve the peaches once they've cooled down a little, with a puddle of cold cream or a dollop of lightly sweetened sour cream. Unsweetened shredded coconut is available at health food stores.

2 tablespoons unsalted butter
6 medium-small ripe peaches, peeled, halved, and pitted
⅓ cup water
juice of ½ lemon
¼ cup sugar
1 large egg white
¾ cup slivered almonds
½ cup unsweetened shredded coconut or
  sweetened flaked coconut

Preheat the oven to 375°. Melt the butter in a 9-inch ovenproof skillet. Add the peaches, rounded side down, then cook them over medium-low heat for 3 minutes. Mix the water and lemon juice, then pour the liquid down the side of the pan—in other words, not on top of the peaches. Sprinkle 2 tablespoons of the sugar over the peaches. Cover the skillet and cook for 5 minutes undisturbed.

While the peaches cook, whisk the egg white and remaining 2 tablespoons sugar together in a bowl. Stir in the almonds and coconut. After 5 minutes, uncover the peaches and spread the topping over them. Bake the peaches for about 20 to 25 minutes, until the topping is nicely browned. Cool the peaches in the skillet on a rack for at least 10 minutes before serving.

The Jelly Cupboard:
Easy Fruit Spreads, Sauces, and
Some Pantry Items for the
Breakfast Table

There is a mystique about people who make their own fruit preserves and toppings, not unlike the mystique that follows bread makers around: others quickly assume you possess superhuman cooking skills; have advanced degrees in both home economics and food science; live in the country; and have abundant free time on your hands to indulge such niceties. I don't know anybody who falls into all those categories. But I do know that any willing cook who can read a recipe and takes pleasure in handling the fragrant, sun-drenched raw ingredients can make fruit spreads in small batches and tuck that fun into a small corner of one weekend. All you need is access to good produce—from a farm, farmer's market, or other outlet—and a modestly outfitted kitchen.

Why bother? There are plenty of reasons. Variety, for one. Here you'll find an assortment of fruit spreads and savory toppings you aren't likely to find on the shelves of your local grocery. Cost, for another. If you wait for the peak season, the low cost of ingredients makes your own quite inexpensive. But most of all for quality and flavor. You just don't know how good fruit toppings can be until you've produced your own with the pick of the crop.

Naturally there are at least as many uses for homemade fruit spreads as there are spreads themselves. There's the obvious—on biscuits, toast, and muffins. But there are also sweet fruit omelets, crepes, blintzes, and coffee cakes that use these spreads as fillings. A dollop of Chunky Vanilla Pears or Cider Jelly is incredibly good with breakfast ham, as is the Citrus Salsa Verde. Use these sweet toppings on plain yogurt, hot cereal, or French toast. The aromas alone will suggest all sorts of possibilities; you'll see once you start cooking.

I think you will find these recipes—be they sweet or savory—simple and accessible. I'm not one to put up huge batches of this or that, and I don't assume you are either. But if you can spare a small block of time for terrific toppings to brighten up your breakfast fare, then have a look around.

Blueberry Lime Preserves

Makes about 2 cups

Karen, my wife, doesn't like blueberries or blueberry preserves, but tasting these homemade preserves radically changed her point of view; she loves these. So do all of my kids. I never bother to put these up because we finish them off so quickly. (If you would like to do so, consult a good canning book about the proper procedure.) Good local blueberries are a must; I get them right from the organic garden of my friends Mike and Nancy. If there are berry farms in your area, wait until the crop is at its peak. Many fruit farms let you pick your own, and the price is about half what you'd otherwise pay.

1 quart ripe blueberries, picked over and rinsed
¾ cup sugar
finely grated zest of 1 lemon
juice and finely grated zest of 1 lime

Put the berries in a large, heavy nonreactive pot. Cover and cook over medium-low heat for several minutes, until the bottom layer of berries starts to give off juice. Mash down on the berries with a potato masher, cover for another couple of minutes, and do this again. Partially cover the berries and cook at a low boil for about 7 minutes more.

Uncover the pot and add the sugar, zests, and lime juice. Return to a gentle boil and cook for another 8 minutes, stirring often. Remove from the heat and let the mixture cool for about 10 minutes, stirring occasionally. Ladle into clean jars, cover, and refrigerate. These will keep for at least several weeks in the fridge.

Cranberry Orange Marmalade

Makes about 1½ cups

This sweet-tart fruit spread is especially nice when you want to brighten up a breakfast platter with a splash of color. Served cool, it's right at home with hot, savory breakfast dishes—eggs, spoon bread, fried apple rings, hash, and other breakfast meats. We love it on Cornmeal Biscuits (page 149) and scones. To reduce the overall amount of sugar—and add another layer of flavor—I have added some apple juice concentrate to the spread.

> 1 navel orange
> ⅔ cup sugar
> ½ cup water
> ⅓ cup frozen apple juice concentrate
> 1½ cups fresh cranberries
> juice of ½ lemon

Cut the orange into quarters, then cut each quarter in half. Place the pieces in a food processor with the sugar and process until the orange is cut into small pieces. Scrape the mixture into an enameled or stainless-steel pot and add the water and apple juice concentrate. Without cleaning the bowl of the processor, process the cranberries until finely chopped but not pureed, then add them to the pot. Bring to a boil over medium heat, stirring occasionally. Boil, covered, for 5 minutes, then uncover and cook for another 3 or 4 minutes. There should be liquid in the pan, but it should be syrupy, not thin. Remove from the heat and stir in the lemon juice. Scrape into small jars, cover, and cool. Refrigerate. This will keep up to a month or more, refrigerated.

Cider Jelly

Makes about 2 cups

Few people know about the wonderful jelly made by the simple boiling down of apple cider. Commercial apple jellies are but a shadow of the intense apple flavor of real cider jelly. Cider jelly is easy to make at home if you have a big pot, a candy thermometer, and good preservative-free cider. It's sensational on biscuits, with a bit of dry, extrasharp Cheddar, on toast, muffins, hot cereal, and crackers. My friends Mike and Nancy Phillips make and sell organic cider jelly from their Lost Nation Cider Mill in northern New Hampshire. You can write them for a current price list (see Sources) or try making it according to Michael's instructions:

"The best cider jelly is boiled down as rapidly as possible. The cider should be freshly squeezed from sound, ripe apples of mixed varieties. A true New England cider jelly comes fully puckered with no sugar added to lessen the tangy apple flavor. The natural sugars and pectin in the apples are all that's necessary for the jelling process. One gallon of cider yields just over two 8-ounce jars of jelly.

"Boil the cider in a nonreactive pot to the jelly boiling point of 220° and then pour it directly into hot sterilized jars. Judging the proper set without a temperature reading is tricky. Home versions of cider jelly are often boiled down too slowly, making the final jelly much darker with less apple bouquet."

Chunky Vanilla Pears

Makes 4 cups

Pears are one of my favorite fruits to cook with, much more versatile and adaptable than many folks realize. Here is a breakfast condiment that I think you will love: chunks of pears cooked briefly and then packed in a wine-based vanilla syrup. You can use this as a topping for yogurt, garnish pancakes and waffles with it, and serve it alongside breakfast meats; it's exceptional with ham. The pears are not at all difficult to prepare; plan to spend a small part of a winter afternoon in the kitchen, cutting up the pears and boiling down the aromatic syrup you pour over them. These improve with time, as the flavor from the vanilla bean is gradually drawn out and into the syrup. Before you begin, round up and clean the necessary jars; they needn't be canning jars. Any small jar with a lid will do. This makes a wonderful present.

juice of ½ lemon
6 large, firm, just-ripe Anjou pears
2 cups dry white wine
⅔ cup sugar
1 vanilla bean

Squeeze the lemon juice into a mixing bowl. Peel, quarter, and core the pears. Cut each quarter across the width into ¼-inch slices, letting the pieces fall into the bowl. After you cut each pear, gently toss the pears in the lemon juice.

Bring the wine and sugar to a boil in a medium-size nonreactive saucepan. Add the pears and bring back to a boil. Lower the heat and simmer for 3 to 5 minutes; the pears should not become soft but retain a little firmness. (Reserve the poaching liquid.) Using a large slotted spoon, transfer the pears to a shallow casserole. Cool to room temperature, then pour them into a colander and drain well, pressing them ever so lightly with the back of a large spoon to express excess liquid.

When the pears are drained, spoon them into the clean jars, leaving about ¾ inch headroom. Bring the poaching liquid to a boil and reduce it to about ⅔ cup, give or take a hair; keep a heatproof glass measure handy and just pour it in to check.

Spoon or pour enough of the hot syrup into each jar just to cover the pears. Cut the vanilla bean in half lengthwise and widthwise. Loosen the seeds slightly with the tip of a knife, then stick a part of the bean down into each jar. Seal and cool to room temperature. Refrigerate for at least a couple of days before serving, periodically tilting the jar to spread the syrup around. These will keep for at least 3 weeks in the fridge.

Cranberry Maple Sauce

Makes about 2½ cups

I've cooked enough with maple syrup to know that it is possible—and a real shame, considering the cost—to cancel out its delicate flavor if you combine it haphazardly with too many or otherwise overpowering ingredients. For my money, cranberries are the near-perfect match for maple; they temper the sweetness of the maple but by no means obscure the flavor, at least not in this sauce. This is a blend that works well on the obvious—pancakes, waffles, French toast—but you'll also want to try it stirred into plain yogurt and with breakfast meats, especially ham.

1½ cups fresh cranberries
½ cup water
½ cup maple syrup

Combine the cranberries and water in a medium-size nonreactive saucepan. Bring to a boil, lower the heat, and cover. Simmer the berries for 5 minutes, until they soften and make popping sounds. Stir in the maple syrup and heat through. Serve warm on pancakes, waffles, and such; cold on yogurt.

. . . .

Cranberry Applesauce

Makes about 1 quart

Good applesauce and applesauce recipes are common enough that it would be fruitless, if you'll pardon the pun, to offer one here. This excellent cranberried version is another story, however. Not too sweet, this sauce is a gorgeous, soft shade of red. The texture is slightly rough from the cranberry skins, though just enough so to add some body to the sauce. Of course you can do a million breakfast things with a good sauce like this: serve it with a dollop of yogurt, on the side with pancakes and breakfast meats, sprinkled with your favorite granola or toasted wheat germ, or as a little something to fancy up a piece of pound cake. We like this with muffins too, where it usually ends up as the filling in muffin sandwiches—a clever idea that in all fairness I must attribute to my kids. This is a dish to make in the fall, when the apple and cranberry seasons overlap.

> 7 cups (about 2½ pounds) peeled, cored, and roughly
>   chopped apples
> 2 cups water
> 2 cups fresh cranberries
> ½ cup sugar
> juice of ½ lemon
> ¼ teaspoon ground cardamom (optional)

Put the apples, water, cranberries, and sugar in a large enameled or stainless-steel pot and bring to a boil over fairly high heat. Reduce the heat slightly and cook at a low boil, covered, for 15 minutes. Uncover and cook the sauce for 5 minutes more; the texture will be thickish, but there will still be some loose liquid in the pot. Remove from the heat and cool for 30 minutes.

Transfer the sauce to the bowl of a food processor and process to the consistency of your liking; I like it just a little on the coarse side, but you can make it smoother, as you wish. Add the lemon juice and the cardamom if you're using it and process for another few seconds. Transfer to a bowl (or jar) and cover. Cool to room temperature, then refrigerate. This will keep for at least a week in the fridge.

Sweet Tahini Sauce

Makes about 1 cup

Many of us know tahini in savory dishes and sauces—think of hummus and baba ghanoujh—but you may not have realized that the same sesame seed paste makes an excellent all-purpose sweet breakfast sauce. For example, we use this on pancakes, waffles, hot cereals, granola, and even split muffins—sometimes in place of maple syrup and sometimes along with it. It has a consistency something like heavy cream, though the taste isn't easy to describe; if you can imagine such a thing as melted halvah, you'll have some idea of how this tastes.

½ cup tahini
3 tablespoons maple syrup or honey
2 to 3 tablespoons water
¼ cup plain yogurt

In a small mixing bowl, whisk together the tahini, maple syrup, and 2 tablespoons of the water until smooth. Whisk in the yogurt. Adjust the sauce to a heavy creamlike consistency using the remaining water if necessary. Cover and refrigerate until needed. This thickens as it sits, so it may need a small addition of water before each use.

Vanilla Custard Sauce

Makes about 3 cups

If I had to choose one all-purpose breakfast sauce for all of eternity, this would be the one. It can turn a baked apple into a gift from the gods, provide added moisture as a waffle topping, or make a cool, creamy sauce for fruit crisps. One of my favorite uses for it is with the Phyllo Apple Crepes on page 30; the slight dryness of the phyllo layers is just the right contrast in texture, and the apple-cinnamon-walnut filling is a made-in-heaven match for the sauce. I recommend using a candy thermometer the first couple of times you make this.

6 large egg yolks
⅔ cup sugar
2½ cups milk
1 teaspoon vanilla extract

Using an electric mixer, beat the egg yolks with the sugar for 2 minutes, until the mixture becomes thick and lemon colored. Set aside.

Heat the milk in a medium-size, heavy saucepan until quite hot. Remove it from the heat and pour into a large glass measuring cup. Gradually whisk the milk into the beaten eggs.

Pour the custard back into the saucepan and cook over low to very low heat, stirring continuously for about 8 to 10 minutes. When the custard coats the back of a spoon—or reads 180° on a candy thermometer—remove it from the heat. Don't be tempted to speed the process by increasing the heat; the sauce will curdle. Strain the custard into a bowl, whisk in the vanilla, and set aside to cool. Cover and refrigerate until needed. This will keep in the refrigerator for 3 days.

Variation: *Custard Sauce with Bourbon:* Stir 1 tablespoon bourbon into the sauce just before serving. Excellent with the Maple Bread Pudding on page 189.

Chipotle Sauce

Makes about 1½ cups

Chipotles are dried smoked jalapeño peppers. And are they ever hot—plenty hot for my taste. Canned chipotles are available in an adobo sauce, made with vinegar, tomatoes, salt, and spices. If you simply dump the whole can into a blender and puree it—as I do here—you have the perfect flavor enhancer for a versatile smoky-hot tomato sauce. This is good with omelets and scrambled eggs—most any eggs for that matter. You can use it with breakfast burritos or with Garden Huevos (page 109) too.

1 tablespoon flavorless vegetable oil
1 small onion, finely chopped
1 garlic clove, minced
1½ cups canned chopped tomatoes in puree
¼ cup minced parsley
salt to taste
1 7-ounce can chipotle peppers in adobo sauce

Heat the oil in a small saucepan and stir in the onion. Sauté over medium-low heat for 5 minutes, stirring often. Stir in the garlic, cook for a few more seconds, then add the chopped tomatoes and parsley. Cover, lower the heat, simmer for 5 minutes, and add salt.

Pour the contents of the pan into a food processor and process to a fine puree. Transfer back to the pan.

Pour the can of chipotle peppers and their sauce into a blender and puree. Stir 2 tablespoons of the puree into the tomato sauce and heat the sauce gently. Taste, adding as much more of the pureed chipotles as you like. Cool and refrigerate in an airtight container.

Citrus Salsa Verde

Makes about 3 cups

My family and I put salsa on just about everything, including scrambled eggs, omelets, hash, and breakfast burritos; for folks who like big breakfast flavors, it's the only way to fly. Even though there are some good commercial salsas out there, the better ones are pretty expensive, and it is often the case that they could stand a little more or less of this or that. So we tailored this salsa just to our liking—that's what cooking is all about, after all—and now I can't keep enough of this around. It has lots of chopped onions and peppers, and a base of pureed tomatillos, those little green tomatolike fruits you often see in salsas. To give this a perky, morning personality I have added a whole peeled orange, ground up in the food processor. But if you would rather, you can just add the juice of an orange.

½ cup finely chopped onion
½ cup finely chopped green bell pepper
½ cup finely chopped pickled jalapeño peppers
½ cup chopped cilantro, lightly packed
½ cup chopped parsley, lightly packed
1 garlic clove, peeled
1 18-ounce can tomatillos, drained
2 tablespoons fresh lime juice
1 navel orange

Combine the onion, green pepper, and jalapeños in a bowl. Pile the cilantro, parsley, and garlic on your cutting board and mince thoroughly, or do this in the food processor. Add to the peppers and onions. Put the drained tomatillos in the bowl of a food processor and process to a puree; mix with the lime juice and other ingredients. Peel the orange with a paring knife, cutting off all the white pith. Process to a smooth puree in the food processor. Mix with the remaining ingredients. Transfer to a sealed container and refrigerate. This will stay in good shape for at least 2 weeks.

Yogurt Cheese

Makes about 1½ cups

Yogurt cheese is yogurt minus its liquid element, the whey. It has a wonderfully creamy texture, like soft cream cheese or mascarpone cheese. Yogurt cheese has many uses at breakfast, especially as a spread on toast, bagels, graham crackers, or English muffins. Because it's on the tart side, I like to combine it with a little honey or preserves as well. Blended with other cheeses and herbs, it makes a wonderful omelet filling. I also like it as a tart topper for pancakes and waffles, in place of butter. It really is incredibly versatile.

To make about 1½ cups of yogurt cheese use 1 quart of plain yogurt. Line a colander with several thicknesses of cheesecloth. Place the colander in a large bowl. Stir the yogurt and pour it into the colander. Place a piece of plastic wrap over the yogurt and refrigerate overnight. Scrape the yogurt cheese into a widemouthed jar, discarding the whey. Cover and refrigerate until needed.

DRINKS HOT AND COLD

I'M AS GUILTY AS the next person when it comes to taking breakfast beverages for granted; you know, the frozen OJ, a cup of coffee at the 7-Eleven, that sort of thing. I have these lapses; we all do. I don't know any people who religiously squeeze fresh OJ every other day, use their juicer on the days in between, and quaff only exotic coffee from home-ground beans. (If I did, I probably wouldn't like them anyway.)

On the other hand, life is too short not to enjoy such good breakfast beverages on a regular basis. Maybe not every day, but often enough to leave a clear taste of the good life in our mouths. Constantly settling for compromises gradually begins to water down our outlook on life, does it not? To settle for second best is to be less than fully alive. You've heard the expression "Wake up and smell the coffee"? That's not cheap instant coffee they're talking about; there's no ritual with instant coffee, no aroma, and little flavor. It's freshly ground, home-brewed coffee they mean. Real life is home-brewed, freshly squeezed, real strawberries and yogurt buzzed in the blender to make a rich and satisfying smoothie.

Here's a section about just that—things you brew, squeeze, and buzz— breakfast beverages worth aspiring to. Some you drink with your meal; others *are* the meal. In the latter category is an assortment of fruit smoothies: drinks based on fresh fruits and yogurt. I make these year-round, but summer is their real season because without drop-dead fresh ripe fruit, the flavor payoff just isn't there. Smoothies are like fruit pies in that they're best when you don't tinker too much with one, perhaps two, basic flavors. Beyond that you quickly reach a point of diminishing returns. The natural sugars in the fruits often add just the right amount of sweetening to a smoothie, though I sometimes add a touch of honey or maple to balance the acidity of the yogurt. Your other option is to use half milk and half yogurt, which will keep the smoothie on the sweet side.

We also examine here what it takes to make a good cup of coffee. Only a

COFFEE CONSIDERATIONS

Of all the food legends I've ever heard, the one about the origins of coffee has to be an all-time favorite.

The story goes that an Abyssinian goatherd by the name of Kaldi noticed one day that his normally laid-back goats were hopping around the field with uncharacteristic verve. Kaldi was perplexed, so he went to investigate, whereupon he discovered that the herd had been munching on the bright red berries of what turned out to be—you guessed it—a coffee bush. Not one to draw premature conclusions, Kaldi tasted some berries himself, and before long he was hopping around with his goats.

There's more. About this time, the abbot of a local monastery happened by, and after talking with Kaldi, the religious man saw in the same berries a possible solution to his monks' bothersome habit of nodding off during evening prayers. So he steeped the berries in water, only to create a delicious and stimulating brew, the news of which quickly traveled to monasteries across the land.

The rest, of course, is history. Were he around today, Kaldi might be surprised to learn that coffee is one of the most important commodities in the world, second only to petroleum. He'd also be interested to hear that 25 million people depend on coffee for their livelihood, that the Japanese bathe in it for its health-giving properties, and that the Turks search for omens of the future in its dregs. Coffee has also provided inspiration for some of history's most famous intellectuals, poets, and musicians. It moved Bach to write his Coffee Cantata.

Coffee literacy is a matter of tasting, sampling, using different brewing methods, and still more tasting to come up with a formula that works for you. Only by comparison can you begin to explore the range of flavors, the nuances that make up a good cup of coffee. Most commercial canned coffee is at the low end of the pleasure scale; it is made primarily of inferior-grade robusta beans. Robusta beans aren't without their good graces, but they can't offer the flavor that fine arabica beans can. Arabica beans are less prolific, not as easy to grow, and slower to mature than robusta beans. Consequently, they're higher priced.

Gourmet coffees—the Blue Mountains, Sumatras, Konas, and other exotic-sounding varieties— vary in their flavors, acidity, and body. *Acidity* in coffee refers not to pH factors but to more subtle mouth sensations; low-acid coffees are described as soft and velvety, high-acid as crisp and bright. *Body* is the sort of "feel" the coffee leaves in the mouth, from rich and full to light. And *flavor* means just that: those unique characteristics that distinguish it from others.

Coffee is a competitive business these days, and dealers aim to please. Find one in your area (or see Sources) who can give you the answers you need and point you toward a brew that works for you.

BREWING GREAT COFFEE AT HOME THE **STARBUCKS** WAY

Disappointed with your present cup of joe? If so, consider these four fundamentals of home brewing from Starbucks:

Proportion: Accurate measurement is the most important step in brewing good coffee. Use 10 grams (2 rounded tablespoons) of grounds for each 6 ounces of water.

Grind: Using the right grind for your particular coffee maker is essential: too fine a grind causes overextraction and bitterness; too coarse a grind results in a watery, underdeveloped brew.

Freshness: Fresh beans, fresh water, and fresh brew—at every step of the brewing process freshness is a cardinal element. Coffee can be kept over a warmer for about 20 minutes before the flavor becomes unpleasant. For the best cup, make it fresh each time you serve it.

Water: Always begin with freshly drawn cold water. Heated to just off a boil (195° to 205°), that water has the best chance of coaxing from grounds the full flavor and aroma you're looking for.

generation ago coffee was just coffee: our parents bought it at the A & P, and nobody gave much thought to the type of grind, place of origin, or brewing methods. Today that's all different, and we're more likely to search around till we find what we consider the ultimate cup of coffee.

Finally, I've also included some comments about juicing, and a few miscellaneous recipes for a special hot chocolate, mulled cider, and one or two others like a Shaker-style lemonade my friend Jeff Paige serves at the Canterbury, New Hampshire, Shaker Village.

Mocha Coffee

Makes 2 servings

Here's a special coffee for holiday mornings or when times are tough and you need a little self-indulgence. Mocha coffee is a combination of chocolate and your favorite brew, decaf or regular. The drink is topped with a mound of whipped cream, then dusted with a little cocoa and cinnamon. Serve piping hot, in tall mugs, with a plate of Sam's Hot Chocolate Dunkers (page 185).

> 1 tablespoon unsweetened cocoa powder plus ½ teaspoon
>   for garnish
> 1½ tablespoons sugar
> 1½ cups brewed coffee
> lightly sweetened whipped cream
> ground cinnamon for garnish

Combine the tablespoon of cocoa powder and the sugar in a small saucepan and whisk briefly to mix. Add the coffee and heat, whisking, until not quite boiling. Divide the mixture between 2 mugs and top each with a generous dollop of whipped cream. Put the ½ teaspoon cocoa into a fine sieve. Hold it over the coffee and tap gently once or twice to dust the top. Sprinkle a pinch of cinnamon over the top and serve.

Banana Maple Smoothie

Makes 1 serving

Chilling the banana gives you a frostier, thicker smoothie; if you prefer yours a little thinner, just use the banana at room temperature.

1 large frozen banana in its skin
1 cup plain yogurt, regular or low-fat
2 to 3 tablespoons maple syrup to taste
⅛ teaspoon vanilla extract (optional)
pinch of ground nutmeg for garnish

Put the banana in the freezer before you go to bed or freeze it for at least an hour in the morning. Let the banana sit at room temperature for 5 minutes, then peel it with a paring knife. Cut the banana into big chunks and add to the blender with the yogurt, maple syrup, and vanilla if you're using it. Blend to a smooth puree and pour into a tall glass; a frosted glass is a nice touch. Sprinkle some nutmeg over the top and serve.

Alison's Strawberry Rose Water Smoothie

Makes 2 servings

All of my kids have uncommonly sharp food instincts, to the point where their observations are sometimes uncannily perceptive. Case in point: I'd been playing around with strawberry smoothies but hadn't yet hit on a formula worth writing home about. One day I passed a sample of the latest experiment to my six-year-old daughter, Alison, and asked what she thought. Without missing a beat she quipped, "It needs rose water"; I swear it was that quick. I immediately tried it, and, man, was she ever on the mark. The rose water—available at health food stores and drugstores—just wraps itself around the sweet berries, squeezing out every little bit of nuance they have to offer. Only the choicest fresh summer berries will do. Incidentally, Alison's middle name is Rose.

1½ cups ripe fresh strawberries, washed and hulled
¼ cup milk
¼ cup honey
1 cup plain yogurt
½ teaspoon lemon extract
½ teaspoon rose water
mint leaves (optional)

If you have the time, put the berries on a plate and place them in the freezer for 30 minutes; cut them in half if large. Freezing them will give you a good frosty smoothie with a lot of body. Chill your serving glasses.

Put the berries in a blender followed by the remaining ingredients in the order listed. Process until smooth. Serve in chilled glasses, rubbing a mint leaf around the rim if you have one.

Peach Smoothie

Makes 2 servings

Ripe, sweet, flavorful peaches make one of my favorite smoothies. The flavor of peaches is delicate, which is one reason I don't like mixing them with other fruit in a smoothie. I do use a touch of vanilla extract, however, because I think it gives the peaches a little lift; if you have one around, scrape some seeds from a vanilla bean instead. The skins of peaches are usually so soft I don't even bother peeling them. If you prefer to peel, however, go right ahead.

> 3 or 4 small ripe peaches, sliced
> 2 tablespoons sugar or honey
> ¼ teaspoon vanilla extract
> juice of ½ lemon
> 1 cup plain yogurt
> ¼ cup milk
> a small handful of ice cubes or cracked ice

Combine everything in a blender and puree until smooth, thinning with a little extra milk if you like. Serve in a tall glass.

Grapefruit Mint Cooler

Makes 1 large or 2 smaller servings

Here's a light, warm weather libation for those times when you prefer something crisp and clear to the creamier and more substantial feel of a smoothie. Even though this is made with grapefruit sections—not just juice—there's no unpleasant pulpiness to speak of.

> 2 large grapefruits (choose hefty, juicy ones)
> 2 tablespoons maple syrup or brown sugar
> 1½ teaspoons dried mint or 1 tablespoon chopped fresh
> 1 teaspoon fresh lemon juice
> ½ cup cracked or shaved ice
> fresh mint sprigs for garnish

Halve the grapefruits, section them, and squeeze the sections and juice into a blender. Add the remaining ingredients, then mix on high speed to a smooth consistency. Serve at once, garnished with a sprig of fresh mint.

Watermelon Berry Slush

Makes 2 servings

This is essentially a fruit smoothie without any yogurt. I love the cold, slushy combination of watermelon, raspberries, and strawberries early in the day during the occasional heat wave we get in July and August. A big guy like me could drink this all himself, but do share it if the occasion warrants.

2 cups watermelon chunks with no seeds
1 cup cold ripe strawberries
¼ cup cold fresh raspberries
1 tablespoon fresh lemon juice
1 to 2 tablespoons honey
water or milk

The night before—or at least an hour in advance—put the watermelon chunks on a plate and place them in the freezer. When you're ready to proceed, combine the frozen watermelon, berries, lemon juice, and 1 tablespoon of the honey in a blender. Blend for about 30 seconds, until smooth; you may have to push the mixture down into the blades to get things going. (Do this carefully, with a rubber spatula.) After 30 seconds, taste and add more honey if you like. Blend for another few seconds, then thin the drink, if desired, with a little water or milk. Serve at once.

. . . .

Shaker-Style Lemonade

Makes 5 to 6 servings

My friend Jeff Paige, chef at the Canterbury Shaker Village here in New Hampshire, serves a lemonade like this to visitors fortunate enough to catch one of his lunches or dinners. Shaker cooks were way ahead of their time in the imaginative use of herbs, both medicinal and culinary. And in the summer almost all of their dishes included fresh herbs from their huge gardens. Jeff's recipe—which I have adapted here—uses fresh spearmint, but if you have access to other mints, try them as well; I even include some lemon thyme in this version, but unless you grow it, you may have trouble tracking it down. On really hot summer days there's no finer breakfast beverage than this. Jeff has written an excellent book called *The Shaker Kitchen* (Clarkson/Potter, 1994) in which he shares some of his most popular recipes from the Canterbury Shaker Village kitchen.

⅓ cup loosely packed fresh spearmint leaves
1 tablespoon loosely packed fresh lemon thyme leaves (optional)
½ cup sugar
½ cup fresh lemon juice
3 cups water
ice

Bring a little bit of water to a boil in a kettle, then turn it off and remove from the heat. In a food processor, combine the herbs and sugar. Process for about 30 seconds, until the herbs are broken into small pieces. Measure out ½ cup of the boiled water, then pour it down the tube of the processor with the machine running. Process for 10 seconds more, then pour the contents into a pitcher.

Stir the lemon juice and water into the pitcher. Top with ice and serve. (Hold off on the ice if you aren't serving right away.)

. . . .

Yogi Tea

Makes 1 serving

I asked my friend Sandy, who knows about such things, how to make a genuine yogi tea. She went on to describe a two-hour affair of boiling and steeping, from which I gathered that a genuine yogi tea is probably as rare as a genuine yogi. No matter. Playing with the basic ingredients, I came up with a 5-minute version that makes up in flavor and aroma whatever it may lack in authenticity. This is a wonderful winter tea, the ginger giving it just enough heat to warm you all the way down. If you're making more than 1 or 2 cups, do this in a teapot, multiplying the ingredients by the number of cups needed. For a hotter, more intensely flavored tea, don't strain it; pour slowly from the teapot, so you don't disturb the settled ginger.

    1 tablespoon freshly grated ginger
    a 1-inch sliver of lemon zest
    boiling water
    honey to taste (optional)
    2 pinches of grated cardamom seed or 3 or 4 crushed
        cardamom pods

Put the ginger and lemon zest in a mug and add enough boiling water to make a full cup of tea. Stir in honey to taste, then add the cardamom. Stir, then steep for 2 to 3 minutes. Strain and serve.

The Best Hot Cocoa

Makes 2 servings

Why is it so difficult to find something as straightforward as a good cup of hot cocoa? Seems like every diner or restaurant I go to uses those silly machines that spew watered-down cocoa topped off with canned whipped cream. Homemade is so much better, and takes but a minute or two to make. If you're feeling in the spirit, whip up some cream and top the mugs off with a big mound of it, dusted with a bit of cocoa powder.

> 2 tablespoons unsweetened cocoa powder
> 3 tablespoons sugar
> ½ cup water
> 1¾ cups milk
> ½ teaspoon vanilla extract

In a small saucepan, whisk together the cocoa and sugar just enough to mix it slightly. Add the water and bring to a boil, whisking. Reduce the heat to medium, then whisk in the milk. Heat almost to the boiling point, stirring continuously. Remove from the heat, then quickly stir in the vanilla. Divide between 2 mugs, topping the hot cocoa with whipped cream and a dusting of cocoa powder if you like.

• • •

Breakfast Menus Throughout the Year

Breakfast is my favorite meal for getting together with friends, for the simple reason that I'm not dog tired as I usually am at night. If you aren't in the habit of entertaining at breakfast, why not try it? Everyone will admire your daring, and you'll get to see your friends in a new light. People tend to be more relaxed in the morning, not so guarded about what they say and how they behave. That can be fun. And interesting.

Don't be intimidated by planning or executing a breakfast menu. Just keep it simple and do as much advance work as possible. Mix dry mixes; prep and cut vegetables; make hashes—stuff like that. Keep the season in mind. Try to feature a fruit if it's at its peak, in a simple compote, a fruit salad, a shortcake, or something baked. Serve something hot in winter, something cool if it's oppressively hot. Have plenty of coffee, including decaf, on hand. Don't bite off more than you can chew, either; you want to have fun too, and you can't if you're tending to too many of the details.

Here are a few menu ideas to consider. They're just suggestions, an inspiration to build on. If something doesn't look appealing, simply make a substitution that sounds better to you.

A SLUMBER PARTY BREAKFAST

Blueberry Banana Pancakes with maple syrup (page 12)
Cranberry Applesauce (page 226)
Freshly squeezed OJ and hot chocolate

SUMMER VACATION BREAKFAST

Creamed corn on toast points
Blueberry Peach Cobbler (page 172)
Coffee and tea

WINTER WEEKEND BREAKFAST

Gratin of Potatoes and Bacon (page 93)
Baked Ham and Turkey Loaf (page 78)
Baked Stuffed Apples with Red Currant Glaze (page 217)
Coffee and tea

SOMETHING LIGHT FOR THE LADIES

Rose-Macerated Oranges (page 201)
Blueberry Lemon Scones (page 145)
Coffee and herb tea

A TRENCHERMAN'S BREAKFAST

Barbecued Chicken Hash (page 83)
Poached Eggs (page 64)
Cornmeal Biscuits (page 149)
Coffee

A BREADBASKET BREAKFAST

Pecan Maple Oat Muffins (page 138)
Banana Wheat Germ Soda Bread (page 150)
Sam's Hot Chocolate Dunkers (page 185)
Crumb Buns (page 164)
Coffee

AN EASTER MORNING BREAKFAST

Vanilla Bean Custard (page 195)
Stewed Figs with Fennel Seed (page 213)
Whole Wheat Poppy Seed Pound Cake (page 159)

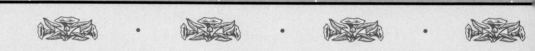

A Juice Story

Juicers and juicing have been around for quite a while, but nobody took the idea too seriously until (a) the price of juicers dropped dramatically and (b) the likes of Jack LaLanne began touting juicers on TV "infomercials"; I saw him myself, a human, juice-powered tug swimming with 75 occupied rowboats tethered to his muscular body. Go, Jack, go!

So I bought a juicer, on sale at Ames department store for $29. The price was right; I had always wanted one of those big Champion juicers, but with a price tag of about $250 it wasn't a priority. Even as I inspected it in the store, it was clear

my juicer was no beefy Champion; it was light, all-plastic, delicate. And compact; owning a Champion is like buying a major appliance. It takes up lots of counter space, and you don't so much move it as you wrestle with it. So I went for the cheapie and hoped for the best.

How has it worked? Not bad, with one major design flaw of the sort you'd expect when you buy an Escort when you wanted a Mercedes: it makes juice, but instead of just flowing into the plastic receptacle as it should, a lot of it flies out through gaps where there should have been tight seals. Using two hands, I've discovered a way

to hold the juice and pulp containers firmly in place while my kids feed the juicer with carrots and apples. This minimizes the messy sputtering but doesn't eliminate it completely. Draping wet dishrags over the machine helps too. If I weren't so lazy, I'd probably return the juicer and get my money back. But since I have lots of kids and dishrags, the arrangement isn't entirely unworkable. Besides, I like the juice, and I still wouldn't fork over $250 for a good model like the Champion.

Fresh juice is a charm, especially for breakfast, but I'm not convinced it makes sense to juice everything in sight. Juicing removes valuable dietary fiber, for one thing.

The way I see it, it makes sense to juice only stuff that's really boring plain, like carrots. I never eat a raw carrot, but I love carrot juice. And if it isn't boring plain, it should at least be cheap. I juice apples all the time in the fall because I can get local apples for next to nothing. But I'd never trade a handful of ripe strawberries for a few sips of strawberry juice. Or the pleasure of biting into a sun-soaked ripe peach for a little peach juice. Tomatoes make a fine juice in late summer, when you have so many ripe tomatoes you know you'll never eat them all or turn them into sauce. Throw in a cuke or stick of celery if you want. Be creative, juice wisely, and think twice before you buy a cheap juicer.

. . . .

Mulled Cider

Makes ½ gallon

Hot spiced or mulled cider is a winter staple at our house. From the time the first apples start coming in and then through the holidays, we enjoy this as often as we're in the mood, which is pretty often. The kids love it for breakfast, especially with pancakes, waffles, or muffins. Sometimes in the winter I'll awake to the smell of mulled cider if my son Ben wanders downstairs before I do and the woodstoves are out; it's a good warmer-upper for times like that. The best mulled cider is made from fresh, preservative-free cider. If there is an orchard in your area, see if they press their own—many do—and buy it direct.

½ gallon fresh cider
5 cinnamon sticks
5 cardamom pods, crushed
10 cloves
zest of ½ lemon, cut into strips
orange slices
ground nutmeg for garnish

Put the cider, cinnamon sticks, cardamom pods, cloves, and lemon zest in a large nonreactive pot and bring to a boil over medium heat. Reduce the heat and simmer gently for 15 minutes. Line a colander with cheesecloth, then strain the cider through it. Put the cider back over very low heat and float a few orange slices on top. Serve hot in mugs, with a dusting of nutmeg on each serving.

Variation: *Cranberry Mulled Cider:* Add 1½ cups rinsed fresh cranberries to the pot. Bring to a boil and simmer as directed. Just before straining, mash the cranberries against the pot with a potato masher. Strain, pushing the cranberries against the strainer with the back of a big spoon to squeeze out as much juice as possible. Put back over low heat and serve hot.

SOURCES

HERE ARE SOME NAMES and addresses for specialty breakfast items mentioned in the book from food producers whose products are in my opinion some of the best available. I suggest calling or writing for a listing of current products and prices.

MEAT AND FISH

S. W. Edwards and Sons
Box 25
Surry, VA 23883
800-222-4267

This fine company sells what many believe is some of the best bacon and country ham in the nation; I agree.

The Harrington Ham Company
Main St.
Richmond, VT 05477
802-434-3411

Harrington sells several kinds of bacon, and it's famous for its corncob- and maplewood-smoked hams.

Ducktrap River Fish Farm
57 Little River Dr.
Belfast, ME 04915
207-338-6280

Ducktrap's wonderful smoked salmon, smoked trout, and other smoked fish products are widely available in the New England area and elsewhere by mail order.

Aidells Sausage Company
1575 Minnesota St.
San Francisco, CA 94107
415-285-6660

Its motto is "a link ahead of the rest." These award-winning sausages are made by Bruce Aidells, a cookbook author and Ph.D. His sausages are full flavored, with a minimum of salt and fat.

COFFEE

Starbucks Coffee Company
2203 Airport Way South
Seattle, WA 98124-1510
800-445-3428

I'd walk to Washington for Starbucks coffee; fortunately it is available by mail. An excellent assortment of rich, dark-roasted coffees from around the world.

Green Mountain Coffee
33 Coffee Lane
Waterbury, VT 05676
800-223-6768

A big name in coffee in my part of New England.

. . . .

PRESERVES AND SPREADS

American Spoon Foods
1668 Clarion Ave.
Petoskey, MI 49770
800-222-5886

Owner Justin Rashid and his small staff are dedicated to making the best preserves in the world, using the top-quality fruit Michigan is blessed with. I love all his products, but my first pick is the chunky New Haven Peach Preserves.

Muirhead
43 Highway 202
Ringoes, NJ 08551
908-782-7803

Muirhead makes a Pecan-Pumpkin Butter that's great on biscuits and toast; I also use it in cornmeal mush and on top of hot cereals.

Running Deer Ranch
Box 100
Paso Robles, CA 93447
805-434-3494

Running Deer Ranch sells fine homemade preserves; its raspberry is a personal favorite.

GRITS

Hoppin' John's
30 Pinckney St.
Charleston, SC 29401
803-577-6404

You haven't tasted grits until you've tasted Hoppin' John's. He also sells a stone-ground white cornmeal that's sensational.

SOURCES

· · · · · · · · · · · · · ·

CIDER JELLY

Lost Nation Cider Mill
RD 1, Box 275
Groveton, NH 03582

My friends Mike and Nancy Phillips make two types of cider jelly, Certified Organic and Orchard Spice. Write them for a current price list.

ENGLISH MUFFINS

Wolferman's
8900 Marshall Drive
Lenexa, KS 66215
913-888-4499

Wolferman's makes twelve flavors of what many think are the best English muffins available in this country.

INDEX

almond(s):
  apple apricot granola, 41–42
  apricot coffee cake, 153–54
  baked skillet peaches, 219
  cherry crumble, 169–70
  sponge cake, 158
  toasted, crepes with cherry preserves and, 35–36
  toasted, orange French toast with, 27–28
apple(s):
  apricot crunch, 168–69
  apricot granola, 41–42
  baked stuffed, with red currant glaze, 217–18
  coffee cake, Lost Nation, 151–52
  oatmeal fritters, 20–21
  pancake, Gail's baked, 19
  and pear tarte tatin with oatmeal crust, 181–82
  phyllo crepes with vanilla custard sauce, 30–31
  rhubarb crisp, 166–67
  walnut crumb muffins, 141–44
apple cider:
  jelly, 223
  mulled, 246
  -syrup-glazed Canadian bacon, 81
applesauce, 15
  cranberry, 226
  warm, gingerbread corn cakes with, 14–15
apricot(s):
  almond coffee cake, 153–54
  apple crunch, 168–69
  apple granola, 41–42
  stewed dried pears and, 204–5
  strawberry croustade with vanilla sauce, 208–9
artichoke heart and leftover pasta frittata, 75–76
asparagus and scrambled eggs on toast, 125–26
avocado:
  grapefruit, and feta cheese, 207–8
  guacamole omelet on a bed of lettuce, 60–61

and hard-cooked eggs with Gorgonzola, 105–6
olive cream cheese, and egg on toast, 131–32

bacon:
  -braised kale with poached eggs, 103–4
  broccoli, and egg croissant sandwich, 126–27
  Canadian, cider-syrup-glazed, 81
  creamy scrambled eggs with sun-dried tomatoes and, 64
  egg, and potato pie, 108–9
  gratin of potatoes and, 93–94
baking ingredients, 136
banana(s):
  blueberry pancakes, 12
  coffee trifle, 177
  cream, 29
  Foster, maple, with custard sauce, 216–17
  maple smoothie, 235
  -stuffed French toast with banana cream, 28–29
  walnut hotcakes, 13
  walnut muffins, 144–45
  wheat germ soda bread, 150–51
basil:
  bagel with smoked Cheddar, eggs, tomato and, 129
  pesto, 71
  poached eggs on pesto bruschetta, 70–71
  poached eggs Provençal, 66–67
  stovetop potatoes with pesto and Parmesan cheese, 97
bean(s):
  black, chili, 112–13
  chilaquiles for a crowd, 118–19
beef:
  open-face steak sandwiches with Roquefort, 123
  rarebit breakfast Reuben, 124
  red flannel hash, 84–85
  roast, hash, 82–83
biscuits, 134. See also shortcakes.
  blueberry lemon scones, 145–46

INDEX